The Ascenders
From Darkness to Light

Joseph Inbar

The Ascenders
Written by Joseph Inbar

Published by
Saba Stories
3330 Reservoir Rd NW
Washington DC 20007

For information, contact Saba Stories at
sabastories@gmail.com

ISBN 0692960856
EAN 978-0692960851

DEDICATION AND APPRECIATION

This book is dedicated to my editor, Christine Poolos, without her continuous support, encouragement, and helpful comments, this project would have never reached fruition.

I am thankful to the following friends who reviewed the manuscript and provided me with invaluable comments.

Dr. Debra Bergoffen
Julie Fitzpatrick
Lea and Hal Gluskoter
Leslie Hantman
Yuki and Richard Henninger
Robert Lanman
Illana Levin
Jane Ellen Ramsey
Suzanne Richardson
Roberta Shapiro

Special thanks to Patrick Stuard who designed the cover and the book format.

TABLE OF CONTENTS

INTRODUCTORY NOTES

1. The story contains foreign words. These are italicized throughout the book and explained at the end, in a section titled Important Words. Where possible, a short clarification is provided in parentheses after the first use of the word.

2. Conquering empires, from the Greeks to the British, called the area at the southern tip of the Fertile Crescent, Palestine. Its border, while vague and constantly shifting, roughly covered the area of modern Israel and parts of western Jordan.

The Jews, from Samuel, the last of the Hebrew Judges, to the creation of Israel, called the area *Eretz Israel* (literally the land of Israel). It has been as ubiquitous in Jewish conversations and thoughts as the *Torah* (The first section of the Jewish Bible).

The Roman conquest terminated Jewish independence, and the area came under a succession of foreign governments. It would see no indigenous government until after the UN adopted Resolution 181 (establishing two states in Eretz Israel), when on 14 May 1948, Mr. Ben Gurion proclaimed the creation of the state of Israel. (The Arabs rejected the resolution and invaded the newly proclaimed state.)

Before the first Jewish presence in the area, which dates back to the dawn of history, nations rose and perished there. Since the arrival of Abraham, only members of *Am Israel* (the Jewish people or the Jewish nation) persisted in *Eretz Israel* to the modern era.

After the Roman conquest, there had been a continuous and creative Jewish habitation of *Eretz Israel* throughout the nineteen hundred years since Emperor Titus destroyed the second temple, putting an end to Jewish independent existence as a sovereign state. Two most famous examples of Jewish creativity in *Eretz Israel* are the compilation of the Jerusalem *Talmud* and the immense contribution to the *Kabbalah*.

During the Diaspora, the majority of the Jewish people protected and maintained their Jewish identity. Not only did they survive the many adversities of the forced exile from their ancestral home, they never ceased yearning to return nor ever stopped attempting to do so. Alas, rulers of many nations choked their aspirations. Challengers even scuttled Jewish attempts to follow numerous incarnations of false Messiahs on their return journey to *Eretz Israel*. Routinely, the despots of Europe confined their Jewish inhabitants under oppressive laws and frequent physical maltreatment, to Ghettos in Europe and the *Pale of Settlement* in Russia.

The bond between the Jewish people and the ancient land of *Eretz Israel* received four international recognitions.

- The first, 27 November 1917, with the Balfour Declaration.
- The second, July 1922, in the League of Nations Mandate for Palestine, which embraced and incorporated the Balfour Declaration.
- The third, 7 July 1937, in the Peel Commission which recommended a two-states solution to the conflict between the Jews and the Arabs who lived in *Eretz Israel* (Palestine, in the international lexicon).
- The fourth, 29 November 1947, in the United Nations Resolution 181 for the partition of *Eretz Israel* (a.k.a. Palestine) into Jewish and Arab states.

3. On Saturday, throughout history, Jewish communities everywhere read the *Torah*. Congregants are invited to recite a portion of the day's reading. They are invited to ascend to the *Torah* (*Aliyah La'Torah*). *Aliyah* does not differentiate between synagogues that are internally flat from those that contain a stage that requires a physical climb to reach the *Torah.*

Similarly, a Jew never immigrates to *Eretz Israel.* The term 'immigrate' is flat, devoid of emotional sparks, and spiritual connotations. Therefore, no Jew uses it. A Jew makes *aliyah* (ascends) to *Eretz Israel,* using the same word that describes the act of accessing the *Torah.* Here, too, *aliyah* ignores the fact that *Eretz Israel* shares a sea level with the rest of the world's coastal zones.

Aliyah conveys what immigrates lacks: an intense and unique emotional, spiritual, and historical bond of biblical magnitude. Furthermore, the word embraces a behavior that springs from antiquity, demonstrates incredible commitment, and connotes unbounded dedication. There is no other nation on earth that holds such a concept.

4. Once a member of *Am Israel* ascends to *Eretz Israel,* he or she becomes a member of the Jewish community, the *Yishuv.* We distinguish between the new *Yishuv,* the one that begins with the advent of *Zionism* in the late 19th century, and the old *Yishuv,* the one that has persisted in the land since Titus.

In the modern era, we recognize six waves of *aliyot* (plural of *aliyah*) that preceded the establishment of the State of Israel. Members of these *aliyot* made up the new *Yishuv.*

Aliyot during the Ottoman rule:

- First *Aliyah* – 1882 – 1903.
- Second *Aliyah* – 1904 – 1914.

Aliyot during the British Mandate:

- Third *Aliyah* – 1919 – 1923.
- Fourth *Aliyah* – 1924 – 1929.
- Fifth *Aliyah* – 1929 – 1939.
- *Aliyah* Bet – 1939 – 1948. This *Aliyah* was a long and sporadic wave of illegal immigration that was organized in protest to the British White Paper of 1939.

5. During the Mandatory period (1920 – 1948), *Eretz Israel* was often in turmoil. One contributor was British insensitivity to the needs of the *Yishuv*. Another was ceaseless Arab belligerence to the Zionist's project. A third was the deep political division within the *Yishuv.* During most of the Mandatory period, the *Yishuv* reacted to British insensitivity and Arab belligerence in two contradictory ways that reflected the internal political division:

A) The policy of restraint, practiced by the majority of the *Yishuv*. It was the official policy of the governing body (the Jewish Agency) and its paramilitary group, the *Haganah*. The primary reason for the restraint was the commitment of the *Yishuv's* leadership to rely on Great Britain for the realization of the Zionist goals.

B) The policy of retaliation, practiced by the Revisionists, a minority section of the *Yishuv,* with its own governing body and paramilitary organization, the *Irgun*. This policy was punctuated by counter-terror attacks, primarily random, with no proven connection to specific assaults on specific targets of the *Yishuv*. The Revisionists did not believe that reliance on Great Britain was a productive policy for achieving the Zionist goals.

1 MISGUIDED FAITH

"And we further order in this edict that all Jews and Jewesses of whatever age that reside in our domain and territories, that they leave with their sons and daughters. Their servants and relatives, large and small, of whatever age, by the end of July of this year, and that they dare not return to our lands, not so much as to take a step on them nor trespass upon them in any other manner whatsoever..."

Alhambra Decree March 31, 1492.

The Friday ten days before Passover of 1903 began like any other Friday, but it would end with a profound impact on Itzhak's future. On that day he would celebrate his ninth birthday. He was a precocious boy, the youngest of five children of Bella and Gershon Hacohen. He was, at that young age, an advanced student of the Bible and a beginning student of the *Talmud*, a complicated companion to biblical sacred lore usually reserved for older students. People in the Jewish community called him *gaon* (genius).

Itzhak started that day as he did any day of the week. He woke up before sunrise and went to synagogue for the first of three daily prayers. On his way, he played his favorite game. He closed his eyes and dragged his hand along the wall at the side of the narrow alleyway, counting his steps and stopped in front of a door. Before opening his eyes, he declared, "Butcher shop." He was always right. He never missed an important address like the doctor's office or the barbershop. When he reached the bathhouse, he lingered. He could smell the fire burning and the sweet incense. Unlike the doctor's office that served everyone in Gordov, the bathhouse was exclusively Jewish. Itzhak loved the place. It was a treat like no other.

Today is Friday, he reminded himself as he anticipated his afternoon at the bathhouse. There, he would immerse his body in hot water and hide behind a curtain of soft, aromatic steam that would peel the accumulated dirt from his skin and soothe his soul. *Stop dreaming,* he commanded himself, and hurried to synagogue.

After the morning prayer and before the beginning of school, he rushed to the market on the Christian west side of Mayakovskogo Street. This was a wide, unpaved road that separated the Jews from the Christians of Gordov. He was alone at the street crossing, a rickety contraption that spanned the dusty road. Everyone called it "the Bridge," but it was just a wooden footpath. Itzhak always enjoyed walking across it because it swung from side to side. When no one was waiting to cross, he deliberately rocked the bridge for fun.

Mayakovskogo Street was the north-south highway corridor that dissected the *Pale of Settlement*, that infamous part of the Russian Empire that was designated for Jewish habitation. In the rainy season, soon after the first rain, the street became a raging tributary of the mighty Dniester. On occasion, the bridge was washed away, slowing—and at times halting—pedestrian traffic for days between east and west Gordov.

The footpath was about ten feet above ground. Only one person could cross it at a time, because it was so narrow and flimsy. Sometimes, but not that day, the lines of pedestrians on both sides of Mayakovskogo Street swelled to a dozen or so, none of whom wanted to walk through the dust and the rubbish that accumulated on the surface of the street. Tempers rose as people competed for the right of way.

Upon seeing another pedestrian approaching the footpath from the west, Itzhak stopped playing. He rushed forward and climbed down to the ground. A maze of narrow alleyways wove through the other side. No matter how many times he walked to the market, he invariably lost his way. Usually, it was the fault of the pigs. Pigs meandered in the open spaces, snorting as they went in search of scraps of discarded food, and blocked his way. He always tried to avoid them. The Bible treated pigs unfavorably.

But pigs were not his only nemesis. Local children playing in the narrow streets taunted him as soon as they saw him coming off the bridge. They mocked his dark clothes and his long, curly sidelocks.

It was often a chaotic scene as he tried to escape the bullies who could easily outrun him. He was usually unsuccessful. Most times, he continued his trip to the market with a torn lapel or a few missing buttons. On many occasions, he escaped into an unfamiliar alleyway and lost his bearing.

Once he escaped the pigs and the bullies, he had to contend with chicken shit. There were chickens everywhere. Chicken shit covered his path and he did his best to avoid stepping in it. At last, he emerged from the foul smelling alleyway into the filthy market square. No one had ever praised West Gordov for its hygiene.

He bought vegetables his mother needed for dinner and rushed home. Itzhak never lingered on the west side of Gordov.

Like the bridge that connected them, the residents of the tightly knit and somewhat isolated Jewish east side, maintained fragile, precarious relations with their western neighbors. Was it the prevailing perceptions among the *goyim* (non-Jews) that Jews were unwanted, mere beings to be tolerated but not befriended?

Jews in Gordov, like most places in the *Pale*, were constrained by an ever growing volume of oppressive laws and regulations. There were laws against mobility beyond the *Pale*, tight restrictions regarding ownership of property, limited access to higher education, prohibition of trade with Christian neighbors on Sunday, and more. Unlike their Christian neighbors, the Jews did not farm. Laws against ownership of land kept them away from agriculture and pulled them toward non-farm jobs. Some were artisans and others made their living as shopkeepers, peddlers, or petty traders who traveled from town to town selling in one locale whatever they acquired in another.

There were a few highly visible Jews who held important managerial positions at the local estate. They managed the books, took care of inventory, conducted commerce, and represented the estate's owner in all disputes involving his estate and any claimant, far or near. In the eyes of the local *goyim*, they were the estate. And consequently, the hate, the aggression, and the malcontent the locals felt toward the estate were directed at the Jews and not at the princely owner.

Reb Gershon Hacohen was the only teacher in Gordov. He taught only Biblical subjects, with one exception: he educated his son Itzhak in an expanded curriculum of modern Hebrew, more than was needed to read the Bible. Reb Gershon also permitted him a glimpse into the few Zionist pamphlets he received from visiting peddlers and hundreds of years of Jewish literature he kept in his library.

People did not look kindly upon the expanded training. They whispered behind his back. "Hebrew? Why teach the boy Hebrew? No one uses it anyway. No one buys and sells using Hebrew. No one greets friends or conducts a conversation in Hebrew. The language is not for the mundane aspects of life. Yiddish is! Hebrew is a holy language to be used only in a synagogue or during religious studies!"

With all the imposed rules and regulations, life was hard in the *Pale*. There were constant fears of anti-Semitic agitations that led to numerous deadly pogroms. Despite the harshness of life in the *Pale*, Itzhak was happy with his lot. It was enriched with a wonderful and unique Jewish rhythm, punctuated with an unquestionable love of *Torah*, unbounded reliance on God, infinite patience to await the promised coming of the Messiah, and an absolute pursuit of orthodoxy as the way of life. That rhythm was common to all the residents of the Jewish east side.

The pulse of Jewish life in Gordov emanated from the one synagogue, the pride of Gordov's Jews. It was a beautiful building, well-maintained, and always full with the sound of prayers or the recitations of religious lessons. Itzhak spent most of his day there.

On that *Erev Shabbat* (Friday night) Itzhak and Reb Gershon strolled to the bathhouse to prepare themselves to receive the Queen, as they affectionately named the *Shabbat* day. The synagogue came into view. "My son," asked Reb Gershon, without changing the leisurely pace of their walk, "tell me please why do you think we love and revere the *Shabbat*?"

"I love the *Shabbat* because it gives me a quiet way to escape Gordov. But I think for our people the *Shabbat*, which God gave us on Mount Sinai, reminds us, till the end of time, of the creation story, of the fact that God rested after he labored for six days to create the universe. I think the *Shabbat* is the soul of our people. Without it, we risk our enduring connection with the Holy One."

They paused before the synagogue, where Reb Gershon asked another question; "And why is the synagogue so critical to our life?"

The boy thought for a long while before replying and then he said somewhat hesitantly, "While the synagogue is constructed with earthly things, it is an everlasting spiritual connection to our ancestral homeland in *Eretz Israel*. As long as we have synagogues, we will never forget our bond with Zion."

"Wonderful answers," said Reb Gershon. "Let's continue to the bathhouse. I can already smell the sweet aroma that seeps into the street."

They entered and undressed. They walked to the hot pool where they met many friends and engaged in everyday talk. They cleansed their bodies and souls from the accumulated dirt and worries of the past week. After a long time of delighting in the steam, the conversations with friends and the aromatic incense, they were ready to leave. Cleansed and relaxed, father and son would dress in their finest and go to synagogue. After the evening prayer, they returned home for a joyous *Shabbat* dinner to welcome "the Queen." There was lots of good food, more praying, and cheerful music and discussions, mostly of biblical topics. *Erev Shabbat* was cherished as a time that separated the mundane from the holy and spiritual world. The Jewish quarter changed into a quiet, slow-moving world. Jews turned inward and spent the day with family in and out of the synagogue.

Now, the prayers were over. Night engulfed Gordov. The synagogue fell silent. The Hacohen family rushed home to welcome *Shabbat*. One by one, the guests entered. There were a few of Itzhak's friends, his parents and four siblings—Avram, the eldest, Yaakov and the twins, Shlomo and Rachel—and an assortment of guests from the *yeshiva* (a Jewish religious school) of Domsky. Bella Hacohen's reputation for cooking *Shabbat* dinners and Reb Gershon's standing as a gracious host did not escape the students of the *yeshiva*, who welcomed an occasional free meal. Everyone knew that his house was a warm home, a refuge from the harsh reality of Jewish life in the *Pale*.

Domsky sprang out of the gray land some twenty kilometers north of Gordov. It was a small town, as nondescript as Gordov. But its rabbi, Reb Mendel, whose fame as a *Torah* scholar reached the far corners of the *Pale*, made Domsky a magnet for advanced Jewish students. Reb Gershon sent him a special invitation for Itzhak's birthday. He declined because of illness in the family. He did, however, send a congratulatory note, ending it with a line that pleased Itzhak no end: "Itzhak is a smart boy. One day I shall welcome him as my student at the *yeshiva*."

After Bella blessed and lit the *Shabbat* candles, Reb Gershon turned to Itzhak, looked at him with a loving expression and asked, "Itzhak, will you please recite the blessing for the *Shabbat*?"

The boy responded eagerly, singing in a euphonious voice.

"The sixth day: And the heavens and the earth and all their hosts were completed. And God finished by the seventh day His work, which He had done, and He rested on the seventh day from all His work, which He had done. And God blessed the seventh day and made it holy, for on it He rested from all His work, which God created to function..."

The boy closed his eyes. His voice was intense, full of reverence. He came to the last sentences with a louder, more robust sound.

"...You have chosen us and sanctified us from among all the nations, and with love and goodwill gave us Your holy *Shabbat* as a heritage. Blessed are You Lord, who sanctifies the *Shabbat*."

Reb Gershon looked at his son and his heart filled with joy. Itzhak was the brightest child in Gordov. He shared his father's love for Hebrew. He was an insatiable reader of Hebrew literature and poetry. While Reb Gershon was listening to the prayer that resonated above the underlying hum, his thoughts floated freely around the room. *I hope this boy will grow up as a good Jew who thinks and acts for the advancement of his people.*

After everyone said Amen, Reb Gershon took a sip of wine, cut and distributed the *challah* (traditional bread), and invited everyone to enjoy dinner.

The house resounded with merriment. Clinks and clangs filled the air as everyone sipped Bella's delicious chicken soup with *Matzah* balls. In between courses, they sang and talked, and even danced around the table. When Bella headed to the kitchen to bring out her famous dessert, Reb Gershon interrupted her. "Not now, Mother. I want to tell everyone the story of the Hacohen family. Then we shall eat your delicious dessert, dance, and sing more *Shabbat* songs."

Silence fell upon the room.

After she returned to her chair, Reb Gershon began to speak. "My grandfather told me this story and vowed that his grandfather told it to him." He paused to collect his thoughts. "For a fleeting human moment, while Europe was engulfed in the barbaric darkness of the Middle Ages, Jewish life thrived in the Islamic world, especially in Spain, where Jews enjoyed an unparalleled freedom. They basked in the glory of emancipation and erudition as they rose to the pinnacles of power and prestige. Medicine, commerce, and sciences were just a few of the subjects in which they excelled.

But, a brief historical moment later ushered in the Christian world. Islam was being pushed out of Spain and the horrors of the Inquisition permeated the land. With it came the final blow to an unprecedented Jewish golden age."

Itzhak was perplexed. He looked around and noticed puzzled expressions everywhere. *Why is father talking about history rather than the Bible and the sages?*

Reb Gershon immediately detected the confusion. "There is a purpose to my story," he said and without further explanations, continued.

"My ancestor, Reb Moshe Hacohen, lived in the eye of the storm. Ignoring the struggle around him, he expanded his business and provided excellent service to the community and beyond. Prosperous, well-liked by his neighbors and clients, he ruled over a large empire of garment production in Toledo. Four of his children were boys ranging in age from twelve to eighteen. All were well-educated. Saadia, the youngest, displayed a sharp mind and a keen interest in all subjects of Jewish religion. He was the only one to devote his life to study at the local *yeshiva*. Everyone adored him and called him *gaon*.

"The transition from Muslim to Christian rule was hard. In spite of the rapid deterioration of conditions in the Jewish community, Reb Moshe maintained a cordial relationship with the various members of the church. They liked his work and consistently purchased their garments from him. Business was booming. On one occasion, a few weeks before the La Guardia trial, Torquemada, the Grand Inquisitor, visited his shop, to purchase his most regal robe.

"Ah, yes, the trial. For days, it was the only topic of conversation after the evening prayers. A few weeks earlier, the Inquisition charged seven people, two Jews and five *Marranos* (Jews who converted to Christianity under the pressure of the inquisition, but secretly remained faithful to Judaism) with a horrid crime of *blood libel*. People said that those seven abducted a little Christian boy in the town of Laguardia, killed him and used his heart, some say his blood, for a nefarious anti-Christian sorcery act.

"Saadia thought that the allegation was stupid. He reminded his father that Jews did not use any blood in their rituals! Even animal sacrifice was prohibited. He quoted the prophet Hosea who proclaimed, 'For I desire mercy, and not sacrifice, and the knowledge of God rather than burnt-offerings.' Besides, Saadia added, the rabbis, after the destruction of the Second Temple, nullified sacrifices and replaced them with prayers.

"Reb Moshe agreed. But he told his son that Hosea did not prevent the Inquisition from alleging that the seven committed *blood libel*."

Rachel hesitated a moment before interrupting her father. "Father, today is Itzhak's birthday. We should be dancing and singing. Why are you talking about Spain?"

"We are because it is important. It is our history, a part of our soul!" He smiled at Rachel and continued.

"A great calamity was threatening the entire congregation. Fear seeped into the remotest communities. One Friday in October 1491, a few weeks after the trial began as Jewish life throughout Spain continued to deteriorate, the Jewish notables of Toledo assembled at Reb Moshe's house. The next day Saadia would be thirteen, a special day on the Jewish calendar throughout the ages. At thirteen a Jewish boy publicly reads the *Torah* and becomes a full member of the community.

"In the presence of the tensed guests, Reb Moshe presented his son at a sumptuous *Shabbat* dinner party. They ate and drank, sang and danced, pushing aside all the hardship that flooded their life. Much as we do at home some four hundred years later," said Reb Gershon.

After a short sip of wine, he continued.

"Just before the dessert, Reb Moshe called for quiet and asked Saadia to talk to his guests about that week's *Torah* reading.

"The boy, seated at the head of the table, rose slowly and looked at the elders. He was cognizant of the misery and fear that swept through his community, gripping everyone with anxiety, carrying on its dark wings the seeds of social turmoil with potentially devastating effects. He was convinced that they were pursuing a misguided faith and was determined to share his thoughts. He spoke. Hesitantly, at first, but quickly regained his confidence. He spoke about the story of Cain and Abel, which was his Bible reading. After he alluded to the unfolding menace, he quoted Bereshit, (Genesis) 4:10, 'The voice of your brother`s blood is crying out to me from the land.' He asked a rhetorical question: where was God during the clash between the brothers? He replied with a parable that Rabbi Shimon Ben Yochai told about the conflict. 'Once two athletes were wrestling before the king. If the king wanted, they could be separated; but he did not intervene. One overcame the other and killed him. The loser cried as he died, "Who will get justice for me from the king?' Or, in the Bible's words, 'the voice of your brother`s blood is crying out to me from the land.'

"Saadia insisted that Rabbi Ben Yochai raised a very important question, namely, who was to blame for the murder? God was the king in his parable. The dying wrestler, Abel, knew that the king was to blame for his murder for he had the ability to stop the fight and prevent the slaughter. But he did not. Did Ben Yochai suggest that God was to blame for the murder of Abel?

"Everyone was stunned. They all understood the parable. It seemed that the boy was blaming God for their predicament."

Itzhak, who was listening assiduously, protested silently. *Ben Yochai was wrong! God was not responsible for what had happened in Spain nor is he responsible for our predicament in the Diaspora!* Then doubts swept his mind. *But if God was blameless, whose fault was it? Is it?*

"Saadia had more to say. He quoted Genesis 4:9 'And the LORD said unto Cain: Where is Abel thy brother? And he said: I know not; am I my brother's keeper?' Saadia explained Cain's reply by using a parable told by another sage: 'I, your God, watch over all of creation and you are blaming me? This is like a thief who steals things at night and gets away with it. In the morning the watchman grabs him and says, why did you steal those things? The thief replied, I am a thief; I have not been remiss in doing my trade, but you are a guard. Why did you fail in your duties?'

"Saadia said that the second sage dismissed Cain's argument that God was the watchman and therefore He was responsible for the murder. The sage suggested that putting the blame on God was to abdicate the idea of man's responsibility for his actions. God asked Cain in an accusatory tone: 'What have you done?' Then He put the blame squarely in Cain's hands. He, Cain, had a responsibility to act in a moral way. And if he did not, that was not God's fault.

"Saadia paused. He looked at the astonished elders and added that he believed their faith was misguided. Cain was the Inquisitor! He was evil. He made the choice to be evil. God wanted them to act, to assume responsibility for their future, to leave the inhospitable land and neither wait for Him to act nor judge His inaction.

"Saadia sat down. There was total silence in the room. They looked at one another in disbelief."

Itzhak was no longer listening. He was stunned and confused. *On a misery scale*, he thought, *the status of the Jews in the Pale is similar to their life under the Inquisition; we are hated guests.* Conflicting thoughts buzzed through his mind. *I have always believed that our life is in the hands of God; if we follow his path we will be rewarded. But maybe the path we have been following for two thousand years is the wrong path? Maybe Saadia was right. They tell me that the Messiah will extricate us from this evil land. But we have been waiting for him in vain, for two thousand years. Waiting for the Messiah is a passive way not God's way. Acting actively is God's way.* He thought about the bullies of Gordov. *Surely God will not send an angel to save me from their bullying. Running away from them is cowardly. Did God want David to run away from Goliath? What shall I do? Perhaps God wants his people to assume responsibility for their life! Perhaps He wants me to be responsible for my own fate! Yes. I was wrong! God expects me to defend myself against the bullies, to assume responsibility for my own destiny. Yes! That is exactly what I must do.*

Reb Gershon noticed Itzhak's expression but decided to continue his tale, making a mental note to talk to him later, in private. "No one heeded Saadia's advice," he continued. "They did not understand the meaning of personal responsibility. 'It is all in the hands of God,' they would say and go about the business of existence. Everyone was hopeful that life would get better. Months passed. When the trial ended the Inquisition proclaimed the verdict throughout the land: death by fire. The seven were burned alive. Anti-Jewish riots swept the country.

"A few months later, The Monarch of Spain brought the terror campaign of the Inquisition to its most sinister end. She issued the infamous Alhambra Decree in which she declared her resolve to order all the Jews to depart and never return. Of course, they were given a way to circumvent the order. Convert to Christianity and stay, otherwise leave, and leave all of your property for the Queen. Some did convert but most left.

"My ancestors, with meager belongings, began a long and painful exodus from Spain. Eventually, one of my ancestors arrived in Moscow, where he established a modest garment business. Years passed in moderate peace. The business grew and provided his family with a comfortable living. Then Catherine The Great rose to the throne. Once again whispers and false allegations simmered. The Jews were the targets of vicious lies. '*They are the enemies of Christ. They spread evil among the people,*' cried the Priests. *'Get them out of town.'* The banners of the local papers proclaimed daily the conspiracy of the Jews to dominate the economy. *They must go,* said the merchants of Moscow.

"Virulent words spread throughout the land, quietly at first but eventually reached the loudest pitch. Catherine the Great established the *Pale of Settlement* and ordered the Jews to leave their dwelling and migrate to the *Pale.* Once again, thousands of miles away from the Spanish expulsion order, Jews were compelled to march to a new home.

"She imposed discriminatory rules over the Jews in the *Pale* that brought a quick decline in the economic and psychological well-being of the Jewish population. Darkness fell upon my people.

"That was the time that my Grandfather's great, great grandfather Reb Yossel Hacohen settled in Gordov, where I was born." He took a sip of wine. It was time for dessert but no one savored it. No one was in a mood to dance and sing. They ate hastily and hurried home.

That night Itzhak tossed and turned in his bed, arguing with himself about which path was the right one to follow. He fell asleep, dreaming about personal responsibility and the challenges that God would present to test his resolve.

***

Everyone was up in time for the Saturday Morning Prayer. After breakfast, they strolled in their finest toward the synagogue. The air was still. The beloved *Shabbat* the Queen enveloped them with tranquility. Reb Gershon and Itzhak walked a few steps ahead discussing the story of Saadia. Reb Gershon said, "My son, it is time for our people to take their destiny in their hands and wait no more. It is time to be free in our forefathers' land. Saadia was talking to us. Today, his voice resonates the truth even though it emanates from faraway Spain. That is the will of God. We must leave the *Pale.*"

"You have read my mind, Father," replied the boy.

Suddenly, the doctor emerged from the synagogue. He moved aimlessly, crying to heaven. His voice pierced the calm air, interrupting the majesty of *Shabbat* and the conversation between father and son. "Oh God, King of the universe," hollered the doctor, "redeem us from the devastation of the Diaspora."

Reb Gershon stopped abruptly and asked him, "Dear doctor, are your wife and children, may they live to a ripe old age, in good health?"

"Yes, thank God, they are. But we have horrific news from Domsky. Earlier this morning I found Reb Mendel's son in the synagogue. He was alone praying intensely, calling for God's help. He mumbled about the police arresting his father. He did not know why. They cursed Reb Mendel for committing horrific deeds."

Other worshipers followed the doctor to the synagogue and heard new versions of the story. Ugly rumors came and faded away to make room for new ones. "There is talk of a pogrom," yelled one panicked voice.

"Thank God the police warned Reb Mendel," rejoiced another.

"The police came to conscript Reb Mendel's son. Our children are next," lamented a third.

A dark cloud descended on the little synagogue at Gordov. *Shabbat* lost its luster. Everyone wondered if the rumors foretold a calamitous future. They tried to sift through the story in order to understand what really happened in Domsky, but all their efforts were for naught.

2 HATED GUESTS

"The anti-Jewish riots in Kishinev, Bessarabia, are worse than the censor will permit us to publish. There was a well laid-out plan for the general massacre of Jews on the day following the Russian Easter. Priests led the mob and the general cry, "Kill the Jews," was taken up all over the city. The Jews were taken wholly unaware and were slaughtered like sheep. The dead number 120 and the injured about 500. The scenes of horror attending this massacre are beyond description. Babes were literally torn to pieces by the frenzied and bloodthirsty mob. The local police made no attempt to check the reign of terror. At sunset the streets were piled with corpses and wounded. Those who could make their escape fled in terror, and the city is now practically deserted of Jews."

Jewish Massacre Denounced, New York Times, April 28, 1903, p. 6.

"Heaven, ask mercy for me!
If there is a God in You and He, a path in You
And I have not found it –
Then You pray for me."

Bialik, On The Slaughter, 1903 (after Kishinev Pogrom).

On the same Friday, in Domsky, the police barged into Reb Mendel's house. Terrified guests and family watched helplessly as the police hauled him from his seat. At the door, the chief of police barked at the people, "Filthy *Yid*. Even Christ will not forgive the rabbi's evil deeds."

His frantic wife clutched the chief's coat, begging for an explanation. Her anxious voice rose into the heavens, "Why? Why? Dear God, protect my Rebbe."

The chief pulled away, dragging the woman through the open door, causing her to lose her grip and fall to the ground. Her screams pierced the calm night. The presence of two officers of the Tsar added a great deal of fear. One of them bellowed at her, "Pig, *Yid*, you will all pay for this crime."

Panic engulfed the Jewish quarter of Domsky. *Erev Shabbat* festivity came to an abrupt and horrifying end. People rushed into the street in their finest, asking:

"What happened?"

"Who was screaming so desperately?"

"Who disturbed God's rest?"

"The Rebbe was taken away," shouted a guest at the Rebbe's home.

"Why?"

"Was he hurt?"

People roamed the dark street searching for answers but found none. Finally a neighbor of Reb Mendel shouted, "It was the Rebbe's wife whose scream disturbed God's rest."

"To the synagogue!" commanded someone.

They rushed to the synagogue. In the confusion, women entered the men's section and took their seat in a forbidden place. A horrified man shouted, "To the women's section. Go!"

One of the elders tried to calm the tumultuous gathering."Quiet! Quiet, in God's name, quiet."

The nervousness subsided slowly to reach a tense silence.

"We must pray for the safety of the Rebbe," said the elder.

Murmurs filled the hall. They prayed without a leader. Each person made his own appeal to God. After a few intense minutes, the elder said, "Someone should go to Gordov and alert them."

"It is forbidden to travel on *Shabbat*," protested a man who stood at the center of the synagogue shaking profusely.

"But it is written that a threat to body and soul supersedes the law of *Shabbat*. I shall go now," said the Rebbe's eldest son. He left promptly for the trip. He reached Gordov just as the first worshippers assembled for the *Shabbat* morning prayer.

At the same time the elders of Domsky went to the police. The chief met them at the door. His hateful look meant trouble. He did not wait for their questions. Instead, he yelled in an accusatory voice, "Your Rebbe stabbed and killed Yavgeny Lombrowsky. We found the boy in a cave. There was no blood left in his veins. *Yid* pigs use the blood of Christian boys for Passover ritual!" Then he slammed the door in their faces.

The news of the blood libel accusation quickly traveled through town. People in Domsky braced for a major catastrophe.

In Gordov, the troubling information shook the community. Reb Mendel's son asked Reb Hillel—the rabbi of Gordov—to come to Domsky and help calm the congregation before Passover.

Later that afternoon, another messenger from Domsky arrived to relay the latest details about the arrest of Reb Mendel. Tension and fear replaced the majesty of *Shabbat*.

Itzhak reacted indignantly to the devastating news. *Again,* he thought, *we face what Saadia has faced in Spain. People still use this horrid allegation to bring pain and suffering on their Jewish neighbors. Those who propagate such nonsense must have a burning hate in their soul. They should all rot in hell. One day I shall escape this madness. I shall leave this accursed country. Saadia's advice to the people of Toledo was right.*

On Sunday morning, Reb Hillel, his wife, two of his oldest children, one of his students, and his helper, Itzhak, set out to spend a few days in Domsky. Their plan was simple: ensure that the synagogue was functioning as usual, and to assist Reb Mendel's wife in managing her household affairs

Four days later, the two Tsar officers who helped stoke the charges left Domsky on their way to Kishinev. After an intense search for evidence, a motive, and a suspect, the police could find nothing to incriminate Reb Mendel in the murder of Yavgeny. They released him. An uneasy quiet replaced the initial confusion and fear.

Early Thursday morning, Reb Hillel and his group left Domsky to return home. On the road, their progress was slow but steady. The cart squeaked and shook monotonously. Soon the children fell asleep and, moments later, the adults succumbed to the boredom of the ride. The sound of snoring rose to the air. Even the driver nodded. For a split second, he fell asleep as the wagon veered slightly off the road and the right wheel descended into a trench, hitting a large stone and breaking in two. The jolt of the collision woke everyone.

The driver was angry. He walked around the wagon, cursing, but the wheel remained broken in two.

"Sit under tree," he told Reb Hillel "I replace the wheel."

Hours passed. The sun was already beyond its midpoint, racing westward. Night was fast approaching. Reb Hillel felt an imminent danger from being on the road. But he was unable to avert his discomfort short of praying for help. He thought God had heard his prayers when an empty cart approached.

He asked the driver to take them to Gordov, but the driver refused. "I take you to the inn," he said.

"Thank you," said Reb Hillel. *I pray to God that this man heard nothing of the troubles in Domsky,* he thought. *In the inn, we can wait for our transport until tomorrow and be home before Shabbat.* They transferred their belongings. "We shall wait for you at the inn," he told his driver as the new cart began to move to the relative safety of the inn.

Itzhak felt good about going to the inn. He knew the innkeeper, a gentle and a kind man, who always welcomed the Jews. A few months earlier, Itzhak and his father had arrived late on Friday, too late to continue their journey to Gordov. The innkeeper sent his wife to the market to buy fruits and vegetables for them as he knew that their Bible prohibited certain foods.

***

Far to the west of Domsky, beyond the mountains, the sun raced toward the western horizon as if wanting to escape the pain and suffering of the *Pale*. The receding sunlight collided with the poplar trees along the road, casting long shadows that dissected the parched land with symmetrical black lines and gave the scene an eerie air. A lone carriage raced on the empty road toward the inn. The passengers paid no attention to the interplay between sun and trees. The passengers, two officers of the Tsar's army who supervised the arrest of Rabbi Mendel, were oblivious to the contrast of colors visible from the window. With a local farm girl, who joined them at Domsky, they engaged in the triple pleasure of wine, women and song. Merriment alone occupied them, not the imprint of a beautiful sunset or the havoc they had left behind. Liquor flowed like water, hands intermingled with hands, flesh with flesh.

Thick, menacing clouds crept from the eastern horizon. "Could rain be on its way?" grumbled the driver. He cursed the two horses in a vain attempt to push them forward at a quicker pace. He was desperate to reach the inn before nightfall. "Faster, you lazy beasts!" he screamed at them, cracking his whip. But they refused to speed up.

Meanwhile, Reb Hillel and his entourage arrived at the inn. The innkeeper came out to welcome him like an old friend. "You are lucky, Reb Hillel" he said. "I have three rooms for you and your family."

"God bless you," said Reb Hillel. He instructed his wife, "We shall rest here until tomorrow. Let's have dinner." She promptly began preparations for the meal at the far corner of the dining hall. Reb Hillel went upstairs to inspect the rooms. He took the largest room overlooking the creek for himself and his wife. The children stayed in an adjacent room. The student and Itzhak shared a smaller room at the end of the corridor.

The skies were starless. A lone lamp that dangled precariously at the right side of the doorway cast a dim light over the yard. The large courtyard was dark and deserted.

The sound of an arriving carriage alerted the innkeeper. He came out to greet the arriving guests with an apology. "Sorry," he said to the driver at the gate, unable to see inside the carriage. "The inn is full. You can stay at the servants' quarters." He turned and rushed toward the inn to escape the blustery wind.

The officers, rowdy and inattentive, heard nothing of the bad news. They did, however, recognize that the carriage had come to an abrupt stop.

"Move the carriage forward, idiot!" shouted the senior officer. "We must get to the inn before nightfall." The driver, bewildered and somewhat frightened, approached the carriage door, knocked, and waited for the reply.

"What now, pig?" shouted the younger officer trying to stay on par with his elder.

"We are at the inn, your highness," answered the driver, keeping a safe distance from the officers' hands. "The inn is full. Only the servants' quarters are available," he added meekly.

Instantly, the weight of the news sank in. The senior officer pushed the local farm girl away and disentangled himself from the body mass. Somewhat shaken, he kicked the door and presented himself before the frightened driver. The innkeeper, who was midway between the carriage and the inn's door, heard the commotion and turned around.

"What the fuck is the matter with this pigsty?" shouted the senior officer. "We are officers of the Tsar's police!" he belched and then yelled at the innkeeper whom he could not see. "Just in case you are blind, you fucking imbecile."

The innkeeper froze. "Yes, your highness," he said. But before he had a chance to explain his predicament, the officer shot his pistol into the air and shouted, "Get us a room, you son of a bitch. If there are any *Yid* pigs in this inn, throw them out. Their room is the one I want."

Servants and guests huddled at the door, anxious to follow the unfolding encounter.

"Right away," answered the alarmed innkeeper. He was overcome with fear for Reb Hillel's well-being and his own. "I'll tell the Jews to leave one room at once." He turned and walked hastily to the door.

"Stop! You bastard!" screamed the officer. "Who is the *Yid* pig that stays here?"

"The Rebbe of Gordov and his family," replied the frightened innkeeper.

"Fuck," said the senior officer. "Throw the bastards, all of them, out to the pigs. Human pigs belong with pigs. Then bring us food and clean their rooms."

Reb Hillel and his entourage, fearing for their safety, withdrew to the far corner of the dining room. Shaking and sweating with fear, they huddled together. Hands locked with hands they fell on their knees. Voices whispering an urgent prayer rose to the heavens. "The Lord is my light and my salvation." Reb Hillel's voice rose above the rest, muted but intense. "Whom shall I fear? The Lord is the strength of my life. Whom shall I dread?" Everyone prayed in his own rhythm as the sound of their affirmation rose through the air and left the inn at the top of the hill on its way to the heavens.

Itzhak's voice rushed ahead of the others. Loud and with a sweet soprano sound he cried to heaven: "O you gates: open wide you ancient doors! Have mercy on us O glorious king." The others, shaking involuntarily, continued with unsteady voices: "When evildoers draw near to devour me, when foes threaten, they stumble and fall."

Their words floated in the stifling air of the entrance hall. Chaotic words. Unsynchronized. Intense. "Though armies be arrayed against me, I have no fear. Though wars threaten, I remain steadfast in my faith," wept the student. Occasional cries interrupted the prayer. Panicked children squeezed their bodies to their mother's. The little one took refuge behind her apron. "O Lord, hear my voice when I call," exclaimed Itzhak, his voice growing steady, reassured, composed. "Be gracious and answer me. It is you that I seek, says my heart. It is your presence that I crave."

"Shut up, you pigs," screamed the young officer.

The story of Saadia Hacohen flashed in Itzhak's mind. He heard a command vibrating in his inner ear: *God expects us to assume responsibility*. A mighty, unforeseen hand grabbed his shoulder and lifted him off the ground. He was small and thin and no match for the young officer. Nevertheless he stood before him proud and self-assured. The prayers vanished from his lips. His little cheeks filled with blood and turned crimson red. His eyes fired anger at the officer, and his voice rose above the heartbreaking prayer.

"You shut up, pig," he yelled at the young officer, who was taken aback. Never before had a little *Yid* boy dared to challenge him, an officer of the Tsar. Reb Hillel and his wife looked at each other, astounded, and then they looked at the thin young boy, standing barely a foot away from the officer. It was as if David had come from the depth of history to challenge a new Goliath, ready for the fight of his life. Reb Hillel's wife cried out with anguish "Come here, Itzhak. Join our prayer, child."

Disregarding his immediate surroundings, the boy did not heed her plea. Instead, he continued in a soprano voice, "We have done nothing to harm you, so leave us alone."

The young officer regained his focus and smacked the boy's face so hard that the boy lost his balance and fell to the floor. Overcome with rage, the officer rushed after the falling boy and kicked him toward the praying group. "Don't ever speak to a Tsar officer, you son of a bitch. Thank your false God that I did not kill you for your disrespect," he shouted, after the bleeding body that came to rest near Reb Hillel.

Reb Hillel's wife held Itzhak in her arms, rocking to and fro as if trying to console the boy, as the rest of the group frantically rejoined in prayer. "Who is the glorious king? The Lord of hosts: He is the Glorious king," they called out in a unified sonorous voice, drowning the vulgarity from the other side of the dining hall. The officers, laughing in a drunken stupor, left the huddled Jews to their prayers.

The stable boy attended to the horses. The servants unpacked the officers' luggage while the senior officer barked a barrage of orders to the servants and slurs against the huddling Jews. He belched and spat as he commanded the servant to carry his luggage to the rabbi's vacated room. "But make sure you scrub the floor and clean the air. The smell of a *Yid* makes me sick," he said.

Servants moved in all directions. Light was brought out to help the newcomers find their way to the table. The driver rushed ahead of his passengers. He stood near the table with his head slightly down and said, "Sit, your highness. I go to kitchen, I bring food."

The officers moved rapidly toward the table. They looked like shadows of themselves unshaven and dirty. Food stuck to their gray beards. The buttons of the senior officer's shirt had been torn. The shirt hung over the back of his trousers as he staggered forward, leaving in his path a trail of unpleasant odors. The younger officer, looking just as disheveled as his senior, staggered after him. Gay but unsure of his footing, he moved a step forward and two sideways, burping and farting. He glanced menacingly at the frightened group by the wall and walked right into their center. Not to be outdone by his elder, he kicked and cursed. "Move away, you dirty pigs. Clear the ground so that my shoes will not be soiled from your diseased presence."

They rolled on the floor, never interrupting their prayers. "Deceivers have risen against me, men who breathe out violence. Abandon me not to the will of my foes."

Itzhak looked at his disgraced rebbe. A growing sense of shame bolstered his resolve. He grabbed the junior officer's shirt, trying in vain to halt his motion. "The room is ours. *You* go and sleep with the pigs," he yelled just before he was thrown against the wall. His struggle was over but his determination to replace prayer with action grew stronger. *That is God's will,* he told himself.

"Go out to the stable, quickly," the frightened innkeeper ordered the rebbe's group. To his servants, he said, "Get the room ready for our honored guests."

Food was delivered to the soldiers' table. They ate hurriedly, slurping the soup, shoving potatoes into their mouths as if they were rushing to fill a sack with looted gold. A belch or two added a new dynamic to the drunkards' dinner.

When they had their fill, the senior officer snapped his fingers at the innkeeper, who stood ready to fulfill any of the officer's demands. "Bring us more vodka," he ordered. Then he called the farm girl who had ridden with them to the inn. "Ludi, or whatever they call you, come here." The memory of the gold coins he'd given her earlier made her act promptly.

"Go get your friend for my young officer here," he ordered. She left to look for her friend, the laundry maid.

The merry officers burst into song, missing the pitch as their voices, corrupted by liquor and frequent hiccups, attempted the patriotic lyrics.

Ludi returned with Olga, her young friend, and fell directly into the senior officer's arms. He reached for his pocket and threw two gold coins on the table. His voice stammered, "H-here, one for you and one for y-your friend." She collected the coins and hid them in her bosom. She covered the officer's face with kisses and motioned to her friend to be nice to the younger officer.

The younger man shoved the table away with his boot and tried to stand. He swayed like a tree before an approaching storm. Olga came to his rescue before he could fall. She picked up the bottle and put his hand around her shoulder in an effort to move him forward. But she, too, was slightly drunk. Both staggered as they tried to reach his room. The innkeeper came from behind and gently guided them forward.

"G-get your f-f-filthy hands off me!"

The senior officer, a bit steadier than his inexperienced junior, came to his aid. Finally, the four staggered into their room. They collapsed on the bed, passing the bottle and pouring drink into the women's mouths.

Olga, giggling nonstop, pushed the young officer off her. He was relentless and tore at her clothes. The four mingled in a violent orgy. The younger officer, overcome by lust, attempted to silence the giggling girl. He covered her mouth with his hand. With his other hand, he grabbed her with all his might and pulled her toward him. She gasped for air. Her eyes filled with blood, but he saw none of that. He kept pulling her toward his waiting body and crushed her underneath his weighty frame. Her shaking stopped and she lay motionless under him. When he was satisfied, he rolled over and soon fell to snoring. Ludi and her companion kept on rolling and drinking. Eventually, they, too, fell into a deep sleep.

Early morning on Friday, menacing clouds hung overhead. The driver of Reb Hillel's cart was waiting in the yard. Everyone in Reb Hillel's entourage was eager to escape another encounter with the two officers. The innkeeper did all he could to assist them.

"A big storm is coming," he said, attempting to persuade them to wait. But the coming *Shabbat* added urgency to their haste. When they insisted on leaving, he wished them well and followed their repaired carriage to the gate of the inn.

In the afternoon, clouds collided in a violent storm. The officers woke to exploding thunder. In the receding rays of the setting sun, they could see their surroundings. The room was a mess. Clothes were strewn everywhere, empty bottles littered the floor, and a young girl lay still on the bed beside them When the young officer realized that only three of them were up and about, he shook the girl, gently at first. Panic gripped him when she did not move. His shakes grew more and more violent. She remained motionless. He bent over her heart but heard no beat. "She is dead," he said. "What should we do?"

Ludi fell to the floor screaming in despair. The senior officer seized her and covered her mouth in the middle of a scream. "Be quiet, you bitch, or you will end up just as cold as she is."

Ludi trembled wildly, gasping for air. He locked her between his arms, pressing her frame. She understood the message and did her best to regain control. Still holding Ludi in his arms, the senior officer barked at his companion, "Throw the body out. The river will take care of it."

The younger officer, visibly shocked, opened the window. A ferocious storm raged outside. He lifted Olga's cold body and pushed it through the window. It tumbled over the cliff and into the raging river below.

A chorus of thunder rumbled from the dark skies. The first rain of the season swept the region with the fury of hell. No one wanted to leave for fear of being swept away in the flooding. The storm hung relentlessly over the inn for the rest of the Friday night through late Saturday night.

The officers ordered their food in. They spent Saturday eating and drinking behind closed doors. Early Sunday morning, they ordered their driver to prepare to leave at once. "We cannot wait here any longer," explained the senior officer to the astonished innkeeper. "State business requires us to be in Kishinev on Easter Sunday."

"But, your highness," pleaded the innkeeper, who was fearful for his family should any harm befall the two officers. "The Dniester will be flooded. You won't be able to cross. Stay here for safety." But they would not listen. The two, accompanied by Ludi, jumped into the passenger cabin. The carriage sped away.

***

Mayakovskogo Street in Gordov was like a mighty river. Debris brought in by the flood lay everywhere. Later on Easter Sunday morning, the rain stopped. Warm sun lit up the clear blue skies. A few people chose to skip the church service and headed to the river to fish for their family dinner, but most of Gordov's Christians emerged from their homes and rushed to church.

After the service, they flocked to the tavern. Word got out at church that a stranger had come to town before the storm, bringing news from Kishinev. By noon the tavern was overflowing with people. Everyone was anxious to hear what the new arrival had to say. A tall, handsome man with a well-groomed royal beard and a mustache, which gave him a distinctive look, especially in the company of the local farmers, sat alone at a corner table. People pushed to get a closer glimpse at him. At last he stood up.

He was impeccably dressed. A beautiful gold chain adorned his left pocket. He pulled it out and glanced at his gold watch. "Ivan," he looked at the bartender. "Ivan," he repeated, even though he did not know his real name. "Give the good people of Gordov some vodka. I want to celebrate Easter Sunday and the news I bring them from the city."

He climbed upon his chair and raised his hands to signal quiet. "Listen to what our paper says," he said, and then repeated his invitation to ensure total attention. He unfolded a copy of *The Bessarabian* and began to read: "*Yids* are corrupting the country folks. They spread evil stories about our savior because they want all Christians to abandon the church. *Yids* want to control you, good people."

The door swung violently, and two officers of the Tsar's army entered. People moved to make room for the pair. They looked as if they had just ascended from hell: disheveled and messily dressed, their pants partially buttoned, their beards soiled, and hair uncombed. They ordered vodka and moved toward a table in the corner of the tavern. Those who occupied the table quickly moved away.

"Please sit, your honors," they said. The pair sat and listened to the man reading the latest articles from *The Bessarabian.*

"They also compete unfairly with our wine merchants. They invented a secret way to make wine better with fewer grapes, and now they begin to sell cheaply causing the local merchants and our farmers staggering losses. That is part of their conspiracy to control the wine business in the country. Only ten days ago, a child disappeared at Domsky. Where did he go? Our paper knows from good sources that the Jews killed him. They used his blood for the Passover holiday. Let me assure you," said the newspaper man, "that we at *The Bessarabian* believe that our government must act urgently to save our children, our farmers, and our merchants from those conniving *Yids*."

Someone shouted, "Even here in Gordov the *Yids* spread evil thoughts. They whisper to our children that our Lord Jesus Christ was not the son of God. God had no children, they tell them."

The handsome man ignored him. He continued to read. When he finished, the senior officer rose and said, "Good people of Gordov. Let me tell you in confidence that your government is working to solve the hideous crime that occurred recently, in Domsky. It was reported that the boy Yavgeny last visited the rabbi's house. He was helping his mother, who did the laundry for the rabbi. Some informants told the authority that they saw the boy entering the rabbi's house, delivering clean clothes.

One witness told the police that everyone knew that *Yids* need the blood of a young Christian for their holiday's rituals. He added that he was sure the boy never came out of the rabbi's house." Then he ordered the bartender, "Fill up the cups of all the good people of Gordov!"

The bartender was happy to comply. "God save the Tsar!" he cried.

"Amen," the crowd answered, enjoying their free vodka.

The young officer rose and said, "Good people of Gordov, during our voyage here we have stopped at the inn. There we heard that a girl disappeared. We saw her visit the rabbi of Gordov. I would not be surprised if he and his family are responsible for the disappearance of that girl. You know today is Passover."

A few sober men laughed at the hint but said nothing. Many others grumbled or shouted to demonstrate their displeasure, "Revenge! Get the rabbi."

The young officer, pleased with the reaction, continued, "We know from our investigation at Domsky that the *Yids* can be very conniving. They act innocently, but their evil heart rejoices in misleading the investigators. We have seen that in other places, too. What I am telling you is that we must be thorough in the investigation of the disappearance of that girl. You must report to us any suspicious action or—"

The door was thrown open with great force, bumping someone's back. A fisherman stood bewildered at the doorsill, looking pale and terrified as if he had just met the ghost of a hated relative. His mouth opened but not a sound was heard.

"Have some vodka, man, then tell us what has frightened you so," said the fellow who stopped the door with his back. He handed the confused man a glass of vodka. The man emptied it in one gulp, wiped his lips with his sleeve and entered the tavern. "I saw it. I swear on my... my grandmother's grave. I... I saw it in in the water," he stammered.

"Saw what?" shouted the senior officer.

"I was there. Another vodka," he demanded. That one went down as quickly as the first. "There were no fish. The water was fast and by the bend, near the big tree where I stood, I saw a body pressed against the tree." A rumble swept through the tavern.

"Out of the way!" commanded the senior officer. "This is a matter for the investigating authorities. Let's go. Show us where you found the body." He moved forward through the crowded room with the younger officer at his heels. People at the back pushed toward the door. A mass of drunkards made its way to the narrow opening following the two officers, who grabbed the fisherman and dragged him outside. "Go!" barked the senior officer. "To the body."

In the ensuing pandemonium someone left unnoticed and ran to the Jewish quarter. He made the distance between the tavern and Reb Hillel's house in such a short time that it left him breathless in front of the gate. He rushed in and banged on the door.

The alarmed rebbe rushed to the door. Before the rebbe could ask him what had happened, the man burst into an account of events in the tavern. "Slow down, man. I cannot make sense of what you say. What body? What authorities? What are you trying to tell me?"

The man regained his composure and retold his story more slowly, adding, "No good will come of it. Be careful."

The disquieting news spread through the Jewish quarter. No one knew what to do, and so they gravitated toward the synagogue and began to pray. Only Itzhak did not pray. He thought about Saadia. He stood on his chair and shouted, "God wants us to defend ourselves against evil." No one listened. They continued to pray.

Meanwhile, at the river's bend, near the large tree, the officers discovered the body. "It's a state matter," declared the senior officer to the astonished local policeman who had been dispatched to the scene.

"This is the girl. She was with the *Yid* at the inn. Let's go to the *Yid* pig and arrest him so that we can interrogate him," commanded the young officer.

The agitated locals moved like a swarm of locusts. No one was bothered by the conclusion that had neither a beginning nor facts to support it. The word of the Tsar's officer was all that was needed to pronounce a guilty verdict, especially in light of the lengthy update they received earlier from Kishinev and Domsky. They raced to the east side, picking up sticks, stones, and any useful debris from the river's bank.

Disregarding the safety of the bridge, they stormed the Jewish quarter, smashing windows and breaking doors. Anyone who was in their way was shoved aside with brutal force. The sound of broken glass mingled with the tormented sound of the wounded. There was no place to hide. Women, infants, the old and the young were mown down by the swelling mob. Yesterday's neighbors tuned into vicious animals. The mob ransacked Jewish homes and took whatever valuables they could find. They attacked each other in the frenzy of looting. Everyone wanted a piece of the Jewish "riches."

They shouted, "Avenge the murdered girl! Death to the *Yids*! Christ killers! Child killers! Give us the killers! Give us the rabbi!" They swayed from side to side drunkenly.

The butcher pleaded for calm. "Remember, we are friends. We have lived in peace for all these years. You know that Jews do not use Christian blood or any blood for Passover."

But no one paid attention. The rising wave moved forward, propelled by the pressure of the surging mob. They were unstoppable. In their haste they pushed Reb Gershon, who fell to the ground and cut his head. The local police watched from the sidelines.

No member of the Jewish community offered resistance except Itzhak. He stood by his wounded father. He was livid at the frightened congregation, who had been led to the altar with no resistance. He moved away from his father and shouted at the mob, "We committed no harm! I was with the rabbi the whole time. He did not commit any crime. He is a holy man. We are forbidden to use blood of any kind. I saw this girl. She was with the officers of the Tsar."

He lifted a broken piece of wood and launched it at the crowd. Someone pushed him out of the way. So violent was the contact that Itzhak struck his head against the wall of a house and fell unconscious to the ground.

The assault continued unabated. Itzhak's attacker threw a torch into the broken window then rejoined the rampaging mob on its way to the synagogue. At the synagogue's door they repeated their demands for the rabbi. They threw stones, breaking the windows of most of the buildings in the square. Two men entered the synagogue and dragged the rabbi behind them.

The senior officer climbed the steps of the synagogue and shouted at the raging crowd, "Enough! We have the guilty man. The Tsar does not want lawless behavior. We shall deal with the rabbi. You go back home."

To reinforce his command, the local policemen rushed to the synagogue steps and echoed the senior officer's demand. "Go home, people. We have our prisoner. He will be put on trial."

As if to show everyone how serious he was, the senior officer pulled his pistol and fired into the air. That brought an immediate halt to the destruction. Most of the crowd turned and began a slow march home, but a few remained behind to assist the wounded. Itzhak regained his footing.

Then heaven opened its gates and drenched torturers and tortured alike. The deluge cooled overcharged tempers. Quiet reclaimed the street behind the retreating mob. The rain put out burning fires but was too late to save Reb Gershon's library.

The Hacohen family stood shell-shocked near their charred house. Reb Gershon moved to a door without walls. Dried blood covered his temple and sidelocks. Sadness forced tears out of his eyes and kept them flowing freely. He approached the burnt shelves and picked up a partially charred book. He held it gently in his hands. The author was Rabbi Alkalai. His book, *The Third Redemption*, was a present from his grandfather when he was thirteen. It was the precursor for his evolving thoughts about the Jewish nation.

Like Rabbi Alkalai and many after him, Reb Gershon became gradually convinced that the security of his people could only be achieved in an independent, free life, on their ancient land. At that moment he felt fully convinced that Rabbi Alkalai was right. He resolved to leave ignorance behind, to leave Gordov in search of redemption from the yoke of the Diaspora.

His hand caressed the shapeless cover as if caressing his own son's head. He paused for a silent moment. The image of the old cemetery filled the room. He closed his eyes. His father's tombstone floated in the air toward him. *Is that a protest? Is his father angry with him for leaving him behind? Once I leave, the fate of my father's grave, indeed the fate of the many generations of the Jews of Gordov, will be similar to the fate of the Jewish quarter. Will it survive the onslaught of the locals, who most likely will pillage the east side and reshape it in their own unsavory image?*

He recited the Mourner's Prayer, placed the volume on the floor, and withdrew from the burnt library and the books that were like old friends. They had shaped his beliefs and helped him instill the love of his people and their ancient language in his children. All the dead Jews he left behind would one day rejoice when they watched from heaven as his children marched to freedom with their oppressed people.

The Gordov police released the rabbi after Ludi testified and implicated the two officers. The two officers were far from the scene of the crime, on their way to Kishinev, where a most devastating crime, the Kishinev pogrom, was underway.

Kishinev forever altered the precarious sense of being of the Jewish masses in the *Pale*. Two days of unimaginable atrocities led to an uncoordinated mass exodus. Millions began the perilous march in search of freedom, civil rights, and redemption in the unfamiliar world beyond the *Pale*.

Once again, people without a home were on the move toward an uncertain future, opening a new chapter in the repeating story of "Hated Guests."

Gordov's Jewish quarter was empty. It looked like a ghost town, a shadow of its ancient self. Most of its residents left, scattered throughout the *Pale*, determined to reach the shore of a new Promised Land where they would no longer be hated and persecuted. Many embarked on the perilous journey to America.

The Hacohen family chose Odessa as an intermediate stop. A few Christian friends came to bid them farewell. Reb Gershon left the door to his house open, thinking that the house was exposed from the library side anyway so what purpose would be served if he closed the door. Then he and his family marched forward toward a new beginning.

3 BETWEEN HEAVEN AND HELL

"Zionism seeks to establish a home for the Jewish people in Eretz Israel secured under public law. The Congress contemplates the following means to the attainment of this end:

1. *The promotion by appropriate means of the settlement in Eretz-Israel of Jewish farmers, artisans, and manufacturers.*
2. *The organization and uniting of the whole of Jewry by means of appropriate institutions, both local and international, in accordance with the laws of each country.*
3. *The strengthening and fostering of Jewish national sentiment and national consciousness.*
4. *Preparatory steps toward obtaining the consent of governments, where necessary, in order to reach the goals of Zionism."*

The Basel Program, 1'st Zionist Congress 1897.

Itzhak, who had witnessed so much senseless cruelty, recalled Saadia's advice to the elders of Toledo. Right there, on the road to Odessa, a few days after Passover 1903, he repeated his vow never again to pray for his protection. He reaffirmed his decision to take responsibility for his own safety, to become the ruler of his own destiny. He paused to look at the only home he knew. Gordov was receding beneath the horizon. As it slipped away from his consciousness, a part of him crumbled, making room for the seed of personal responsibility to take roots. He turned back and strode energetically forward.

Fleeing Jews crowded the roads leading away from the *Pale.* They traveled by train, by carriage, in primitive farm carts and even on foot. The rich, the poor and those in between. The young and the old, singles and families, they choked the arteries of odious western Russia. The Southern route to Odessa was no exception.

For the multitude, irrespective of whether they were familiar with or had never heard of *Zionism*, the destination was America—the land of the free: a new Promised Land in which they hoped to live in peace and freedom from hate. Those who possessed the needed funds for the journey, would linger in Odessa for a few days, just enough time to secure a place on the next departing ship. Others looked at Odessa as a temporary shelter, a place to work and earn money before embarking on the journey to the unknown.

A small minority of the mass exodus, who were cognizant and adherents of *Zionism*, had an alternative destination: *Eretz Israel* (the Land of Israel). But few were willing to select it. Life in America seemed seductive, easier and more promising both economically and socially. It was a person-centric life where the act of making a living, pursuit of happiness and living freely was the central theme, the key for a comfortable existence. Whereas in *Eretz Israel*, life was cause-centric. The purpose of existence was to replace the old, derelict patterns of the Jewish persona with national pride, creativity and independence. The life of a person was subservient to the cause.

Those people viewed Odessa as a pause in a long journey toward a national revival. Reb Gershon was among them. While he was determined to go to *Eretz Israel*, he was fully aware that his talent and skills were unfit for the task. *Eretz Israel* needed strong young people, builders of roads, agricultural workers, industrial workers and more. It needed people who could accept unequivocally the hardships that were born from the hostile conditions of an untamed land.

Religious teachers, tailors, petty merchants should stay home. One day, maybe, he reasoned, *there would be Hebrew schools that would need teachers like him: teachers who could blend the secular Jewish literature with religious studies; teachers who could help revive his beloved Hebrew language and adapt it to everyday life, literature and higher learning.* His knowledge of the facts on the ground wasn't up-to-date. He was not cognizant of the education progress in *Eretz Israel*. Deep inside his soul, he knew that he was too old to move to the land of his dreams. He decided to wait. Perhaps his five children would go there and, in time, invite him to join them. In the meantime, he resolved to set roots in Odessa and guide his four boys and one girl in the Zionist way.

Odessa was one of the four largest cities in Russia; its port, one of the biggest. It was a modern town dotted with exquisite architectural monuments attesting to its growing wealth. Jews were treated in Odessa like in no other place in Russia. The restrictive anti-Jewish laws that suffocated life in the *Pale of Settlement* were ignored in Odessa. The city fostered a profusion of economic opportunities, in the grain trade, in the crafts, finance, medicine and more, that were harnessed by the growing Jewish population of the late nineteenth century.

When Reb Gershon and his family came to town, they entered, unknowingly, a center of Jewish renaissance. The city was a magnet for Jewish culture, businessmen, intellectuals and artists. At that time, Jewish control of the grain trade was considerable. There were more Jewish craftsmen in town than gentiles, more bankers, and more medical professionals. The manifestation of Jewish wealth and power was everywhere. Fabulous private and public buildings stood as testimonial to their affluence. Evreiskaia Ulitas—the Jewish Street—was vibrant and alive with the business of living well. Later, when Reb Gershon explored the town he stood in awe before the Brodsky synagogue. He had never seen such a building for the glory of God.

In spite of the cosmopolitan nature of the city, the majority of Jews observed the traditional Jewish religious life of the *Pale.* Rich and poor prayed side by side in magnificent synagogues. At the end of the service they parted company. The poor returned to crowded apartments, tucked away from the main boulevards. The rich strolled leisurely to their sumptuous homes.

The vibrancy of the Jewish community was diametrically opposite to the misery of the *Pale* and the life of those who flocked out of it. In those perturbing days, after the infamous Easter Pogrom in Kishinev, the population of Odessa swelled at an alarming rate. Most newcomers arrived with few possessions, hardly enough to afford minimal comfort and necessities. They were destitute, in danger of hunger and maladies. The vagaries of the climate, lack of clothing, paucity of shelter, and the absence of basic human hygiene added to their misery.

The sages, who had left their imprint on the Jewish psyche, said, "All Israel are guarantors for each other." Indeed, this adage did not escape the consciousness of the Odessa Jewish community. It rallied energetically to meet the growing challenge presented by brothers in distress. The wealthy merchants were generous. Illustrious members of the community created and supported a committee that governed the life of the Jews in Odessa. It attended to the educational and health needs of the community and supported the less fortunate of its Jewish brothers.

With the rapid rise of immigrants in town, the committee's efforts doubled. Volunteers joined a myriad of groups to tackle the growing sense of destitution. There were groups to feed the hungry, to shelter the homeless, to educate the children, to heal the sick and more.

Reb Gershon and his family, who came to town with only a few cherished possessions, not necessarily useful for daily life, benefitted immensely from that generosity. Within a few days he was offered a teaching position at one of Odessa's *Yeshivot.* His family received a small apartment, enough clothing and an adequate budget for food to bridge the period preceding his first salary. With its future unfolding positively, the family began the slow process of adjusting to their new life.

Odessa was also the most Jewish city Reb Gershon had ever seen. Jews, all kinds, were everywhere. The juxtaposition between modern and orthodox Jews was a reality he had never experienced before.

Orthodox Jews dressed in dark suits crowned by black hats, made in part from rabbit fur, crowded the streets. Their sidelocks waved freely in the light breeze as they rushed forward, looking away from the unavoidable females in modern clothing who crossed their path. They were determined to avoid temptation. They protected their innocence and piety. But the collision between heaven and hell was unavoidable. Those pious Jews projected an alien image on the main streets but a familiar sight in the Jewish quarter, where they mingled reluctantly with modern Jews who looked and talked like educated Russians. Reb Gershon was not one of them but his soul was bubbling secretly with the modern influence of *Zionism*.

Women in ankle-length dresses, their heads covered with large headscarves looking much like Russian *babushkas* (grandmothers), moved freely in the Jewish quarter but were rarely seen outside its boundaries. They, too, moved with a special rhythm on the way to or from the markets alongside modern women who were dressed in the latest fashion. The Devil was lurking on every corner in Odessa.

In the Jewish neighborhood, the streets were abuzz with sound. Children played unattended, rejoicing in a few moments of freedom from a long and arduous day of studying. Mothers summoning their children by name, vendors announcing their wares, wagons ferrying people from one point to another, all combined to form ceaseless waves of disharmonious sounds.

When he was not teaching, Reb Gershon meandered around town in search of the right Jewish neighborhood, the right synagogue, a larger apartment for his family and a place to open his school. In his search he occasionally strayed from the Jewish path and wandered into the other Odessa.

There he saw the city in its full glory and decadence. His nostrils inhaled the stench of raw sewage from exposed sanitation trenches along his route. A short distance away they delighted in the scent of flowers growing in abundance in the median strips of the main boulevards.

His eyes soaked up the many colors and shapes of modern architecture and brought him dismay when the masses that filled the sidewalks swept him into their chaotic march.

His ears unsuccessfully attempted to calibrate the din of traffic and the incessant calls of vendors who were hawking everything imaginable.

Odessa had a most prevalent and visible hedonistic side. Inebriated people staggered in and out of bars, invading his space. They spewed vulgarities as if conducting a dialogue with an unseen enemy, or perhaps with themselves. Dance halls dotted certain streets. Ladies of the night strolled seductively in plain view, day and night. He was horrified and offended by the other Odessa he saw, by its decadence and disquiet, by its hellish features. He traversed those sections unintentionally but vowed to avoid them in the future.

After a few weeks he found a place to live in an orthodox Jewish neighborhood. The synagogue was small but pleasing to the eye. Like most synagogues in Odessa it was named after a working guild. His was the teachers' synagogue. He moved his family to a larger apartment, made friends in the synagogue and soon resumed his *Shabbat* dinners in the company of friends.

What his new neighborhood lacked in material symbols, it had in abundance of piety, reverence and spiritual purity. He found his heaven and avoided the hell that was light years away from his consciousness yet only a few blocks away from his neighborhood. To separate heaven from hell he imposed restrictions of movements on himself and his family.

One Friday evening he lingered on after the prayer. He was anxious to ask his rabbi a question about that mysticism point the rabbi discussed during the evening service. The question led to another and soon the two engaged in a long and erudite conversation about the infinity of God and the ten Sefirot—those creative forces that emanate from God. Each one points to a different aspect of God's creative nature, and together they compose the world of divine light. Many worshipers gathered around them. They stood in silence and listened to the conversation. They were spellbound by the depth and breadth of knowledge Reb Gershon displayed in the discussion. He spoke eloquently. He was mild-mannered, never attempting to outshine the rabbi, who was visibly elated with the addition of a new scholarly member to his congregation.

Soon after that dialogue the rabbi approached Reb Gershon and asked him to teach the subject to those who were willing to study. "Of course we will reward you handsomely for your work," he added. Reb Gershon agreed. He felt that his family's days as outsiders were coming to an end. It was the right time to find and establish his school. He resumed his search.

Within a few weeks he was able to find a suitable place to open the school. His reputation preceded him; students flocked to his school from his and other neighborhoods. He even accepted the son of the richest grain dealer in town.

With his teaching obligations, a growing circle of erudite friends and the piety of his daily visits to his synagogue, Reb Gershon had little time to exit his heavenly part of town. His disdain for Odessa abated somewhat. He was among his people. He felt secure in his little enclave. He was ready to settle down in his new home. But he remained on guard for the spiritual health of his youngest son, Itzhak.

After they moved to the new apartment, Reb Gershon's relaxed attitude, which had informed Itzhak's childhood in Gordov, took a dramatic turn. His brief encounter with the other Odessa troubled him enough to formulate a special strategy regarding Itzhak's freedom of motion. He became rigid and defensive. He limited Itzhak's range of exploration to a narrow strip of roadway. His two older children, Yaakov and Avram, were granted much more freedom. They had to venture daily outside the Jewish enclave to enter the labor market, first to look for a job and then to get to and from it. Rachel and Shlomo attended a school nearby and had no need to enter the hellish side of town.

"Itzhak should stay close to home at all times. We'll wait until the boy grows up a bit before we allow him to roam the streets," he told his perplexed wife, who had no clue of the other Odessa.

Even though Odessa could have been an enchanting new world to the nine-year-old, Itzhak neither saw nor heard any of its wonders. He lived in relative isolation. For him, Odessa was a narrow corridor of black asphalt that meandered among unattractive apartment houses. He thought of Gordov. He often wondered aloud while walking to school, *it looks as if some mighty hand covered the dirt roads of Gordov, lifted them from their ancient place and carried them to my neighborhood so I shall remember the hated place for as long as I am here.*

That familiar ribbon of black tar that was in perpetual ill repair was his Odessa. It led from his dwelling to his father's school, about one kilometer away. The synagogue was midway between the two. There was neither a tree nor a playground in sight. Dull gray was the dominant color. Itzhak always thought the place drab.

"Life is boring in Odessa. It was much more fun in Gordov!" he complained one evening after a long and particularly challenging day in school.

His father chided him, "Remember the exodus from Egypt. There the Israelites were toiling under the yoke of slavery, when God, blessed be his name, took them out of bondage and led them into freedom, on a return journey home. And what did they do after a short time in the desert?"

It was meant as a rhetorical question. But Itzhak did not wait for the answer. He exclaimed, in Hebrew, "And the children of Israel said unto him: 'Would that we had died by the hand of the LORD in the land of Egypt, when we sat by the flesh-pots, when we did eat bread to the full; for ye have brought us forth into this wilderness, to kill this whole assembly with hunger.'"

"Correct," said his father, stroking his son's hair.

"I apologize, Father, for comparing my life to that horrid place. I am happy we have left Gordov. I know that Odessa is only a temporary stop on our way home."

"Your apology is accepted. I love you, Itzhak. You are our youngest. And like Yaakov shielding his youngest, Benjamin, we may at times be overprotective of you. I limit your motion for your own good. Odessa can be hell, the dwelling of the devil, and you are too young to make his acquaintance."

"I trust you, Father. I love you, too."

Life flowed monotonously and uneventfully forward. Itzhak awoke each day before dawn. After breakfast, he walked with his father to school, where he spent a few hours at his father's new library.

At nine, when the rest of the students arrived, Itzhak joined them in the schoolroom and spent his entire day in prayers and study. After the evening prayer he returned home for supper and bed. In time, he learned to enjoy his limited life. He settled into his routine and put all his energy in his study and his books. Time flew by rapidly. Habit and the pressure of studies coupled with his inherent will to excel pushed the clock forward as if it was carried on the wings of wind. Itzhak's curiosity about the other Odessa, the one beyond the limited and sheltered boundaries of his world, weakened with the passing of time.

All four of Itzhak's siblings were members of a local Zionist club. Reb Gershon encouraged their participation even though he was torn between two opposing forces. On the one hand his orthodox leanings pulled him away from contact with the secular, modern world. On the other, he was emotionally attached to the modern ideas of *Zionism*. In Odessa there were ample opportunities to engage, to meet other Zionists and assemble in study and cultural groups. He was aware that men and women mixed in such gatherings to discuss events, to learn Hebrew, to sing and dance together, but his strong devotion to the coming renaissance of the Jewish nation overcame his natural aversion to the modern world. He trusted that his children could balance Jewish secularism with the Jewish religion. But the non-Jewish Odessa remained a hellish place, and he did all he could to limit his children's contact with that world.

The four other children were good and loyal children but lacked Itzhak's brilliance and voracious appetite for learning and reading. Itzhak's sister, Rachel, attended a special school for girls. She was a curious young lady who loved to converse with her young brother and learn from him whatever she could. In spite of his natural orthodox inclinations to shelter females from men in general, Reb Gershon encouraged her independent thinking and, with great emotional upheaval, permitted her to join her brothers at the Zionist club.

Itzhak spent the first two years in Odessa becoming, to his father's delight, a deep thinker and an accomplished user of the Hebrew language. Life ebbed and flowed. He dedicated his weekdays to his scholastic efforts and, on the holy *Shabbat,* he enjoyed the purity of spirit that took over his life. It began on Friday night with the jovial mood at his father's table, where the entire family gathered to welcome *Shabbat.* And it continued during the day, as he joined the congregation at the synagogue, always dressed in his finest attire. There was nothing that disturbed his routine. All was quiet. All was normal. But it was only skin deep.

Far to the east, at the edge of Russia, the Tsar's army was engaged in a deadly and a losing war with Japan. Jews, unless conscripted by force, did not partake in the conflict. The war adversely affected the life of thousands of families. It had a drastic impact on the Russian economy. The Tsar kept a tight control over the lives of his subjects, and the travails of the war heightened their misery. There was great unease across the land.

At the same time the country was divided between the many who sought more freedom and those who were determined to oppose and suppress liberty. People marched in protests, and the Tsar's army suppressed them. Protests grew more and more vocal, and the government response grew more violent. Early in 1905, St. Petersburg exploded in bloody repression when the Tsar's army massacred unarmed protestors.

Close to home, in Odessa, the economy was in terrible shape. Many were unemployed. Those who worked were threatened with reduction in salary. Prices of everyday goods and food staples climbed daily. Crime was on the rise. In addition to the economic hardship that gripped the city many were overtaken by the revolutionary fervor that swept the country. Workers at the port staged daily walkouts and demonstrations.

All of that seemed irrelevant to Itzhak's daily routine. Then, one day in June of 1905, an event rocked the port of Odessa and reverberated throughout Tsarist Russia.

In the midst of the continuous turmoil, the crew of a Russian warship mutinied in response to the killing of one of their members who, representing his comrades, protested the foul food on board.

The mutineers steered their ship to the port of Odessa where a swirl of revolutionary fervor exploded in reaction to their travails. Drinking, incendiary speeches, and looting followed. A large section of the port was set on fire. In spite of the government's declaration of martial law, unstoppable rage engulfed the city for six days. The inevitable carnage ensued when the Tsar's army fired and killed or wounded thousands of protestors.

At the height of that revolutionary tension, and after the end of the Russo-Japanese War, Tsar Nicholas issued his October Manifesto in which he outlined a plan to improve the conditions of the masses. He promised the creation of an elected legislative body as well as to institute civil liberties such as freedom of speech, press and assembly.

People on the right united against the liberal provisions of the Manifesto. Once again agitators took to the streets of Odessa blaming the Jews for the unpopular liberal content of the Tsar's decree and the persisting economic turbulence.

The echoes of the agitation banged violently on every door in the Jewish quarters. The local newspapers added oil to the conflagration. They unleashed an unrelenting campaign to expose a Jewish conspiracy to dominate the economic life of the city. They blamed the Jewish bankers for acting against Russia in the war with Japan; they blamed the Jewish craftsmen and merchants for crowding out the local merchants; they blamed the Jewish grain dealers for inflating prices and causing economic stress in the city.

A great sense of fear swept the community. Itzhak couldn't escape the intensity of the anti-Jewish sentiment that rolled incessantly through the streets of Odessa, like thunder through a dark sky. The fresh wounds of Gordov reopened, replaying the horrors of the inn near Gordov and the mayhem that swept his community in its aftermath.

During the months of unrest, Itzhak's elder brothers, Avram and Yaakov, volunteered with the Odessa Committee to patrol the Jewish neighborhoods. Itzhak, in spite of his desire to join them, stayed home.

On the eve of the festival of Sukkot—the holiday that commemorated the forty years during which the children of Israel stayed in temporary dwellings, known as Sukkah, while wandering in the desert on their way from Egypt to their ancestral home—Reb Gershon's family waited for the two brothers. The family dressed in their finest and prepared to move into the Sukkah to celebrate the holiday with prayers, merriment and good food. The sun sank below the western horizon. The first stars were visible overhead. It was time to begin the festivities but Avram and Yaakov had not returned.

Later that evening, Yaakov returned home alone. Words flowed out of his mouth like water out of a broken faucet. "Avram and I took part in a Jewish defense force. We fought the marauding mob on the street that led into our neighborhood. Avram was brave. He stopped the attackers although his only weapon was a broomstick. He used it magnificently well.

"He smacked and beat at the approaching mob, moving aggressively forward to push back the attackers. We followed him, and the assailants retreated, stunned. It was the first time they'd experienced the power of a Jewish defense. Avram was our leader, our strength. He was no longer a single person; he was *us*. He moved like a large body of men with a single focus: to defend the people. We looked into his fiery eyes, and we knew that, thanks to his bravery, no harm would come to our streets.

"As the aggressors retreated in panic, someone lingered on and shot Avram. He fell to the pavement, bleeding profusely from his chest. I know he did not suffer. His face lit. He died as a happy and a proud Jew. Finally, the idle police intervened. They dispersed the crowd and took Avram's body."

Itzhak's mother fell to her knees screaming uncontrollably. Reb Gershon crouched silently beside her, rocking forward and backward as if engaged in an angry dialogue with his God. The children, Yaakov, Rachel, Shlomo, and Itzhak dropped to the floor near their parents, adding their mourning wails to their parents' trauma. Agony descended upon their broken life. The planned merriment of Sukkot banished. For seven days the house was in mourning. The mirrors were covered in black. Everyone spoke in a hushed voice. Friends came to pray and share in the family's anguish.

In spite of his overwhelming grief, Itzhak made a gallant effort to overcome his sadness and think proudly about his brave brother. *He was murdered while defending his people. He was a new Jew, no longer led, like the Jews of Kishinev, to the slaughter without resistance. He was a brave Jew.* Such thoughts brought him temporary solace.

Ten days later, on October 18, 1905, the earth under their feet shook violently. No force of nature rattled the streets, no angry God unleashed his wrath upon his flock, and no Japanese soldiers marched on Odessa in a bid to reignite the belligerence that had ended a month earlier. Ignorance propelled by unrestrained religious and economic hatred wreaked havoc in the Jewish community of Russia. Odessa, too, was shaken to its core.

After three days, a tense quiet descended upon the city. The many wounded suffered in the local hospitals. The dead—four hundred Jewish men, women and children, and about a hundred non-Jewish men—were taken off the streets and buried. Glass from Jewish storefronts littered the sidewalk, and the embers of burned-down houses still flickered in the gray autumn sky.

Once again the Jews were on the move. Wave after wave of destitute people streamed to the relatively open borders of America. But Reb Gershon persisted in his decision to stay. In spite of the recurring turmoil in his life, in the face of his personal loss, he did not want to compromise. For him, the only destination was *Eretz Israel*. And he was not ready to uproot his family and move there.

A few weeks later, when a semblance of normalcy pushed away their mourning, Yaakov, who seemed agitated for days, informed his parents of his decision to leave for America. "That is the land of opportunity. A land in which a Jew can be free and live unmolested."

Rachel glared at her brother accusingly. "You are wrong, Yaakov! The only solution to our misery is when we take responsibility for our collective future. Individuals can run on and on, but they will never be free unless they are anchored in a free nation. A nation like all other nations."

Reb Gershon stared at his daughter with admiration and bewilderment. "This is an amazing idea, Rachel. How did you come up with it?"

"Itzhak told me about Pinsker's Auto Emancipation. With his help I read it in your library. We also talked about it in our youth group only a few weeks ago. I shall become a Zionist, father," she said and added with a shy smile riding on an adult determination. "I will!"

Reb Gershon smiled. "It is indeed a most interesting view of the Jewish problem."

"Yes," said Shlomo, her twin brother. "Pinsker believed that the Jews can neither assimilate nor become an integral part in the nations in which they reside."

"Tell me father, why is it that the Christians hate us so?" asked Itzhak.

"I confess to reading the Christian Bible in the hope of finding an answer to just such a question."

"Did you, father?"

"Yes, I did. The answer is there for all to see. It is written plainly and most directly. Matthew, he wrote one of the four Gospels—the good news—says that the Jews accepted responsibility for the death of Christ by saying 'let his blood be upon us and that of our children.' John, another disciple of Christ, is more accusatory, more virulent. Let me see."

Reb Gershon went to his library and pulled out a few books; behind them he had hidden the New Testament. He took the book from its hiding place and thumbed through it, somewhat apologetically, for the book was not a customary reading for a religious Jew. When he found John 8:44, he told his amazed children, "You see, I am also an educated man besides being an orthodox Jew. So here it is. Jesus is engaged in a conversation with the resentful Pharisees. John ascribes to Jesus these virulent accusations: 'Ye are of your father the Devil and the lust of your father ye will do. He was a murderer from the beginning and abode not in the truth because there is no truth in him.' So, we are not only God's killers, we are also children of the Devil, of a false God. That is one reason why they hate us so much. Another reason is our continuous refusal to accept

Christ, in spite of enormous pressure directed at us over the centuries. Finally, I think they are jealous of our success whenever we are given the opportunity to succeed."

Itzhak was silent. Steeped in thoughts. After a while he said, "I always thought that their hate is a sign of ignorance. Now I can see that it is rooted in a misguided belief. One day they will awake to the truth and see that we are neither better nor worse than them. We are all the children of God."

Reb Gershon reflected on his children's words, on the maturity of their argument. At that moment he knew that he could trust them to choose the right path. Then he addressed Itzhak, "Well-said. Until your brother leaves, if he does, you may join him and the twins on their weekly meetings at the local Zionist club. Listen to what they say. Read their pamphlets. You may discover a new path that will lead you to the true Promised Land."

"Thank you, Father, for your trust."

In an instant Itzhak's narrow universe expanded beyond any image he might have conjured up during his isolation. The club was in another neighborhood. Yaakov resolved to lead his brother from his Jewish isolation into the wide world. He therefore purposely chose a different route each week. He was deliberate in his actions. "You must see that there is another world out there, beyond ours."

His first day out of his regular routine was a watershed day in his life. He was just six months shy of his twelfth birthday. They strolled into the club, a basement in one of the fancier houses in the area—Yaakov followed by Shlomo then Itzhak and Rachel.

"Meet my baby brother," announced Yaakov to Itzhak's embarrassment. "He is stepping into the other side of the Jewish world. Now, treat him with respect because in spite of his young age he speaks Hebrew better than anyone here and he knows the Jewish law better than most." His tone was jovial but held a clear hint of pride.

People came to say hello, each one embracing Itzhak with a hug and a tap on his back. "Welcome to *Habonim* (The Builders)."

I hope my discomfort does not show, he thought as he tried to force a mature smile. They sat in a circle and talked about the last Zionist Congress, the seventh. Itzhak sensed their talk was a continuation of other conversations; they delved into their subject with no preliminaries.

"I remind you that the Uganda proposal nearly destroyed the nascent Zionist movement. Now it hangs upon the integrity of our group like Damocles' Sword. We must make our voice heard. Are we for or against the decision of the Seventh Congress? I urge you to vote 'For' as did the majority of the world's Zionists. I do not want to lose any of my dear friends because of this issue," pleaded the young man with the thick-rimmed glasses.

"Please remind everyone what that decision was," requested Yaakov.

Itzhak blushed. *I can't believe that my brother is so out of touch. No wonder he wants to immigrate to America.*

"Of course," said the young man with the thick-rimmed glasses. He showed no emotion toward Yaakov. Itzhak decided that he was the leader of *Habonim*. "The seventh congress voted against the Uganda proposal. By doing so it reaffirmed the first Zionist Congress' Basel Program, which was at the core of the Zionist movement. Accordingly, the Zionist's goal is '...the promotion by appropriate means of the settlement in *Eretz-Israel* of Jewish farmers, artisans, and manufacturers.'"

A tall, fragile man declared "No! The Seventh Congress was dead wrong. We need a place to rebuild our devastated nation. Any place is a good place. Britain's offer of Uganda is a good one. We should take it. World Jewry needs a place to recapture its breath. It needs the place now!"

"I agree," echoed a young woman who spoke softly as if she did not want her opinion to be heard. But her voice picked up strength and self-assurance when she added, "The main goal of the Zionist movement is to rescue the destitute and create conditions for Jewish independence and national rebirth. We need a land to call our own. Anywhere will do."

"Not true," exclaimed a scholarly looking man. "In any place but *Eretz Israel*, we'll forget the eternal adage *'If I forget thee, O Jerusalem, may my right hand forget its cunning.'* We'll lose our connection to history, to the land of our forefathers. Now is the time to reaffirm the supremacy of *Eretz Israel* over any other land.'"

"We will not forget Dov," protested Mendel, a religious man whose name Itzhak had heard earlier. "Even if we settle in another place we'll regard it as a temporary, emergency shelter for a destitute people. I assure you that we'll continue to pray for the return to *Eretz Israel*."

"Mendel, I mean no offense so please take my words as a simple observation of historical reality. Have we not been praying for two millennia, yet nothing but pain has been our reward?"

Mendel shrugged his shoulders. He elected not to reply.

"I think those who side with the Territorialists are dead wrong," said Rachel "Pinsker, when he insisted that the goal of the Jewish effort must not focus on the Holy Land but on any land that we could call our own, was just as wrong. *Eretz Israel* is the only place on earth with which we have a multi-faceted bond: spiritual, historical, national and emotional. I say we must vote against the Territorialists for whom any land will do."

"I agree with you, Rachel," said the man with the thick rim glasses. "If we ever are called upon to justify our national aspiration and rebirth, what can we say about Uganda? Or Argentina? Or just any piece of land?"

They argued for an hour or so. Itzhak listened attentively. He could not believe the vehemence of their arguments about where to rebuild the Jewish nation. In his mind *Eretz Israel* was it. *Have we not declared at the end of the Passover celebration 'next year in Jerusalem?' No one has ever said anything about Uganda.* He sided with his sister. *Only Eretz Israel is the natural place for the Jews to rebuild the Jewish nation*, he concluded.

They took a vote. Three people voted against the Congress' decision to reject the Uganda proposal, and for that matter any other territorial proposal other than *Eretz Israel*. Those three immediately declared their intent to leave *Habonim*. "We belong with the new Territorialists movement," said Mendel as the three marched out of the meeting with a clear display of anger.

That meeting was an eye opener for Itzhak. On his way home he could not help anticipating the next meeting and those that would follow.

Week after week he went to the *Habonim*'s meetings. At the end of their conversation they sang Hebrew songs and danced the Hora. Itzhak was elated. He absorbed everything: the stories, the songs and the new dance steps. Most importantly, the spirit of the meeting captivated him. Everyone exuded happiness. Everyone's face was ignited with a special fire, the likes of which he had never seen before.

He always returned home full of enthusiasm, full of admiration for the exuberance and dedication of his new friends. Each successive meeting presented him with new lessons and gave him an opportunity to contribute to the group's objectives. His knowledge of Hebrew elevated his status in the group from Yaakov's kid brother to a person. He was often called upon to help in the weekly Hebrew lessons and did so with great pleasure.

In the meetings he learned about the agricultural settlements in *Eretz Israel*, about that rich Frenchman, Rothschild, who supported them, about the weather and the hard living conditions of the new immigrants' life.

Most importantly, each meeting brought him closer to finding his real self. He felt that *Zionism* was the best realization of Saadia's thoughts. It was his calling. Tirelessly he pursued his new interest. His strategy was simple. Read... read... read. He bombarded his father with requests to obtain pamphlets, books and essays on the Zionists' project. At first, his requests were unfocused, general. But with the passing of time he became more precise.

"Father," he said one day, just before the Chanukah holiday, "I have this strange sensation within me. My mind meanders far afield, to a land I have never seen. I feel drawn to it. I feel as if I wander in its hills teeming with flowers and awash with sunlight. I am happy. I want to lie on the ground and become one with the land. It is as if I have found my calling, you know, the answer to the question people always ask 'what do you want to do when you grow up?' I want to be in this land. I want to restore it to its former glory." Then he abruptly changed the subject, "Could you get me literature about *Eretz Israel*? *Habonim* will devote its meeting after the holiday to the *Eretz Israel* vision and reality."

His father hugged him in silence. They stood together for a long moment.

A few days later he received an essay by Ahad Ha'am and a book by Herzel. "Ahad Ha'am is one of the most important Jewish thinkers and writers of our time," said his father. "One of his essays describes his long visit to *Eretz Israel*. Herzl, the father of the Zionist movement, wrote a book. It outlines Herzl's vision of the Jewish state. As you read it you will see that he was not particular about its geographic location. He was urgently seeking a solution to Jewish alienation everywhere they lived. That brought him later to accept the Uganda plan, which threatened the survival of the Zionist enterprise. Given the intense opposition to the Uganda plan, Herzl eventually changed his mind and became a full supporter of the original Zionist program. You have before you the reality of *Eretz Israel*, versus expectations for its future. Read them both. By the way, Itzhak, *Eretz Israel* needs young people to love her dearly."

Itzhak smiled and hugged his father and said with a true enthusiasm, "Thank you, Father. I love you." Then he withdrew to the corner and started to read.

Eretz Israel was at the center of the first meeting after Chanukah. A member of the Odessa Zionist organization joined with *Habonim* members to guide the conversation. He talked about the Ottoman Empire and described how it ruled *Eretz Israel*, or Palestine, as the Turks called it. "It is an economically and socially backward land. Administratively, it is divided into districts that are ruled from Beirut or Damascus by corrupt administrators. Nothing can be achieved without a *Bakshish* (bribe)," he told them.

Everyone was curious about the Governance of *Eretz Israel*, the inhabitants of the land, the Zionist colonies, the climate and more. Many asked questions. He answered in details. Overall, he left them with the impression that *Eretz Israel* was a wild, thinly populated and barely cultivated land. "The few Arabs who live on the land dwell in primitive villages where livestock mixes freely with people and the sanitation conditions are abominable. Each village is a separate and an independent entity. The inhabitants are loyal to the family and the village. Their interest in the Ottoman bureaucracy is minimal. Their interaction with other villages and the few urban centers is limited. This can be explained by the inadequacy of the transportation. Roads are bad most of the year especially in the winter. Two rail lines exist. One connects the little town of Haifa with southern Syria, and the other connects the port city of Jaffa with Jerusalem. Both are narrow corridors that leave the rest of the land isolated. People rarely leave their villages. They are born and they die in the same geographical area. By the way, Jaffa is the gateway to *Eretz Israel*, one day we should talk about that town.

"The few who live in the countryside depend on subsistence farming which is, for the most part, unproductive. Most of them are too poor to own the land. They use it as tenants of rich local Arabs or Arab merchants who live faraway, usually in the large commercial cities of the Ottoman Empire. The locals have neither social nor cultural institutions and certainly no body politic," he said and shifted his thoughts to the Jewish population and the Zionist colonies. "We, on the other hand, have introduced modern agriculture and commerce, schools and social institutions, medical services and improved sanitation. We settle on land that we purchase. We are modern, educated, and deploy modern technology for land and health management that benefits the small indigenous population. In short, we move the land and its inhabitants toward a better future."

Itzhak felt ill at ease with the tone of the discussion. He prodded his sister's arm and whispered in her ear, "Tell him that what he says is not exactly the way Ahad Ha'am described life in *Eretz Israel*."

"I may, later. I do not want to start an argument now. Let's see if anyone else has read the essay 'The Truth from *Eretz Israel*.'"

Dov was the first to speak. "Can you say more about the Zionist colonial effort?"

"Our most critical task is to purchase land. We buy it wherever we can. There are enough rich landowners who are eager to sell. You know," he reflected with an obvious display of contempt, "since we started to colonize *Eretz Israel*, absentee land owners have redefined the essence of greed. They know we want land. The age-old notion that Jews have money propels them to set an exorbitant price to any piece of land they offer to sell us. Speculators rapidly inflate the value of even the most infertile parcels like swamps and stone-filled hilly land. We, somehow, have managed to borrow or solicit donations of the needed funds. After all, we are purchasing our ancient homeland, taken from us by the sword and kept from us by the successors of those sword-wielding thieves.

"We drain the swamps. Dislodge boulders and clear the stones then apply modern agriculture techniques and turn unproductive land into a high-yielding land."

The young man with the thick-rimmed glasses, by now Itzhak knew that his name was Sasha, asked, "What kind of difficulties will we face when we make *aliyah* (immigrate, literally "ascend") to *Eretz Israel* next year?"

"The biggest problem is the gap between knowing the problems and experiencing them," he replied. "Even though we have been introducing modern life to *Eretz Israel*, our evolving enterprise is still hampered by many obstacles. In a nutshell, life is extremely hard for newcomers. The rudimentary services that we take for granted here, such as clean clothes, ample food, a comfortable bed to sleep in, ease of access to neighboring places, medical services, and clean water are seriously lacking for those of us who rise to the challenge and exchange the familiar with the foreign," he said in a serious voice. "Moreover, the Jewish community, they call it the *Yishuv*, is a rainbow of political, religious and economical perspectives. You will not find it easy in *Eretz Israel*. You must be strong, dedicated people who can postpone gratification and endure disappointments while never losing sight of the conviction that a new Jewish nation is being built and you are its builders, *Habonim*, in Hebrew."

There was much more to ask, much more to learn.

"It is late, perhaps we should continue this conversation next week," suggested the Zionist representative. Everyone agreed.

"Do not forget to raise Ahad Ha'am's point next week," insisted Itzhak on their way home. "If we are to aspire to *Eretz Israel* and not to Uganda or Argentina or any other place, we should know the truth about the place."

Rachel nodded.

A week later, Itzhak and Rachel walked alone to the meeting. Yaakov stayed home. The topic was irrelevant to his future life. Mentally, he was already in America. It was only a matter of a few weeks, he estimated, before he'd have the necessary funds for the trip. Shlomo was rapidly losing interest in the Zionist cause also. He was attracted to the glow of America's streets, which according to his brother, were paved with gold and surrounded by freedom and equality for all.

The Zionist representative was already at the meeting when Itzhak and Rachel arrived. After they sang a few Hebrew songs, they settled for the weekly Hebrew lesson, which put Itzhak on center stage. As usual he was ready to help anyone who called for his support. At the end of the lesson the representative said, "Earlier this year our local committee discussed Mr. Vitkin's article, 'Kol Kore.' Itzhak," he smiled at the boy, handed him the pamphlet and asked, "can you translate the title of the article?"

"Of course," answered Itzhak "It means a Plea, or literally, a voice calling."

"Yes, thank you. But having read it, I can provide a more precise translation. It is actually a Voice that Calls for Action. The article is important because it expands on my answer to Sasha's question last week."

"In what way?" asked Estie, who had impressed Itzhak when he first saw her. *She still looks like an angel,* he thought, admiring her long blond hair that cascaded down her shoulders.

"And who is Mr. Vitkin?" she continued.

Rachel rose from her seat before he could reply. "Before you answer," she turned to Estie, "I hope you do not mind if I go back to our last meeting for a minute?"

"No, please do. I want to hear what you have to say."

"Thanks." Rachel turned back to the representative. "My brother and I have read Ahad Ha'am's 'The Truth from *Eretz Israel*.' We would like to share with you and our friends one quote from that essay. I urge everyone to read the entire essay. May we?"

"Of course you may. I have not read the essay so I am interested."

Rachel turned to Itzhak and asked him to translate the relevant paragraph. He stood up and said, "Ahad Ha'am tells us that we who live in the Diaspora are used to believing that *Eretz Israel* is a wild, uncultivated land. We believe that anyone who wishes to buy land can do so at great ease. But that is not so. Throughout the country it is hard to find arable land that is uncultivated. As to the natives, he warns us that our belief that the Arab is a wild desert man—who is, like a donkey, oblivious to his environment—is misleading. The Arab, he says, is cunning, wise and has a clear understanding of our goals in *Eretz Israel*. He warns us to treat the natives with respect, with love and with justice. I liked the essay very much."

"Thank you, Rachel. Thank you, Itzhak. That is incredible. I think we should read the entire essay," said Sasha.

"Thank you for bringing this essay to my attention. I want to read it and share it with my friends. I think that in our preparation for *aliyah* we must be cognizant of all the facts as relayed to us by our best minds. My apology for stating that *Eretz Israel* is sparsely populated but this has been the prevailing opinion among my friends in our committee.

"Now if I may, I'd like to share Vitkin's essay. I must say that he is a superb source. He lives in *Eretz Israel*. He is a teacher, a writer and an ardent Zionist. His pamphlet is a call to Jewish youth whose heart is with *Eretz Israel* and the Jewish people."

It is for me, reflected Itzhak.

"This is also an important essay. Let me just share two points. The rest you can read on your own. Mr. Vitkin tells us exactly what kind of a person is needed for the Zionist cause. Then he paints in vivid colors the obstacles that await that person. It is a good extension of our conversation last week.

"The struggle requires fighters who are not seeking riches, people who can demonstrate an unconditional and unbounded love of the Jewish people and the land. Healthy, strong people, who are disciplined and ready to dedicate their life to the people's business.

"Then he talks about the conditions that his heroic person will meet. The struggle in *Eretz Israel* is akin to a war waged on many fronts: on a personal and interpersonal levels, with nature, with the local Arabs, with the government bureaucrats, with diseases, hunger. Most troubling is the war with a degenerated old Jewish *Yishuv* in *Eretz Israel.* These are quite stringent requirements," declared the Zionist representative and added, "and that is just looking at the tip of the iceberg."

Itzhak's inner voice was adamant. *I will be that person. I am ready to face all obstacles. I must read the entire essay.*

"Excuse me" he addressed the representative, "where can I find the whole essay?"

"Here it is," said the representative and handed him the pamphlet.

On the way home Itzhak asked his sister about Estie. "She looks so young. Is she a member of *Habonim*?"

"No," replied Rachel with a mischievous smile. "She is Sasha's baby sister. She is fourteen. Do you like her?"

He blushed. "Sort of," he said.

Rachel hugged him and said, "You are blushing, brother. Your secret is safe with me."

They walked hand in hand and said no more about the subject.

When Itzhak sat in his father's library to read the pamphlet his heart raced with anticipation. He felt his blood rushing through his veins. When he finished he knew that the essay called on him. He was ready to give *Eretz Israel* unconditional love. *I have an iron constitution,* he thought. *I shall not fail my beloved country.*

The rest of the days of 1906 flowed lazily in a predictable pattern. Itzhak's dedication to the Zionist cause and his vow to accept responsibility for his own deeds did not diminish his willingness to study and partake in religious activities. Life was good. He spent his time studying, reading, attending local meetings of *Habonim* and participating in the Jewish liturgy: *Shabbat* at the synagogue as well as the numerous religious holidays that dotted the Jewish calendar. Itzhak was happy with his lot. But he was also unaware of his father's struggle with a growing emotional conflict between his old ways and a tsunami-like power that was pulling his children toward a new world. Life took a sudden turn for the worse.

Yaakov's growing agitation with his life in Odessa and his frequent affirmation of his will to leave for America dampened Itzhak's otherwise enthusiastic attitude.

One day Yaakov missed dinner. Early morning, before sunrise, the police dragged him home, inebriated. "The boy was drinking with a prostitute at the Always Lustful saloon," he told the shocked parents as he dumped the boy at the door. "You better watch what hell hole he visits. Next time he will be arrested."

Mrs. Hacohen went into mourning as if she had lost a second child.

Reb Gershon rarely confided his feelings with his wife, nor would he open a crack into his soul for his children to peek inside. He locked his feelings—a volcanic rumble that was ready to explode—deep inside him. His fear of losing his daughter and three boys, two to America and two to a cause he considered a spiritual heaven for any Jew, had been jolted up to a calamitous level by Yaakov's behavior.

While the burden of his emotions lay heavily on his heart, Mrs. Hacohen was more transparent. The recent traumatic events intensified her grief over the loss of Avram. Her puzzlement over the changes sweeping through her family was visible in her protective attitude. She neither accepted nor understood it.

Just after Passover, Yaakov, still embarrassed by his recent escapade, made good on his intent to move to America. He declared his departure day, packed his clothes and left. His action was swift, leaving no time for either his parents or his siblings to disabuse him of his decision. For six long and silent months Itzhak observed his parents' visible anguish over Yaakov's fate.

At last, shortly after the Jewish New Year, the first letter arrived. Happiness pushed sadness away. But the delight was short lived. In a few words Yaakov encapsulated the hardships that confronted him in the lower East Side of Manhattan. It was as if each word was written with tears and accentuated with "*Oy*." He described the inadequate, unsanitary living and working conditions: the heat, the high humidity, the lack of electricity and running water and the rampant anti-Semitism.

Itzhak gave a verbal expression to a feeling everyone shared. "Yaakov has returned to Gordov," he exclaimed.

The next letter was still sad yet ended on a brighter note. "I am working in the needle trade. Yesterday I was able to open a savings account in the local bank. I joined a local synagogue. I miss you very much. Your loving son, Yaakov."

Itzhak noted sarcastically, "My brother is a tailor."

Reb Gershon breathed a sigh of relief. "He works for a living and finds time to be Jewish, too. He repented. That is good. That is very good."

A few weeks later Shlomo left to join his brother, who, according to his latest letter, was doing well in his own tailor shop.

Members of *Habonim* followed a different path, a more rigorous road that led away from savings banks and synagogues. They were busy coalescing a group spirit, experimenting with menial labor, which was alien to most Jews. They prepared themselves for a laborer's life. Such life, they were convinced, would lay the foundation for the new Jew who would tackle the hardships of existence in *Eretz Israel* and put the Jewish people on a path to a renewed nationhood.

They were doing all they could to toughen their souls and harden their bodies. They gave up on sweets, consumed less food, and walked instead of using public transport. They traveled to a distant estate, managed by Sasha's father, to till the fields, attend to a large herd of milking cows, and learn the fundamentals of modern agricultural and animal husbandry.

"As Vitkin said, *Eretz Israel* needs strong people who are dedicated to the Jewish project, not to their individual passion," said Sasha, when he first suggested the adaptation of a new, more stringent life pattern for the group. "A simpler consumption coupled with strenuous work will prepare us for our new life."

In early October, a few days after Sukkot 1907, all thirteen members of *Habonim*, nine men and four women, left Odessa on their way to *Eretz Israel*. Itzhak stayed behind; he was too young.

The anguish of parting company with Rachel was written all over his parents' faces. Itzhak hugged his tearful mother and said, "We will soon join her in *Eretz Israel*."

But, for now, Itzhak was alone and lonely.

One afternoon as he meandered away from his neighborhood he came across a store that caught his eyes. At the entrance stood a tall, elderly gentleman, a bit chubby and neatly dressed. His face was adorned with a huge, well-trimmed mustache. He engaged Itzhak in a conversation in barely-comprehensible Russian.

"Name of me is Mr Aziz," he told Itzhak. "You interested pumps?"

"Maybe." Itzhak was not sure of the application of pumps to his life until it suddenly hit him. *Pumps... water pumps... I can use them in Eretz Israel.* He quickly changed his answer. "Yes, of course I am interested."

"In please, have tea, we talk."

Itzhak walked into the store and enjoyed tea with Mr. Aziz. During their conversation he discovered that Mr. Aziz was Greek Orthodox, from Jerusalem and that he spoke fluent Arabic.

Itzhak immediately realized how important friendship with Mr. Aziz could be. Before he left he asked if he could visit again on the following week. Mr. Aziz happily agreed.

And so, during his next visit after they had tea, Itzhak came to the point without losing any time. "I want you to teach me Arabic," he told the convivial man. "I will be glad to teach you Russian."

Mr. Aziz was delighted. "Tea more to celebrate," he said and rushed to fetch the teakettle.

Itzhak was no longer alone and lonely. For the next several years he met with Mr. Aziz twice a week. They spent an hour on the study of Arabic and one hour on the study of Russian. Itzhak dedicated many hours at home to advance his knowledge of Arabic. Mr. Aziz was a lover of books and his library contained many volumes in Arabic. Itzhak loved to read *One Thousand and One Nights*. He read it over and over, honing his reading and comprehension skills. Occasionally he read the Quran.

As he progressed in learning the language, he divided his attention between Arabic and water pumps. He visited local estates as Mr. Aziz's apprentice and soon mastered the intricacy of pump installation and repair. He became an assistant to Mr. Aziz and within a short period of supervised work he was entrusted to be an independent installer and repairman. During his work with Mr. Aziz he acquired important agricultural skills such as tending vegetable gardens, caring for chickens and milking cows and the intricacies of modern orchard management practices.

He earned large sums of money, which he divided between savings for his pending *aliyah*, for his parents and occasional gifts to his sister in *Eretz Israel*.

On his fourteenth birthday he found a new Zionist group. He was happy to return with vigor to his Zionist youth life—the songs, the dances and the long discussions of what it meant to support the cause were to him, like manna from heaven. To his delight, Estie joined the group a few months later. Her long blond hair distracted him. On many occasions, at home, while alone in the darkness of night, he sank into a deep romantic dream about the two of them. He confided in no one.

One meeting, Michael walked in just before they started to sing. Itzhak thought that he looked more rugged than the times they had spent together in *Habonim*. "Tell us about life in *Eretz Israel*," Itzhak asked.

Michael opened his mouth and spouted vitriol about the *Yishuv*. He talked without stop about hardships in the fields, unbearable climate, bad living conditions, malaria, meager and bad food, loneliness, and perpetual sadness. "In short," he said, "the land consumes its inhabitants. It is hell on earth. I am not returning and don't recommend going there. America, here I come!"

The following week only Itzhak came to the meeting. The next week was the same. It seemed that the group had disbanded.

A letter from Rachel came too late. It warned him that Michael was asked to leave the group because he was lazy and a bum. "Do not believe anything he says," she wrote.

Once again he was alone, without the Zionist friends whose company he enjoyed so much. Serendipity brought him to the same street corner with Michael a week before he sailed to America. They talked about this and that. At last Itzhak gathered all his inner strength to ask, just before they parted company, "How is Sasha's sister, Estie?"

"She is fine," replied Michael. "Her family plans to immigrate to America at the end of the month."

Itzhak was crushed. That night he wrote a long and somber letter to his sister.

In her immediate reply to his declaration of unrequited love she simply wrote, "My dearest Itzhak, I am sad for your loss, but, in time, Estie will form in your heart a sweet memory."

After that there was a long period of silence. He was worried. Then another letter arrived. He opened it eagerly and read:

Rishon Le'Zion
December 4, 1911

My Dearest Itzhak,

Please accept my apology for not writing as frequently as I did before. It is simply that I have been overcome with the hardships of life. My existence, my thinking, my feelings are pulled away from the enterprise to which I swore total dedication. I am ashamed. After four years as a devout soldier of the Zionist cause I have begun to doubt my ability to cope. A veil of uncertainty has descended upon my very existence. I feel sad. Guilt ridden. A sense of betrayal of the principles that have brought me to this land and guided my life heretofore.

The principles of selfless and total devotion have been eroded by my yearning for clean clothes, a warm bed, a room to call my own, a meaningful and interesting profession and a lust for learning.

I no longer feel that I do the Nation's bidding with total dedication, that I am no longer able, perhaps want, the burden of self-sacrifice. I am horrified by some of the ME thoughts that penetrate uninvited into my soul.

I am lonely. The hard labor, which is monotonous and repetitive, obscures my view of the broader cause and focuses my attention on the few feet of the Motherland that I see and engage with on a daily basis. My mind cannot leap beyond my limited world and embrace the green mountains, the fertile valleys, the brothers and sisters who toil the land here and in faraway places completely disconnected from my daily reality. I am aware that those people are an extension of me; I know that together we are the builders. We lay the foundation for the rejuvenated Jewish nation but somehow I fail to feel this deep in my consciousness.

Perhaps it is the outcome of my continuous bouts of malaria. Perhaps it is the pain and the delirium that my sickness bring into my daily life. I am lost, dear brother. I have no one to console me. My friends give me all the care they can, but in our primitive surrounding this care does not do much good.

I long for home. Please do not think ill of me for I have decided to return home. I know that this is only a temporary break from my beloved land and friends. I shall come home to heal and then I shall return.

Your loving sister,
Rachel

A few weeks later Rachel appeared. She was frail and in a very poor health. Itzhak used some of his savings to send her to a sanitarium in Crimea. Occasionally, he visited her. Within a few weeks she grew stronger, more energetic, more engaged. Itzhak rejoiced in her progress. "Your skin has lost its anemic yellowish color. Your eyes regained their spark. I tell you, my beloved sister, you will be as good as new before the month is over." He hugged her to demonstrate his happiness. A week later, to the delight of her parents, she returned home.

***

In 1912, shortly before his eighteenth birthday, Itzhak was ready to make *aliyah*. He knew that his journey would be perilous. Crooks, shady characters, immoral men, wolves in sheep's clothing who presented forged credentials were eager to prey on immigrants at every port on their way. Jaffa, his final destination, was no exception. But villainous persons were only a part of the risk. Hunger, seasickness and poor sanitary conditions introduced additional complications. To prepare for the trip, Itzhak paid a visit on the next day to the Odessa Committee office for guidance.

"Only talk with the clerk at the Odessa Committee office when you disembark the ship in Istanbul or Beirut," advised the clerk. He spoke in short disconnected sentences as if he was on an automatic pilot. "You get no food in third class. Only one spigot of water. Take food for two days. Speak to no one when you disembark in Istanbul and Beirut. Beware of Mr. Hardman in Jaffa. He looks and talks like one of us but he is no good. Buy more food in these ports. Always rely on the Odessa Committee Office. In Istanbul get the Red Document. It will save you money in Jaffa. The Jaffa port is full of shady characters. Speak only to the *Eretz Israel* office person. Also, Ottoman clerks expect *bakshish* for every action they render you. Always carry small change. One Ruble or a Frank for the clerk in Istanbul. One for the clerk in Jaffa. That is enough. Oh yes, get a container to hold water, this way you avoid the long lines. Be prepared not to wash your body." He handed him his discounted ticket and bade him well. When Itzhak was near the door he called after him, "I forgot," he said apologetically, "in Jaffa, Mr. Rabinovitch from the *Eretz Israel* Office will meet you at the port plaza."

Itzhak tried to rearrange the sentences in a logical order. *How do I identify Mr. Rabinovitch?* he thought as he reentered the office. The clerk was busy instructing other travelers. Itzhak waited.

When the clerk was free he asked his question. "Do not worry. Mr. Rabinovitch will find you. He will call all the new Zionist arrivals."

"Are there more Zionist on the ship?" asked Itzhak.

"Yes, twelve," replied the clerk.

Itzhak felt happy. *I am not alone. I must find them on the boat.*

A day before he set sail he said goodbye to his parents and Rachel.

"Why must you go now?" asked his father. "You are so young." But secretly he was elated. He reflected on his family. *My eldest died. Two of my children already disappointed me. They settled in America. Rachel has been working for the Odessa Zionist Committee and has been regaining her strength and joy of life. I know she will soon join Itzhak in Eretz Israel. Now Itzhak is ready to fulfill Rabbi Alkalai's assertion that the security and freedom of the Jewish people can only be achieved within our ancestral home. I know he will succeed.*

"Write to us, Rachel and to your brothers in America so we'll know how you are doing. Unfortunately I am too old to go with you. I know that the task is immense, too hard for me, but you, my son, will prevail. I know that." He handed him the last letter from his brother, which Itzhak put in his bag for safekeeping.

"Here," continued his father with teary eyes, after he embraced his son, "take this." He handed him a neatly folded paper. "Read it if the dark clouds of despair obscure your vision of the future."

Itzhak unfolded the paper, looked inside and immediately recognized its content. It was a hand-written copy of 'Blessing for the People,' a poem by the Jewish National Poet, Bialik. His father cherished the poem. It was an ode to the pioneers who carried out the Zionist enterprise in spite of the many hardships and disappointments.

Itzhak folded the paper and put it in his bag for safekeeping. "I shall cherish it more than anything, Father. Thank you."

"Go, my son, and may God be with you," said his father.

Itzhak hugged his parents and said, "Every Passover, for two thousand years, we tell the story of the exodus from Egypt. It is a dream of *aliyah*, a dream of a national rebirth. Fathers tell it to their children and they pass it on to their children adding a link to an ever growing, an unbroken chain of longing to reclaim our beloved land. I am the latest link in that chain. I will care for it, strengthen it, and pass it to my children. I realize the dream by moving away from the darkness of the Diaspora into the bright light of our ancient homeland. I transform aspirations into actions. I love you. I thank you for all you have done to educate me and instill the love of *Zion* within me. I promise you will follow in my footsteps. I fully intend to bring you and mother home, to join me in the Promised Land. And to you, my beloved sister, I can only say 'next year in Jerusalem.'" They stood in a silent embrace, crying.

The next day he left home and did not look back. On his way to the port he stopped at a barbershop. The barber cut his sidelocks. Itzhak tied them together and stored them in a special box. He was determined to reach his goal, the 'settlement in *Eretz Israel* of Jewish farmers…' just as the Basel Program had stated in 1897, fifteen years earlier.

4 HOME AT LAST

"Anu Banu Artza Livnot U'lhibanot ba...(We came to our land to build and be reformed by it.)"

Menashe Rabinah, a song of the Second Aliyah.

On Wednesday at four in the afternoon Itzhak set sail from Odessa to Jaffa. He started the journey alone. He was a lad of eighteen, self-assured, convinced of his destiny and devoted to the Zionist cause. For seven years he had been training himself for a fundamental change: the transformation of a Diaspora Jew, a hated Jew in the *Pale*, into a free, emancipated and independent Jew in the land of his forefathers—his home. He read profusely about *Eretz Israel*. To toughen his constitution, he had spent many days on agricultural farms to learn the fundamentals of farming.

With the help of his father and a few friends who spoke Hebrew, he had sharpened his skills. He spent many hours each week at Mr. Aziz's water-pump store, drinking tea and delighting in his increased command of Arabic and the intricate technology of water pump installation and repair. He enjoyed working for Mr. Aziz, as the man liked him and paid him generously—money he eagerly saved for the journey.

He was ready to go. Intellectually aware of the enormous hardship that would confront him but ready to sacrifice his life for the sake of rebuilding the Jewish nation. For the sake of reshaping his fellow Jews into a proud, free people who would engage in manual labor as well as commerce. He was ready to become a pioneer, a man of ideals and iron constitution. He was ready to face whatever *Eretz Israel* threw at him.

As soon as he boarded the ship he began to look for the Zionist group the clerk at the Odessa Committee had mentioned. His ears were focused on Hebrew and Yiddish sounds. *Where there is Hebrew there are people like me who ascend to the land of my dreams.* It took a short time to push through the passengers that crowded the third-class deck before he heard anyone speaking Hebrew. It was somewhat weak, broken, hesitant, but Hebrew nevertheless. There, at the edge of the deck, he saw eight young men and four young women sitting in a circle and talking. He tiptoed closer. He halted far enough away to be unobtrusive, yet close enough to hear and make sense of the conversation.

"You are correct, Moshe," said a slim young woman. "I know *Eretz Israel* is not a land of milk and honey. But it is not the *Pale* either. It is our land: the subject of our everlasting dreams. Our home. It will be like a lump of clay in the hands of an artist, and we shall be the artists and shape it in our new Jewish image."

Itzhak was impressed. *Nice metaphor.* Instantly she caught his attention. She was attractive and pale looking. She was well-groomed and impeccably dressed. *How odd. She must be a city girl from a well-to-do family, but she is traveling in horrible conditions,* he thought.

"I agree, Sorke" replied Moshe, "but you must remember that the Turks are not giving up the land any day soon. Herzl tried and failed to convince them to sell the place to us. So, we will do whatever the man from the *Eretz Israel* Office in Jaffa tells us to do. We are the clay and *Eretz Israel* is the artist. She will do with us whatever she wants and we shall oblige her."

Itzhak looked at him and noticed the rugged line that carved his determined face. His hair was combed backward and lent a formidable addition to his long torso. Simple khaki pants and a clean white shirt adorned his body; metal-framed glasses completed the look. *He is definitely a socialist,* he thought, *just like my team leader in Odessa.*

"You know, Moshe, I agree with you. We are her servants. It will be our duty to nurture her to life. We shall clear her and tend to her needs. We shall plow and seed her and harvest her bounty. They said in Odessa that she is a wild land lying in ruins," said a short but stocky fellow. "None of that should stand in our way. We bring an iron will and unwavering dedication."

"Nice words, Gershon, but we have not confronted the reality of *Eretz Israel* yet," replied Moshe. "They also say in Odessa that many brave comrades succumbed to the hardships and left her to her derelict state."

"I think that we should expect nothing. We go, we see, and we calibrate our future with the conditions on the ground. Our belief in ourselves and our dedication to the cause are most important," said a small, fragile woman who sat near Gershon.

"Excellent sentiment, Tova," said Moshe.

Itzhak inched closer to the group. "Shalom," he said. "Please excuse my interruption. I am Itzhak."

"That is okay. We talk all the time. We love to hear a new voice. I am Moshe," replied the tall socialist. "I am the leader of this group. We call ourselves *Gesher* (Bridge). We are from Odessa on our way to Jaffa. And you?"

"Odessa," he replied.

"I am Yossel the farmer. Well, actually, I am an Economist, but I helped my father in the farm management of a large estate in the *Pale*," said a tall, muscular man. He rose to shake Itzhak's hand while examining him from hair to toes. *The lad is tall and skinny with a face of a kid but with an expression of an intellectual*, he thought and added with a slight smirk of self-satisfaction, "Are you on a tour with your parents?"

"No! I am on my way to Jaffa, alone but with the blessing of my parents."

"Really," said Alexa in disbelief. "You look so young. I am Alexa. I studied Agronomy. I am an agricultural expert." She smiled and sat down.

"I am eighteen. Do not be confused by my age and my young looking face. I am strong and determined. I have been preparing for this journey since I was nine. I speak fluent Hebrew and Arabic," he said with a hint of hubris. "Can I join your group?"

Moshe was impressed by Itzhak's self-assured manner. "Wait till we bring the matter to a vote by the whole group. Meanwhile I'd like the other members of the group to introduce themselves." he said.

One by one they rose and approached Itzhak.

"Kalman. Before I went to the university I decided to make a*liyah*."

"Gershon. I studied engineering, but gave it up to ascend to our neglected motherland."

"Tova. I was studying to be a teacher, but the call of *Zion* interrupted my studies." She gave Itzhak a bear hug. "What about you?" she asked.

"Wait, Itzhak. Meet the other members of our group first."

"Avram. I am an engineer."

"David, I am a doctor. My father set me up in his practice but I decided to answer the voice of the Zionist movement. I can be of greater value there." He smiled and gave Itzhak a friendly hug.

"I am Sara; everyone calls me Sorke. I studied Russian literature but I did not finish. Like my friends, going to *Eretz Israel* was more important." Her demeanor was honest and her eyes were welcoming.

He liked her and said, "I am happy to meet you, Sorke."

She looked at him with an overt expression of admiration. In her mind's eye she saw a determined young man, a true pioneer, an intellectual.

"Ribi. I studied gastronomy." She smiled and added, "You better tell me when my food lacks salt."

"Baruch. I was prepared to study forestry to help my father's business, but *Eretz Israel* seemed more attractive to me." He shook Itzhak's hand warmly.

"Pinchas, I too responded to the call of the motherland."

"I have already introduced myself," said Itzhak. "I studied at my father's Heder (school) but was educated in his library."

"Friends," Moshe asked in a formal tone, "do we accept this young man to *Gesher*?"

"Of course," they all said in unison. "We'll be happy to have him."

"Come join our circle of friendship and tell us about your studies," suggested Moshe.

Itzhak was happy to tell the group about his friendship with Mr. Aziz. "Not only did he teach me Arabic," he said, "but he also shared with me Arabic newspapers. I've had the opportunity to learn about the Arabs and their customs. My father taught me Hebrew."

Moshe was thinking, *Arabic, knowledge of local temperament, and Hebrew, not bad*.

"Welcome to *Gesher*," said Yossel. "I guess I forgot to tell you that I am just a simple man from the *Pale*."

At that moment Itzhak was no longer alone. He had acquired twelve new friends.

"I like the name '*Gesher*.' It is a beautiful name. It means that we are the bridge between the darkness of the Diaspora and the brightness of the future in *Eretz Israel*," said Itzhak in a warm and reverent voice.

Kalman smiled. "You know, Itzhak, I have never thought of it in this way. But now that you mention it, I like our group's name more than ever."

They sat in a larger circle and continued their conversation. Alexa said, "My father always talked about *Eretz Israel* with love and reverence. He used to tell me that one day we should leave this accursed land and return home to *Eretz Israel*. It has been deserted for too long."

Pinchas added, "You know that there are non-Zionist Jews who live in *Eretz Israel*. They reside mainly in the four holy cities: Jerusalem, Hebron, Tiberia and Tzfat. But they are poor, old and most likely do not know of the Zionist movement, nor will they support it if they know. They are much like our own Jews of the Diaspora. Meek, passive, and trusting their present and future to the will of God and the contribution they get from the Diaspora. They are a remnant of a broken People."

"So is the land," said Ribi. "It is poor and neglected. Yes, there are a few Jewish Farm settlements in the wilderness of *Eretz Israel*, like Rishon Le'zion and Petach Tikva. Eventually our settlement will join them."

"It may be the wilderness," added Gershon, "but it is our wilderness. We shall revive it with our hard work."

"I think we should spend some time in Petach Tikva. I know it is the oldest settlement and most developed," suggested Sorke.

"You know, Ahad Ha'am wrote in his essay, 'The Truth from *Eretz Israel*,' that the land is populated and cultivated. Mr. Aziz told me that there are many Arabs in *Eretz Israel*. For the most part they look askance on the Zionist project. In their eyes we are unwelcome strangers. We better discard the notion that the place is empty and wild," said Itzhak, and then changed the subject abruptly. He did not want to start his tenure with the group by being controversial. "I hope the Ottoman authority will honor our entry card and let us into the country."

"They will," Gershon said, "but your observations about the land are amazing. If you are right, we need to plan how to deal with the locals."

"Ahad Ha'am advised treating them with justice and respect," Itzhak responded.

"We want to build our own farm, till the land, sow and harvest the bounty that she will yield for us, her returning children. I hope the *Eretz Israel* Office in Jaffa will help us buy land."

The passage through the Black Sea was uneventful. Itzhak spent most of the day on the main deck, talking with his new friends about being laborers, about learning Hebrew, about the importance of their mission. They spoke a shaky Hebrew, and Itzhak was determined to teach them as much as time permitted.

On Friday morning the boat arrived in Istanbul. Avram invited Itzhak to walk with him to secure the Red Document from the Turkish authorities. They followed all the instructions they received in Odessa. "Tell me," asked Avram as they walked to get food, "what caused you to make a*liyah* at such a young age?"

Itzhak told him about the disturbances at Domsky, the inn near Gordov, about the pogrom in Gordov. Then he said, "I have seen my people helpless, harassed, abused and humiliated. I have read the dark history of misery and bloody deeds against our people and I could not escape the conclusion of Rabi Alkalai, Pinsker and others, who said that the only remedy for the miserable condition of the Jewish nation is to assume personal responsibility for their fate by the acquisition of a homeland of their own where they can be free to develop their language, culture and national character. *Eretz Israel* is historically ours. But we must reacquire it with money and sweat."

Avram was silent. He was touched by the strength of Itzhak's conviction and depth of knowledge. "Amazing, Itzhak. I came to the same conclusion by a different route. My decision to make *aliyah* is rooted in the horrific suffering I witnessed in Kishinev and Odessa. I vowed, never again. Even though I am not well-versed in Jewish history, I remember my grandfather's conclusion of the Passover meal 'Next year in Jerusalem.' We must be a free nation in our own historical home. Only then shall we be respected by other nations."

They bought fresh food. After a day's rest, the boat set sail through the Mediterranean Sea to Beirut.

Clouds gathered on the eastern horizon. Everyone saw the distant signs of a brewing tempest, but no one thought it was heading in their direction. Suddenly, a massive black cloud veered southwest. Within seconds it hovered above the ship, drenching the surprised passengers with sheets of water. The sea grew choppy. Restless. White crowns adorned its waves as they rolled furiously across the sea. The wind howled ceaselessly. Threatening columns of salty water washed the deck.

"Get all the passengers below deck," barked the Captain at his second mate, who was rushing about pushing people and cursing angrily at those who moved too slowly for his liking. Eventually the deck was clear. People crowded below in a cramped space. There was no place to go. The air was salty. Everything was damp. Bugs moved across the floor like medieval armies swarming the battlefield.

The storm raged for two days, shaking the boat and its passengers. All that time the crew worked feverishly on the most urgent tasks, leaving routine activities unattended. The toilets remained at the mercy of their users, some of whom had no concept of hygiene. Stinky vapor drifted toward the lower deck passengers' quarters. There it hung repulsively overhead, causing nausea and other discomforts. Sleeping was nearly impossible.

It came as no surprise that, under those unsettling conditions where every discomfort was magnified, everything upset the stomach. Everyone walked about in a daze. People who were seasick had no place to relieve themselves and had to use the already unsavory toilets.

The misery lasted for two days and two nights. On the third day the wind died. The sea stretched calmly to the four corners of the skies, swelling gently under the warm eastern wind. The sun climbed slowly across a cloudless sky, bringing with it an end to pain. People felt the change; no one was tossed from one side of the ship to the other.

"Open the doors. Let some good air clear the stench!" shouted one of the Arab passengers.

The sailor who was coming from the upper deck cursed and told him to shut up and wait. Then the captain ordered the crew to let the people out. One sailor rushed to open the door but did not allow the pushing passengers out.

"Stay below until we tell you that all is clear!" he screamed at the swelling masses that pushed toward the door. Crewmembers were the first to enjoy the fresh sea air and the warm sun. They checked the deck for damages.

"Let them out," shouted the first mate, and the guards at the door moved swiftly to the side, avoiding the surging passengers.

Soft, warm sun swept the deck and seeped into the living quarters below, drying the persistent dampness. Hungry and tired passengers scattered throughout the open space. Everyone wanted to escape the bugs and the stench. They sat as if in shock. No one talked. They were just happy to breathe fresh air and soak up the warm sunrays that flooded the deck. Only the steady hum of the motor disturbed the quiet that engulfed their floating world.

For a brief moment, life aboard the ship seemed more tolerable. But, by the next day, Itzhak noted that his food supply had dwindled and what was left was inedible. Hunger ate away at him. He constantly thought about food. The line for the only water supply was long. When he finally reached the front of the line, the spigot produced no more water. For the next two days he and his friends experienced the pain of hunger and thirst. He could see his new friends suffering like him. No one had food or water. They huddled together on a sliver of the deck, squeezed between two large groups of Arabs. Itzhak rested, limiting his activities to conserve energy. He daydreamed about the coming week, about his first day at Home. *What will Eretz Israel be like?* He could not concentrate. His empty stomach rumbled and growled. He felt awful.

After two days of hunger the boat docked at the port of Beirut. Members of the *Gesher* group waited for the passengers to disembark in order to avoid pushing and crowding. At last Itzhak and his new friends disembarked and headed for the Odessa Committee Office. After a good meal at a nearby café they went food shopping. The port area looked unpleasant, but they did not care. Beirut was incidental to their journey. Jaffa—not Beirut—was the place they wanted to feel, smell, and hear.

Many of the Turkish and Arab passengers remained in Beirut; a few Arabs boarded the ship for the journey to Jaffa. Itzhak was happy. Fewer passengers in third class meant more room, shorter lines to the water spigot. After a day's rest in Beirut the ship continued on to Jaffa.

Itzhak was delighted with his new friends. Even though they had led separate lives in Odessa, they shared a past and destiny with him. For them, the journey was the conclusion of years of devotion: living, breathing the cause. His new friends had come to Odessa from all corners of the *Pale*. There, like a blind man searching in darkness, they found each other, formed an association, joined the movement, and spent years together working for the Zionist cause. They were the vanguard of the nascent Zionist movement in Odessa. They, like his brother Avram, went to the defense of their brothers and sisters who lived under a continuous threat of hateful agitation and ignorance that invariably led to terrible Pogroms. Odessa, Kiev and Bialystok were just a few of the many that swept the *Pale* during 1905 – 1906 but those were subjected, unlike the Kishinev Pogrom in 1903, to strong resistance by Jewish groups throughout Russia. But at age eleven, Itzhak was too young to join a self-defense group, or march with his friends who fought for justice and honor for their people.

He and his new friends shared the same politics. They read and talked about *Eretz Israel.* For them, going to *Eretz Israel* was not a simple act of immigration. Unlike many of their brothers and sisters who immigrated to somewhere in the Western world, they made *Aliyah.* They ascended. As if *Eretz Israel* existed in another sphere of creation. As if it did not share a sea-level coast line with Great Britain, the United States, Canada and other countries that absorbed huge waves of Jewish immigration.

They were ready to rise and ascend to the Promised Land in order to take part in resuscitating their comatose nation and its deserted homeland. Those who succumbed to the hardships and left the Zionist enterprise were never emigrating from Palestine. They descended! Those who descended were the weak. The disloyal. The uncommitted. The traitors.

Soon after they left Beirut, Itzhak walked to the eastern railing and eagerly scanned the horizon, hoping to catch a glimpse of the land of his longing. *Eretz Israel* was but a few miles below the horizon.

The rest of the group, just as focused, just as eager as Itzhak, joined him. They stood shoulder to shoulder with anticipation, their eyes glued on the fading light of the eastern skies. They scrutinized the silvery band far to the east searching for any sign of land, when Kalman spotted the Galil Mountains. They were overjoyed.

Tova began to sing in Hebrew, quietly at first, almost in a whisper choked with emotion:

As long as the heart within,
A Jewish soul still yearns

Her voice rose slowly until everyone could identify the words. They gathered around her, held each other's shoulders and with teary eyes burst into song.

As long as the heart within,
A Jewish soul still yearns
And onward, towards the end of the east
An eye still gazes upon Zion:
Our hope is not yet lost
The hope of two thousand years,
To be a free people in our land
The land of Zion and Jerusalem

They sang the Hatikva *(*the Hope*)* in Hebrew. Their feeling, true to the lyrics, captured the yearning of two thousand years of a nation in exile.

Their voices grew louder and then died down slowly, as if refusing to leave the images their breath painted upon the air. Overcome by emotion, they sank to the deck and lay quietly. They were not ready to sleep. Eagerness weighed down their tired minds. Their eyelids remained open. Their thoughts meandered in all directions, while their gazes fixed on the Eastern sky until darkness engulfed the ship and a canopy of bright stars shone upon their voyage.

The silence lasted for a long time until Moshe's voice refocused their wondering thoughts. "Hatikva," he said, "was written thirty-four years ago by Naphtali Herz Imber. He was inspired by the founding of Petach Tikva (Opening of Hope), the first modern settlement in *Eretz Israel*."

"It is interesting to note," interrupted Itzhak, "that the name is anchored in an ever present past. It was the Prophet Hosea who provided the inspiration for the name. He said, *And I will give her vineyards from thence, and the Valley of Anchor for an opening of hope: and she shall sing there, as in the days of her youth, and as in the day when she came up out of the land of Egypt.*

Everyone smiled at their young friend.

Moshe continued. "After the poem was put into music, it was adopted by the sixth Zionist Congress in 1903 as the anthem of the Zionist movement. But let me continue with Petach Tikva, as it marked a significant milestone in the redemption of our land. A handful of orthodox Jews, members of a local society for working the soil and redeeming the land, left the walled city of Jerusalem, a courageous act with no precedent. They headed to the swamp-covered plains near the Mediterranean to usher in a new era—the end of the Old *Yishuv* (the old Jewish community).

"The creation of Petach Tikva in 1878 was the first crack in the wall of dependency and apathy that typified the old Community. From that day on Jews took their destiny in their own hands, and activism replaced Jewish inaction. We no longer wait for the Messiah. We assume responsibility for our own destiny."

Itzhak liked Moshe's comments and wanted to add a few words but kept his thoughts to himself. He did not want to interrupt again. Instead he smiled, hoping that no one noticed.

"Did I say anything funny?" asked Moshe with an obvious hint of annoyance.

"No! Not at all. You reminded me of a story my father told one *Shabbat* dinner, a few days before Passover. I was only nine."

"I wish you would share it with us, as it elicited such a broad smile on your face," demanded Yossel.

"Very well" said Itzhak and told them about Saadia's recitation of Ben Yochai's allegory. "At the end Saadia said Cain was responsible for his own deeds. God wants us to assume responsibility for our own life. And that is exactly what we are doing here."

Moshe was delighted. *Our new friend is somewhat of a scholar,* he thought. "Now let's have some sleep. Tomorrow morning we shall be in Jaffa. We shall need all the energy we can muster," he suggested.

Saadia was right, Itzhak reflected. *And now we raise the banner of his wisdom. We join the new Jewish community. The new Yishuv, independent, self-assured and, most importantly, our responsibility...our destiny.* He felt tired but happy and soon fell asleep with a broad smile on his face.

Before retiring for the night, Sorke opened her diary to a new page and wrote. *"April 15, 1912. A few days ago Itzhak was a total stranger. Now he is one of us. I like him. He is smart. Articulate. Handsome. Young in age but mature in thinking and behavior. I LIKE him!"*

***

She glanced at Itzhak, who was lying on the deck a few feet from her, saw his smile and reciprocated with a smile of her own.

One by one, the group fell into a deep sleep dreaming about the land they had come to rescue.

The sun rose over a calm sea. It flooded the deck with a bright light that nudged the men and the women from their deep slumber. A few jumped to their feet, calling their comrades to shake the web of dreams from their eyes.

"Rise, friends, *Eretz Israel* is on the horizon," rejoiced Yossel, who spotted a distant mountain range.

The boat drew nearer and nearer. A skyline of a small city emerged from the morning haze. Houses that crowded the eastern horizon followed closely the contours of a hill that rose from the shoreline. Two large towers dominated the landscape. One was clearly a minaret of a local mosque; the other looked like a clock tower. People dressed in long, white dresses led a caravan of camels along a narrow strip of the sandy beach.

"Jaffa," proclaimed Kalman.

They gathered at the front deck watching *Eretz Israel* transform from a dream to reality. "Imagine," said Moshe as they pushed forward to get a better view of the city. "Millions of Jews have left the *Pale* on their way West, to America. But we, a droplet of the wandering people, are going home. We come to rebuild our land. To raise her to a new glory. To let her reshape our character. We come to forge the new Jew."

They broke into song spontaneously. *"Anu Banu Artza Livnot U'lhibant ba"* (We came to our land to build and be reformed by it) reverberated throughout the deck: a new sound of faith and conviction. Hands locked around shoulders, feet moved forward, and the entire group began the slow motion that would end in frenzy. Round and around they danced in ever-widening circles of the Hora dance. "Anu Banu" mixed with La...La...La...drowned the hubbub of passengers eager to leave the cramped quarters of the ship. Occasionally the dancers separated, clapped their hands to give their Hora a greater meaning. They swirled without a pause. Every round accelerated their motion. The faster they went, the louder they sounded. Ecstasy engulfed them as they moved at an ever-growing speed, singing louder and louder. The energy was all consuming.

They finally fell to the deck, exhausted and grasping for air. But they were elated.

A cacophony assaulted their eardrums. Confused sounds of Russian, mixed with Arabic, Yiddish, Turkish and a few words of English and French. The air was abuzz with excitement, which soon turned into bewilderment and fear. They had reached the end of their voyage. The ship laid anchor about two kilometers from the shore. Little boats were steered by half-naked oarsmen who shouted in Arabic as they surrounded the ship. More boats raced over the calm sea to reach it.

Sailors threw ladders overboard. An unruly mass of sweaty bodies with strange, dark and menacing faces, climbed aboard in a competitive frenzy, pushing and shoving each other. They surrounded the frightened passengers like a pack of hungry wolves. Like animals in a feeding orgy they raced to snatch any baggage that was within reach as if it was prey. They shouted the price of the journey to shore, but only a few understood Arabic. The oarsmen left the passengers no choice. They grabbed whatever they could, threw their "prey" to the waiting boats below, then pushed the frightened passengers toward the ladders and helped them, roughly, through the descent.

The young pioneers left behind the unsavory quarters of the ship and prepared for the journey toward Jaffa. They waited in the rowboat for the Arab who was still on board searching for more passengers.

The boat rose and fell with the swells. Everyone was anxious and nauseated. The Promised Land was ever so close, yet still untouchable. They waited. The oarsman finally dropped a few more pieces of luggage followed by their owners. Then he jumped overboard. Dripping with water he climbed aboard his little boat and rowed toward shore. Like all the other oarsmen, he zigged and zagged among the many threatening rocks toward the port's plaza.

Itzhak wondered about the danger. He witnessed a boat tipping over and saw its shivering human cargo wade through shallow water to shore, having lost most of their belongings. "They are lucky," he told Moshe. "Imagine what might have happened if they were in deep water. Or, if it was our boat. I can't swim."

Moshe smiled, "I can. I would save you."

Once on land everyone shouted. Fathers became separated from their children, friends lost contact with friends. Chaos was everywhere.

The Jewish travelers fell to their knees, raised their hands to the heavens and filled the air with prayers. Moshe assembled his group. He shouted, "We have arrived. We are home at last! We are here now forever and ever."

"Amen," replied the group. Words of thanksgiving ascended to the morning skies. They rose to their feet and looked around.

The port's plaza was the first sliver of *Eretz Israel* they encountered. It was an alien land. Unsavory. Full of unfamiliar shapes, sounds, and smells. The street that led to the office of the Ottoman Immigration authorities was crowded with people coming and going. People pushed and shoved. Merchants with pushcarts loaded with foodstuffs shouted in Arabic as they thrust their wares, covered with flies, into the faces of the newcomers. Moshe and his team pushed forward next to a long line of Jews who were to board the ship on their way out of the country. Tired people with guilt-laden eyes watched them in disbelief.

"I am just going to visit a sick mother," said one person whose wife and two children looked away.

"Why are you coming here? It is not a good place," said another.

"Go back to Russia. This place is full of Arabs. They hate us. We are unwelcome here."

"There is no work."

"Malaria killed my child."

"Typhus has tortured me for months."

"Look at hands. Are these the hands of a farmer? I am a tailor. So why only work I find digs in orchards?"

Everyone had a story to tell. Everyone felt a need to tell it, as if he was explaining why he was abandoning the Zionist dream. The dream of the Promised Land, the land where Jews would be free and secure, exploded before his eyes as it collided with that savage reality.

Itzhak hesitated. His legs felt weak. He took a deep breath. *I wonder, is my devotion to the project strong enough? Will I survive the reality that is unfolding before my eyes?* He recalled his sister's letters. *Could she have been a part of a similar tired crowd? Probably. But she did not abandon the cause; she fell ill for it! She will return. I am not going to let these scenes affect me,* he resolved. He felt an added strength taking hold of him. *There are always the weak who do not rise to a challenge.*

At the eastern edge of the plaza they encountered pimps and prostitutes, unsavory agents of hotels who tried to lure them to flea infested rooms for inflated fees. Even the infamous Mr. Hardman was there.

Unlike most of the naive passengers who fell prey to the unscrupulous hordes of "well-wishers," Itzhak and his friends were prepared for the onslaught. Itzhak recalled the words of the clerk at the Odessa committee. "Mr. Hardman was once our agent in Jaffa. He was supposed to help the newcomers. Beware of him. He is neither a Zionist nor an Idealist. He is not a friend. He is a greedy hotel owner who takes advantage of people rather than help them. Stay away from him."

Mr. Hardman approached the group and with gentle words tried to lure them to his hotel.

"Moshe," whispered Itzhak who stood nearby, "avoid this man. He is no good."

"I know," said Moshe. "I visited the Odessa Committee office before I left. We should meet the real *Eretz Israel* Office's man outside the Ottoman office."

Twelve days at sea in deplorable conditions left an unpleasant mark on their appearance. They moved like ghosts toward the exit, where a crumbling building served the Turkish immigration office. Unshaven, dirty, tired and hungry, they filed one by one into the immigration office. The haggard clerk asked his questions in a monotonous voice, rarely raising his face to look at the people who stood before him. He spoke in Turkish. Someone translated into Russian.

"Why are you here?"

"To visit relatives."

"Where are you from?"

"Russia."

"You must register with the Russian representative in Jaffa!"

"Yes."

"Give me your Russian and Ottoman documents."

"Here."

"One Frank."

The next in line asked no questions. That was the famous *bakshish* they were warned about. Everyone handed the clerk a Frank.

"Here is your three-month permit to visit the country. When you leave you'll get your documents back."

They could see the logic of his words. But they knew that tomorrow, with a little *Bakshish* their papers would be returned and no Turkish official would bother them again. After all they were Russian citizens protected by the Russian Consul in *Eretz Israel*.

A well-dressed man stood outside the Ottoman Immigration Office calling for the *Gesher* group. "I am Mr. Rabinovitch from the *Eretz Israel* Office in Jaffa. Please follow me," he said once he identified the group.

The street that led out of the port toward the *Eretz Israel* Office and the local hotels was narrow, unpaved and strewn with trash. The walls of a dilapidated structure across the Ottoman's office were covered with bold graffiti. "Go home Jews!" it screamed in a red-hot painted Arabic calligraphy. Itzhak read and fumed with anger. His comrades moved right past the graffiti.

This is my home, he protested quietly to himself, clenching his fist. *This is my home! This is my home!* he repeated. An agitated air streamed out of his closed lips.

They walked toward Bustros Street. Moshe, cognizant of Itzhak's sudden agitation asked, "What is the matter, Itzhak?" Itzhak shrugged his shoulders and said nothing. He did not want to cause alarm among his friends.

They soon got the message without understanding the language. A large group of Arabs gathered outside the plaza. They jeered the newcomers with threatening gestures. "Go home, Jews. Go back to Russia," they shouted in unison. "Allah is great! Palestine is for Palestinians, not for dogs."

Itzhak paused. He understood. Moreover, his friends sensed the unwelcoming gestures.

"What do they say, Itzhak?" asked Gershon. This time he had no choice but to translate. His friends were stunned. A few reacted instinctively. They stopped and picked up debris that lay on the ground; stuff that could serve as defensive weapons: a metal pipe, a stone, and a broken limb of a nearby tree.

Mr. Rabinovitch moved briskly toward them. "Listen, Listen," he spoke Hebrew with a heavy German accent as he tried to calm their anger.

Not everyone understood. "Stop and listen to me," Itzhak translated. "Listen friends, this man is trying to tell us something."

The anger at the shouting Arabs died out abruptly. Fury gave way to an uncertain pause. "Follow me!" commanded Mr. Rabinovitch. "We must get out of here before the excited mob gets out of control."

They lined up behind him and marched briskly away from the port's gate. The hostile mob followed the small group as far as the intersection. Someone threw a stone. Yossel was hit. Fresh blood streamed down his face. Everyone gathered around him in a defensive posture. Eyes burning with rage held the mob at bay. Penetrating gazes scanned the stationary crowd searching for the guilty man.

"This is not Russia," shouted Gershon as he lifted the blood-coated stone. "This is our *Eretz Israel. Am Israel Chai*! The nation of Israel is alive!" Then he hurled the red stone with all his might at the threatening mob. Bedlam engulfed the two groups. Lily-white bodies collided with dark muscular ones.

"Stop!" commanded Mr. Rabinovitch. "We must go before the police arrive." Two people helped Yossel to his feet. They regrouped and retreated beyond the corner. Echoes of discontent persisted in the air of the narrow street.

Their guide led them to Bustros Street, where they settled at a local Arabic coffee house for some orange juice, Turkish coffee and hot tea. David examined Yossel and determined that the wound was non-threatening.

"Eat and rest," suggested Mr. Rabinovitch. "You have had quite a full morning. Be thankful that Yossel is only superficially wounded, as medical facilities are not great here."

"Yes. We are. But I assure you that we will defend our lives and property. This is not the *Pale*," said Tova indignantly.

"The Arab belligerence was quite unexpected," remarked Yossel, who had regained his composure. "Itzhak was right when he reminded us that the locals may not welcome our enterprise. But I say to them, we are here to stay!"

"Land ownership and immigration are major problems here. In time you will understand the issues and their nuances. Let me assure you that there is an aggressive effort to purchase land, mainly from absentee landlords who do not live here. Private people, the Palestine Office, the Odessa Committee Office and others buy land. No one wants to push the Arabs out. There is ample space to accommodate our people and theirs," remarked Mr. Rabinovitch.

"Perhaps," said Sorke, "for now I am most disturbed by all of those emigrants. They are a disgrace to the Jewish nation. I was more distraught from that scene than from the attack by the Arab mob. Here we are, thirteen of us and fifty of them. What a shame."

"Do not be so harsh," responded Baruch. "We have yet to experience the conditions they escape. Who knows how we will react."

"I agree," said Itzhak. "My sister Rachel had to leave *Eretz Israel* because of severe sickness."

"I am not harsh," said Sorke. "I just recalled the complaints of the Israelites on their liberation march from four hundred years of slavery in Egypt. Did they not cry for the food they had there? Imagine wanting to go back to the darkness of the Diaspora."

They ate and drank tea and took in the entire aroma and sounds of Jaffa around them.

"When you are ready I shall lead you to the Turkish bath so you can bathe, then to a good local hotel. Tomorrow I shall show you the town and instruct you about your next steps," said Mr. Rabinovitch.

The visit to the bath felt like a stopover in the Garden of Eden. They cleansed their bodies and rested in the steam room. They lingered, savoring the pleasure of transforming a stinky, dirty body into a clean one. When it was over, Mr. Rabinovitch led them to a clean and welcoming local hotel.

On that day, Sorke's diary note was brief. *4/15/1912. Home at last!*

***

After a good night's rest, even though they slept two to a bed in crowded hotel rooms, they enjoyed a hearty breakfast and, led by Mr. Rabinovitch, went to explore the town. They soon came across an unending stream of Arab women dressed in vibrant clothing, their hair covered. On their heads, perfectly balanced, were large baskets full of local produce. The women strode quickly and confidently. The local market was at the end of the street. Loud noises, unfamiliar scents and colorful stalls filled the street and the narrow alleys that dissected it. The young men and women meandered through the market admiring the colors and inhaling the aroma of spices, citrus fruits and vegetables.

"Go ahead buy an orange. It is the famous Jaffa orange that is prized in Europe," said Mr. Rabinovitch.

Ribi said, "I see beautiful produce: tomatoes, cucumbers, eggplants, onions and many kinds of greens. I see eggs, and chickens, but no meat. No milk products."

"Yes," said Mr. Rabinovitch, "Arabs have few cows and many goats and therefore little butter and cheese. However," he continued, "the German Templars of Sarona and Wilhelma, nearby settlements, provide excellent milk products and meat to the Jewish market at Neve Shalom, one of two Jewish quarters in town."

Throughout the day they realized how far away from Odessa they were. The streets were filthy, filled with foodstuff, papers and camel dung. Except for Bustros Street, the byways, alleyways and streets were unpaved.

Bustros Street contrasted with the unsanitary conditions, dilapidated houses and general chaos. It was a modern urban center: relatively clean, lined with modern houses, shops and coffee houses. It was the business, the administrative and the social hub of the region.

"This is our office," said Mr. Rabinovitch as they passed the *Eretz Israel* Office. "There is the Odessa Committee office. Over there is the Land Development Corporation. Remember that this street is the Zionist's administrative center of *Eretz Israel.*"

Itzhak stopped at an adjacent kiosk to browse through the newspapers. After a short while he bought a Hebrew and an Arabic paper, tucked them under his arm and rejoined the group's leisurely stroll to the hotel. He managed to read both papers before bedtime.

The next morning, at breakfast, Moshe asked him, "Would you please share the key topics of the papers?"

"Sure," he replied. "The Hebrew paper discusses the continuous struggle of the Conquest of Labor. In a nutshell it provides a detailed report on the ongoing struggle of the rank and file, as well as the leadership of the Second *Aliyah, (*second wave of immigration*)* in replacing Arab labor with Jewish labor throughout the *Yishuv's* land. The Arabic paper promotes a strong opposition to Jewish immigration and purchase of land in Palestine."

"We are here, Itzhak, ready and able to join our brothers and sisters in the struggle for the redemption of our national right on our historic land," declared Moshe. "As far as the Arab's opposition, our love for *Zion* and dedication to its redemption will not be diminished. Tomorrow we shall go to Rishon Le'zion to observe one room of our national house."

5 HEBREW LABOR

"We must place Labor at the center of all our aspirations it is the foundation on which to build all our future progress."

A.D. Gordon, About the affairs of Labor.

"... Hebrew labor is imperative for the establishment of our country and the rebirth of our people."

A.D. Gordon, The Labor.

On a bright spring day in 1912, three days after the demoralizing welcome in Jaffa port, they went to explore the countryside. David insisted that Yossel should stay behind and rest; he volunteered to stay with him.

The rest of the group marched southward. Every step they took connected them with the ground of *Eretz Israel*. Their eyes were fixed on the distant horizon where they expected to see the new, albeit nascent, Jewish world that until that day existed only in their imagination.

Their first foray into the reawakening motherland was vigorous and bombastic. They sang, in Russian and, occasionally, in Hebrew, songs they had learned back in Odessa. Their voices rolled through the land with bravado and candor.

The world stands upon the work
Rejoice and sing a song of thanks.
Work is the essence of our life
It will save us from any strife.

They were ready to work the land, to redeem it with their labor, as they were sure all who came before them did. They were a happy bunch, resolutely preparing to follow in the footsteps of their predecessors, the Jews who answered the call of the Lovers of *Zion* movement, and later that of the nascent Zionist movement in the twilight of the nineteenth century and the dawn of the twentieth century, to settle *Eretz Israel*. Those settlers formed the first modern wave of immigrants to establish agricultural settlements across the land.

One was Rishon Le'zion, which awaited the visiting newcomers in the distance. They marched forward in anticipation. Most of them had no idea what they might see. They imagined the encounter in a dreamlike haze. Itzhak and Moshe were thinking about the Conquest of Labor in Rishon Le'zion.

Moshe led the group. He moved forward with outward determination, even though he lacked a real sense of Rishon Le'zion's whereabouts. "How do I walk to Rishon Le'zion?" he asked the clerk at the *Eretz Israel* office before they left.

"Follow the path of the diligence," the clerk replied. "In a few hours, you will get there."

"What's a diligence?" asked Moshe.

"You better get used to it, as it is the best way to travel around unless you prefer to walk. You will see it on the roads outside of Jaffa."

"Thank you. But what is it?"

"It is a coach pulled by two or three horses. It has three benches, enough room for eight passengers and a coachman. Anyway, go to the end of the street, turn right and continue south. You will eventually see the tracks of the diligence."

Moshe did. His friends followed leisurely behind him. Baruch walked at the end of the line. There were little conversations and lots of singing. Unexpectedly Sorke turned around and said, "I tell you, Tova, I feel happiness in my heart. We are the latest link in the ancient chain that bound the Jewish soul to *Eretz Israel* for thousands of years." Her voice reflected the exuberance of the group.

Tova nodded. "Walking on the land is only a tentative link, working it is a permanent one. One day soon, we shall build a settlement. We will work the land and through our work we will forge the real link."

"I agree," interjected Gershon, who was a few feet behind Tova. "Farm labor will be the essence of our success."

Then the three rejoined in the merriment.

Ahead, the land of their forefathers undulated gently toward the distant mountains of Shomron, waiting for them to revive her by the sweat of their brow. They marched south, following the dirt road of the diligence.

Their legs carried them through the gentle terrain. Their bodies were light and their souls intoxicated. A northern wind blowing at their backs propelled them forward as if they were carried on an eagle's wings. They were young and single, enthusiastic, secular, educated, and awash with socialist convictions. But most importantly, they were fiercely in love with the land under their feet. That emotion brightened their perception of the future. Their well-being was yet untouched by the looming difficulties. Their will was iron-strong, their enthusiasm boundless. They were eager to contribute their sweat and energy to the land that caressed their feet.

The road stretched before them as if it had no end. It meandered through a monotonous landscape of rudimentary cultivated fields and open grassland punctuated by dull, gray Arab villages teeming with people. Herds of goats and sheep roamed in search of food. Here and there they saw a solitary figure walking lazily behind a donkey, plowing a small plot adjacent to a single mud hut. They moved forward, enjoying the strange but pleasant aroma of food preparation.

After some time, the landscape changed. The sandy road meandered between citrus orchards alive with Arab workers. Without warning, Moshe's stride lost its energy. He paused momentarily. The song on his lips died down. For a moment he was suspended in mid-step. "The land is full of Arab workers," he reflected aloud. "Maybe this is Arab land?"

The folks who marched behind him neither heard his words nor saw what he saw; the passion of singing mesmerized them. Unprepared for his sudden change of pace they bumped into each other, wondering what had happened. A brief moment later Moshe regained his stride. *It will be different in Rishon Le'zion*, he thought. With renewed vigor a new song reverberated through the air. It started quietly but soon reached a crescendo that matched their previous mood.

Here in the beloved land of our forefathers
All hopes we'll realize
Here we shall live and devise
Glorious and free life...

With a song on their lips, the group marched on. Citrus orchards interlacing with almonds groves and sprawling vineyards blocked the horizons on both sides of the road. Arab men, women and children in their dark attire were all around. At that point, everyone saw what Moshe had seen. Once again the song died.

Gershon was visibly perturbed. He commented with a touch of anger, "The Arabs are everywhere. The Jews are nowhere. Well, almost nowhere. I see a few here and there."

"I am sad to say that I have noticed the same thing," said Tova.

"That is not what I'd expected. I thought Jewish settlements employed Jewish people," said Alexa.

"Let's not be unhappy. First, we do not know who owns these orchards. Second, even if this is Jewish land, maybe there are not enough Jewish workers to work in these fields," said Ribi.

"I agree," said Itzhak. "Wait till we get to our destination. There we shall find the answer. For now, it is too early to be sad, Tova."

"Perhaps." interjected Baruch. "But if this is a Jewish land then I am definitely appalled."

The paucity of Jewish laborer dampened their enthusiasm. But the anticipation of seeing Rishon Le'zion and learning about its life helped them resume their songs and move forward with renewed energy.

They emerged from the orchards marching into a broad, clean avenue lined with beautiful trees. They paused and looked with awe at the first Jewish settlement they had seen in *Eretz Israel*. From afar they could see a great winery teeming with Arab laborers. Further downhill, a few Jewish laborers were visible at numerous orange-packing houses while a caravan of camels crouched on the ground waiting to be loaded.

A large synagogue loomed above them from a low hill not too far west. Beautiful dwellings lined both sides of the avenue. Each proudly displayed a vegetable plot, a flower garden, a chicken coop, a barn for a few milking cows, a shed for farm tools, and a small citrus orchard. Laundry was drying in the light breeze, and children played energetically in the enclosed yard of what seemed to be a school. The reawakening *Eretz Israel* stretched in front of their eyes. This was the world they had been dreaming about, minus the Arab workers. Farmers and a few Jewish workers, who strolled along the main avenue, were but a drop in a drab wave of Arab men, women, and children filling the avenue.

"Now that is what I call progress," said Kalman. He was preoccupied with the rhythm of industry and commerce rather than with the presence of Arab labor, the very fact that offended his friends' sensibilities.

A farmer crossed the road to welcome them. "Hello. I am Mr. Glazer. Are you newcomers?" he asked as he warmly shook each one's hand.

"We are," replied Moshe. "We arrived three days ago."

"In that case, welcome to *Eretz Israel*," said Mr. Glazer.

After a short conversation in Yiddish, the farmer, who had been born in Odessa and was eager for news about his city, invited the group to his house for tea. It was a comfortable house, with three bedrooms, a large kitchen, a social space and a porch overlooking a garden and a little orchard. They sipped tea, ate delicious cookies and talked about Russia, specifically about Odessa. They were so engrossed in their conversations that they paid little attention to Mrs. Glazer, who served them so graciously.

After an hour or so of benign discussion, Gershon abruptly changed the subject. "We have walked through your orchards and vineyards. We saw countless Arabs. I counted only a handful of Jewish workers. Clearly, this is Jewish land that Arab hands cultivate. Did we not come to redeem the land by our labor?" No one but Moshe displayed any hint of displeasure upon hearing Gershon's comment.

"Our main goal is the redemption of the land and that has been extremely hard. It is what we have been doing," replied Mr. Glazer with a forgiving smile.

"That is not enough," protested Tova. "The land must be redeemed with Jewish labor."

"I think this is neither the time nor the place to argue labor policy," interrupted Moshe. "It is late. We must be on our way back to Jaffa."

Gershon accepted Moshe's admonition reluctantly. Tova reacted apologetically. "Pardon my comment, I do appreciate your hospitality. Thank you."

"It is okay," said Mr. Glazer. "I actually agree with you and your friend. I'd like to invite you to come again on Friday. We can have a candid discussion about the Hebrew Labor policy."

"That will be nice," she said. "And thank you for being so kind."

Moshe looked around and tallied the expressions on his friends' faces. Then he said, "I think we would love to spend the *Shabbat* here. Where can we stay?"

"There is a small hotel near the synagogue. Go there before you leave and see if they have a few rooms for Friday. If not, the women can stay in the house and the men in the garden shed."

"We require no preferential treatment," Alexa protested. "What the men do, we do!"

He smiled apologetically. "It will be very uncomfortable for all of you in the garden shed. Maybe we can do a lottery to identify the four who can sleep inside."

"I like that," said Rubi.

"Great. I shall ask Mr. Libovich, the diligence owner, to pick you up at your hotel on Friday. We jokingly say that if you can count eleven people when you see a diligence passing by, you know that it is empty."

"Thirteen," interjected Moshe, "Two of our friends did not come today."

"That is okay, we are used to more people on board. The coachman will be there around noon. Where are you staying?"

Moshe gave him the name of the hotel and they parted company. While they strolled along Rothschild Street, Alexa went to the hotel. There were no rooms available.

"Tell them what you read in the paper you bought," Moshe asked Itzhak as soon as they left the settlement.

"Jewish labor has been a major issue in *Eretz Israel*. There are demonstrations and continuous discussions about the subject. The focus is the Conquest of Labor. That is, to ensure Jewish labor on Jewish land. We should talk more about that when we get home."

The trip back home was somber. Gershon walked gloomily behind. The rest were deep in thought. Baruch slowed down. When he lined up with Gershon he put an arm on his shoulder. They walked together for a while without a word. Then Baruch said, "I know how you feel my friend. I share your feeling."

"Thank you," Gershon said and moved forward to be near Tova. Baruch reclaimed his position at the end of the line.

The next day at breakfast they met a group of workers who came to Jaffa from Gedera and Petach Tikva. One woman was visiting from Kinneret. They bonded and listened to stories about life in *Eretz Israel.* One of the workers said jokingly, "Welcome to *Eretz Israel*, where life is inhospitable, employment is hard to find, the Arabs dislike us, roads are bad, transportation is worse and the Turks do their best to stifle our project. But this is our HOME!"

Yes, Moshe thought. *This is home. How do we move forward in it?* He asked, "We visited Rishon Le'zion yesterday and noticed a handful of Jewish workers. We are planning a trip to Petach Tikva to seek work. Will we see the same thing? What should we expect?"

"You will find that many farm workers complain that the farmers refuse to give them work. "

"And why is that?" asked David.

"Many reasons," asserted one of the workers from Petach Tikva. "There is the issue of our experience..."

"Lack of experience," interrupted another worker from Petach Tikva.

"Some farmers think that we are not tough enough for the local weather," added the man from Gedera.

"Employing the Arabs is cheaper and more profitable," added another worker.

"It is much more complex than that," said an older worker. "I have been in *Eretz Israel* for many years. I have learned much about the people of the First *Aliyah.* They are older, more devout, somewhat tired of the daily routine. They are no fans of our socialist ideas. For years they have struggled with a hostile environment and lack of experience in farming. They have known failure and diseases. Some gave up and left for better life in America. Those who chose to stay failed to become economically viable. They were rescued from a catastrophic collapse by the generosity of Baron Rothschild, who supported the first wave of Zionist immigration. He appointed managers to guide the settlers toward profitability. Few of them controlled the daily life of the farmers, often robbing them of their independence and pride. They offered economic security but contributed greatly to the decline of morale and the rise of dependency."

"Who is this man?" asked Ribi.

"A wealthy Jewish banker from France," replied the older worker and continued. "Life on the farm was hard. At times, nature added unfathomable cruelty to their paucity of experience. First, a large-scale infestation of worms and caterpillars devastated the vineyards, which dominated the budding agriculture of the time. Next came the locust. Misery and despondency ruled the land.

"But the Baron, like a loving father, continued to support them whenever they failed. Eventually, their efforts began to yield economic benefits; prosperity settled among the farmers and with it the desire for easier life, comfort and better future for their children. The original principle of redeeming the land through Jewish labor was relegated to the margin of their daily life. *Eretz Israel* was reawakening not by the toil and sweat of its returning children but by the sweat and muscle power of the Arabs, who resented the presence of the Zionists in their midst. The Arabs were given an ever-growing role in the development of the early settlements. They worked the fields and assisted in all domestic affairs of the farmers, who became lazier and exchanged real work for a supervisory role. That was true for Petach Tikva, Gedera and the other settlements that were established by the First *Aliyah*."

"But things are changing," suggested another worker. "We insist on Jewish labor. We demonstrate and protest. I am glad to say that they open up to it little by little. There are thousands of people who, like us, came on the Second *Aliyah*. 'Hebrew Labor' is our battle cry. We never yield. Never compromise. Eventually we shall conquer the labor in the settlements."

"You see my friends," said Itzhak. "They have laid down the foundation: the redemption of the land. It is our task to launch the next step in the redemption of our people: ensuring Hebrew labor in the fields and orchards that they cultivate."

"Well said," acknowledged the workers from Petach Tikva and Gedera.

"Women must be a viable part of the Hebrew labor," asserted Tova. "What about women as farm hands?"

The woman from Kinneret answered, "That is a major problem. The farmers, even if they agree to employ Jewish workers, shy away from allowing women to work in the fields. They have no concept of our wish to be treated equally to our male comrades.

"I was determined to be a farm hand, to dig holes in a new citrus orchard or to fill holes in a planted vineyard. The spade was my tool of choice. One of my friends convinced his employer to allow me to work in the field. He told him that we would never succeed in the Zionist project if we leave fifty percent of our manpower unengaged. He promised him that I would reach the same daily quota as the men do. It was hard. I had never worked in the fields. But I had never lived in my motherland either. I had come here to redeem the land with my own hands and that was what I was determined to do. So, I was glad to learn. My friend helped me, through great personal sacrifices, to reach the daily work quota. He allowed me to take more rest while he was digging in my place.

"When going to and coming from the fields I had to hide my tracks. Someone else carried my spade. I went to work in a circuitous path to steer clear of other farmers. We wanted to avoid unproductive debates about the role of women in the labor force. Even my comrades displayed a great deal of discomfort when they saw me working with a spade. They were afraid that I might become ill.

"After weeks of exhausting work during which I have never lost my enthusiasm and determination, I began to perform as well as the men. One day the farmer invited me for tea. He announced that he was raising my salary. I was offended. I asked him if he was doing so because I was Jewish and a woman. He smiled at me softly and told me that he was raising my pay because I was well worth it. My happiness was boundless. From that day I no longer hid the fact that I was a farm hand.

"But the struggle had not yet been won. Many farmers remain recalcitrant and refuse to employ women in field work."

"You also must take note of the fact," added another worker, "that even if you get a job, the pay is meager and the living conditions could be appalling. Many of our comrades gave up and left either for the city or for a foreign country."

"You should know that the labor movement is doing much to alleviate our miserable conditions," said a laborer from Gedera. "They built small houses for married laborers, kitchens for all the Jewish laborers and even social halls. I tell you this so you will know that you are not alone. Our movement is supportive. We are making slow but steady progress toward Jewish labor on Jewish land."

"Have you heard about Mr. Gordon?" asked another laborer from Gedera.

"Vaguely," replied Moshe.

Itzhak kept to himself. He had determined during the trip to Rishon Le'zion that learning from people who experienced the daily life in *Eretz Israel* would serve the cause better than his bookish knowledge.

"He is the conscience of the farm workers. He is also the revered voice of the labor movement. I am sure you will meet him eventually."

"He tells us of a delegate to the tenth Zionist Congress who proclaimed that the redemption of *Eretz Israel* is an obligation that is carved with blood and sweat on our heart. He further explains that the redemption is conditioned by our own labor. Nothing else will do. Not everyone agrees with such a position. Among those are many farmers.

"The key question, asks Mr. Gordon, is whether or not the labor of our hands is a primary precondition to the redemption of our motherland?"

"Of course it is,' interjected Gershon.

"I agree," added Tova

"I think we all agree," said Itzhak. "We came to break the Diaspora character of the Jew, the one unused to bonding with nature through working in nature."

"Mr. Gordon preaches that the land we buy will be ours only if we work it," continued the farmer from Gedera. "Mr. Gordon also demands that we put work and he means farm work, at the center of all our future activities."

"And the farmers reject this principle?" asked Baruch.

"Yes, many do."

The hour was late They had a full day ahead of them. After they agreed to reconnect in Petach Tikva, they parted company with warm hugs and went to tour Jaffa's back allies.

Itzhak stayed behind to craft a short letter to his family.

Jaffa April 19, 1912

Dearest parents and sister,

My most pressing interest is to inquire about Rachel's health. You were on the mend when I left, dear sister, are you completely healed?

I am the happiest man. A few days ago we arrived in Jaffa, a chaotic, dirty town with multiple colors and aromas: some pleasant and other nauseating. It is in *Eretz Israel* but it is NOT what *Eretz Israel* should look or smell like. The town is vibrant and alive with local commerce. Arabs are everywhere. Jews are more numerous on the port departing lines than on the arrival line. Only a few are visible on Bustros Street (the main street of Jaffa). I assure you that this will not be the case when you come to live with me.

Your loving son, Itzhak.

Shortly before noon they milled around the hotel, eagerly awaiting the arrival of the diligence. When it came to pick them up Moshe noticed three people already seated. He reflected on the "empty diligence" comment. *Three and thirteen equals sixteen,* he calculated quickly to conclude that Mr. Glazer was not joking. *This diligence won't be empty,* he thought.

"Squeeze more," directed the coachman. "I have to pick up two more passengers." They were eighteen people on board.

"We are packed like sardines but that is better than walking," Moshe said with a snicker.

Everyone managed to eke out a smile.

They rode down the street and turned south on a dirt road. The ride was bumpy, uncomfortable but friendly. In Rishon Le'zion they went to Mr. Glazer's house and were ushered in for refreshments and conversation. Mrs. Glazer glided quietly among them to serve them tea and cookies. This time they were more attentive to the quiet lady who welcomed them with a gentle, warm smile. They thanked her enthusiastically.

After a few exchanges of niceties Moshe, who resolved to continue the earlier conversation with their new friends, framed his question as broadly as he could to avoid inciting their host. "Could you discuss with us the topic of labor in Rishon Le'zion?"

"Of course. I actually want to, as you are newcomers and probably have already heard a few derogatory comments about the farmers who built the first settlements in *Eretz Israel.*

"We, like you, chose to come here instead of going to America, because we wanted to re-forge the bond between the Jewish people and their ancient land. We were full of enthusiasm but constantly ran into obstacles. There were no Jewish laborers to help us build our homes, plow the land, dig wells, plant and tend the fields and harvest the product of our labor.

"The land was brimming with inexpensive, experienced and willing Arabs. We hired them and, with their labor, built the foundation on which your generation must continue to build our national home."

"That is admirable," said Gershon with a hint of sarcasm. "We heard your call and chose to answer it. We are here. But from what we hear, you refuse us work..."

Tova continued his line of thoughts. "More than that. You refuse to accept the essence of the Zionists' notion that our national home must be built with our hands."

"Just to retain the facts for this discussion," Itzhak interjected, "we must be aware that Hebrew labor was not a part of the Zionist initial program. It is ours, the members of the Second *Aliyah.*"

Mr. Glazer seemed fidgety and anxious to address Tova and Gershon's comments. But before he had an opportunity to reply, David asked, "Is it really necessary to build settlements across the land with Jewish labor?"

David's question stunned them. Even though no one doubted his commitment to the concept of Jewish labor, his question strayed far afield from their unanimous position on the matter.

A second farmer looked at David and said, "Many farmers will answer 'No' to your question. They think that in order to acquire land we need money to buy it. The people who have the money want to see that they are investing it in *Eretz Israel* not only as an idealistic deed but also as a deed that can produce a profit. How do you maximize the profit? By employing skilled labor at a minimal cost!"

"I understand that but I would answer yes," said Mr. Glazer to everyone's surprise. "Because as I see the reality of *Eretz Israel,* the settlements serve a higher calling than mere profit. For if profit was the goal then the gates of our ancient homeland could be closed. There is enough cheap Arab labor, experienced and willing to work under the harsh climate conditions. Furthermore, I agree that the redemption of the land by Hebrew labor is the key to our success."

Gershon and Tova looked surprised but pleased. The essence of Mr. Glazer's ideas was as nationalistic as theirs.

"One more thought," he said with a broad smile. "If we want the character of the settlements to remain Hebrew we cannot accept the notion that more Arab presence in our settlements is good. For eventually the character of our settlements may lose its Jewish identity. Moreover, since the Arabs do not like our presence here, in a state of emergency their multitudes may endanger the entire settlement. So, if you want to work, I employ Jewish labor."

Another farmer, who was on the diligence said, "Unfortunately, the majority of our farmers seek to redeem the land of *Eretz Israel* with profitable farms. They fail to see the value of Jewish farm labor as opposed to hiring willing Arab workers. But I agree with you. I take solace in the fact that a key goal of the *Eretz Israel* Office is to expand the number of Jewish settlements. While I am sure they strive to create economically viable settlements, I am encouraged that they disallow economic considerations to trump the national goals of the Jewish people in its homeland."

"Allow me to add a few thoughts," said Mrs. Glazer. Until that moment she was almost invisible even though she sat quietly by her husband throughout the conversation.

When she began to speak, her barely audible voice caught Itzhak's attention. He noticed her plain but neat appearance. Her quiet demeanor exuded gentility and warmth. *A pioneer woman indeed,* he thought.

"It is true that people of my generation," she began, "look askance on you, the new generation. They prefer the Arabs to work in our fields. Why is that? First, you are nonbelievers and we are devout. God plays a larger role in our lives than in yours. We fear your secular influence on our children. Second, you are socialists. I often hear in conversations with my neighbors that they feel threatened by your socialistic leaning, by your aspirations to change our way of life."

"I am afraid you have touched upon a very important topic," said Alexa. "But please believe me when I say that our main interest is the same as yours. We want to revitalize the Jewish nation, not to expand the reach of the International."

Sorke wrote later in her diary: *April 21, 1912. The lesson from Rishon Le'zion is simple. I am convinced that the national interest of the Jewish people trumps profitability of agricultural settlements, especially when they are settled on land that has been acquired by national funds. Our goal should be to redeem as much land as possible in all corners of Eretz Israel and work it with Hebrew labor. How will we grow the Jewish population if we prefer Arab labor to our own?*

***

They spent *Shabbat* at leisure. In the evening they returned to Jaffa. Following their second visit to Rishon Le'zion, they shared a sense of disappointment and rejection. The ride home was mostly in silence. They seemed to share a profound need for reflection. No one was ready to compromise on the principle of Jewish labor. Even though they welcomed Mr. Glazer's position they knew that he was in a minority: most of the farmers did not share his views.

They felt like returning children walking excitedly home, after being absent for many years, to find the door locked and the windows bolted. A big poster had been hung on the door proclaiming, "You are not welcome."

A few days later they embarked on a two-week tour of the settlements around Tel Aviv in search of work. They found none. Physical exhaustion, anger and disappointments made an imprint on their psyche. Pinchas showed signs of resignation. He said, "I am tired. That voice at the port was right. This is a land that destroys its inhabitants."

Moshe and Itzhak tried to console him. Itzhak said, "*Eretz Israel* Office in Jaffa will help us out. Do not despair, Pinchas."

When they arrived at Petach Tikva, their last destination, no one paid any attention to them. Panic permeated every corner of the place. The settlement was without water. It seemed that everyone was in shock after hearing that the messenger, who was sent to fetch the only pump mechanic in Jaffa, returned empty-handed and reported to the chairperson of the settlement committee, "The man is busy and unavailable for at least a week."

"What do you mean busy?" asked the chairman in disbelief.

"We have a life-and-death situation on our hands and the man is busy?" interjected a farmer who stood nearby.

"Couldn't you have paid him extra to bring him here?" asked a third man in a voice full of anguish.

"You do not understand," said the messenger. "The mechanic is in Gedera responding to an emergency. A dispute with the Arab neighbors over grazing rights in Gedera escalated over three days of skirmishes, until at last someone attacked the pump house and damaged the pump."

"What shall we do?" lamented a farmer whose herd of cows had been without water all day. "My cows will die without water. Can't we go to Jerusalem or even fetch the mechanic from Lydda?"

Those questions remained unanswered.

Itzhak descended the diligence and approached the person who conversed with the messenger.

"Excuse me sir," he said in Hebrew.

"Don't interrupt, can't you see that we are dealing with a serious matter?" the chairman berated him in Yiddish. "You young people have no manners!"

Itzhak understood but elected to ignore the scolding and the language in which it was uttered. *If he wants to scold me he better do it in Hebrew*, he thought and then repeated his original question.

A farmer, noticing how persistent the young man was, turned to him and rebuked him, shouting in Hebrew, "Can't you see that we are busy?"

"Yes, I can," Itzhak replied in Hebrew, but everyone ignored him.

Itzhak's friends could not believe their ears. Alexa said, "Itzhak, leave them alone, why are you interrupting their conversation?"

Itzhak looked at her with a boyish smile and said, "Trust me Alexa. All will be well at the end."

Then he repeated his question for the third time, adding in a demanding voice, "Listen to me, sir, I can help you."

This time he captured the attention of the messenger, who addressed his interlocutor in Yiddish, "This boy says he can help. Let me hear what he has to say."

The chairman nodded.

The messenger, bewildered by Itzhak's self-assured manner said, "Really? How can you help? You are only a boy."

"I may look like a boy," Itzhak fired with a steady, unyielding voice, "but I never speak in vain. Do you wish to hear me?"

"Certainly. How can you help?"

"Give me a set of tools, make the diligence ready to go to Jaffa and bring whatever parts I may need, and I shall fix your pump," he said nonchalantly. "I have yet to see a pump I cannot fix."

People milling about nearby were drawn to the conversation. Itzhak's comrades looked at him, astonished. He had never revealed to them his mechanical ability.

The messenger turned to his interlocutor and relayed Itzhak's proposal.

"Wait," interjected one man, "Are you seriously giving this boy access to our pump?"

"What choice do we have?"

"Do as Mottel said. Send an urgent messenger to Jerusalem or perhaps to the Arabs in Lydda. I know they have a reliable pump mechanic."

"Nonsense," replied a man who was new to the conversation, "that Arab knows nothing. I once contracted him to work on my pump and he did nothing but charge me money."

"Let's see what the boy can do. We really have no choice," said the first man.

Itzhak smiled. He understood every word they said. Itzhak looked north, toward Odessa and whispered, "Thank you, Mr. Aziz. I knew your teaching would come in handy for me and my friends."

And so it was. Everyone paraded to the pump house to watch the boy fix the pump and bring relief to the settlement. They walked swiftly as if seeking to hasten the repair process. Itzhak moved calmly, at times lagging behind. At the pump house everyone pushed to get a good view of the proceeding.

Itzhak appealed to the messenger, "Could you please ask them to leave? I need some space to work. I also like quiet when I work."

People were asked to wait outside. Only the messenger remained with Itzhak. The young man folded his sleeves and delved into the challenge in front of him. He thought nothing about soiling his only clean garments.

An hour later, after disassembling the pump and examining the various parts, he declared, "I got it. We have a simple problem. This O-ring is worn out. We need a new one. The sooner you get it the quicker you will have your water flow restored." Even though he could easily speak Yiddish, he spoke Hebrew. No other language was good for him. Yiddish did not belong on the lips of a new Jew. He was the new Jew.

It was late in the afternoon. The likelihood of finding the pump store open was rapidly diminishing.

"Find the clerk if the store is closed. Pay him to open the store. We must have the part today," said the chairman to the driver of the diligence, who left in a hurry.

Then he turned to Itzhak and spoke in Yiddish. "Please stay with us tonight." He was unconvinced that the boy had correctly diagnosed the problem and would be able to fix it. But he felt compelled to keep him on hand until the O-ring arrived.

Itzhak did not react to the invitation. His facial expression signaled that he did not understand. He wanted to remain polite. Little did he know that within less than a year the entire *Yishuv* would explode into the "war of the languages," where Hebrew was touted as the language of education, commerce and social life in *Eretz Israel*.

He said, somewhat jokingly, "We shall come tomorrow and finish the job."

The messenger was alarmed. He implored Itzhak in Hebrew, "We want you to stay. Be our guest. You need fresh clothes. We need you."

"The rabbis said, 'He who starts a good deed must complete it.' I will be glad to stay. But I am with my friends. We have just arrived in *Eretz Israel*. So I ask that you extend the invitation to all of them. The reason we came here is to learn about your great work in *Eretz Israel*. We did so with the hope that we would be able to stay and work for you."

The messenger translated Itzhak's reply.

"We will be glad to do so," said another man. He turned to a group of farmers and, after a short discussion, secured places for the entire group to eat and wash and stay overnight. "Please come to the worker's hall at seven in the evening so we may talk about the settlement and the people who live here."

Rested, well fed and jovial from their dinner at various farmers' houses, they assembled at the worker's hall. One farmer, who looked like a nobleman of old Russia, told them the story of the settlement's remarkable journey from 1882, when it was abandoned due to malaria, to its present greatness. "Petach Tikva is the mother of all the settlements. Its creation was a significant milestone in the redemption of our land," he began.

"Excuse me," said Ribi, "we discussed that during our journey to Jaffa. Could you focus on today's Petach Tikva?"

"Sure," he said with a fatherly smile at Ribi. "Look at us today. We are a town and a village combined. Our main streets have stores that provide us many necessities and even comfort items. On the side streets you'll find our homes. They are surrounded with flower and vegetable gardens and even small orchards. Many of our farmers raise chickens and have a small dairy cowshed. In the past we were a dreary place consumed by poverty and shortages of basic goods. Not anymore.

"We have schools and kindergartens. We have a large and active synagogue, a well-stocked library and a large fleet of diligences.

"Beyond our commerce and dwelling areas you can see a large expanse of citrus groves, almond plantations, wheat fields and more. We have grown in people and riches beyond our wildest imagination.

"We are healthier. Gone are the days of rampant malaria and our inability to receive rudimentary medical care. We no longer endure the tortuous journey to Jaffa through swamps, muddy roads and a swollen river to seek medical care. We have a doctor in town.

"We expand in peace. Gone are the days of a hostile Turkish government that stifled, by brute force or through legal maneuvers, our efforts to thrive and grow. We are secure in our homes unlike the early days when our homes, our property and our people were often subjected to deadly aggression by our Arab neighbors.

"We are independent and proud, unlike the bygone era of poverty and dependence on the Baron Rothschild's charity. Most importantly a growing number of us believe in Jewish labor and always welcome new immigrants who knock on our doors in search of work. Look around you at our worker's hall, we are very proud of it. It has a large social room, six bedrooms that sleep four, a small library and a kitchen."

The returning diligence interrupted their conversation. The joyous driver burst into the hall with the O-ring in his hand. Everyone cheered and followed Itzhak to the pump house. Within an hour the sound of the working pump filled the air to the jubilation of all the residents of Petach Tikva. The friends were invited to stay and work.

Six months later Itzhak and his friends were still working in Petach Tikva. Sorke and Tova worked at the school. Ribi helped in the worker's kitchen. David helped at the doctor's office and the rest, including Alexa, worked in the fields.

Those were six hard and challenging months. Day after day they dug holes to plant new citrus groves or cleared the land in preparation for planting. Some plots were covered with stones and boulders. Each stone had to be dug out and moved some distance away, where it was used to erect a fence around the farmland that emerged from the rock-strewn blanket that had covered it for many years. Sorke wrote in her diary: *October 2, 1912. We are true Zionists. We work the land. It is a backbreaking effort but it is our destiny. We dig holes and move stones. Alexa said today, "Eretz Israel will be revived one stone at a time." I think she is right.*

***

Arabs were everywhere. In the fields, in the orchards, in the small gardens adjacent to the farmhouses. There were a disproportionately smaller number of Jewish laborers among them. Some were transient, others permanent. A few came from the small workers' settlement near Petach Tikva. Others, like members of *Gesher*, lived in the settlement itself. They quickly bonded with the rest of the laborers with whom they found a common purpose. They shared the themes of Jewish labor, free immigration, uninhibited purchase of land, and the sanctity of the Hebrew language.

For them, work—no matter how menial, how boring, how hard it felt—was no ordinary matter. It was elevated to a level of holiness that every laborer could feel. Each shovel they put in the ground erased years of forced national separation from *Eretz Israel*. Each hole they dug was a path to nurturing the revitalized Jewish nation. Jewish labor was at the core of their political universe. On occasion, they took a day off to join a protest march in Tel Aviv, or to demand Jewish labor in Jewish settlements in Jerusalem.

Itzhak's hands were covered with calluses. They sometimes burst, exposing the raw skin to the harshness of the wooden handle of the spade. But he kept digging. His body was always cold; at times, damp and most often reeked with unpleasant odor that accumulated over days of sweat and dirt from his daily toil. His skin was no longer ghost-like white. His hands no longer Diaspora-soft.

Home was a small corner in a barn with empty cans that supported a plank of wood for a bed. He had never acclimated to the stench of the cows that shared a portion of his residence. Loneliness was his burden.

His meager possessions, besides essential clothing, were a kerosene lamp, a small library of books and a selection of local Hebrew and Arabic newspapers. Twice a week the driver of the local diligence brought from Jaffa that week's editions of *al-Karmil* and *Filastin*, which he read attentively to glean information, whether local opinions or global ones, about the Arabs' attitudes toward the Zionist project. He also dedicated a portion of his precious free time to expanding his knowledge of the Arabs.

A monotonous routine ruled his daily life: working, eating meager amounts of food, conversing about essential topics and sleeping. His mind was lucid and actively searched for intellectual, social and cultural stimuli. He broke the monotony of his day by reading from his precious library or thinking about his family, especially about his mother who had endured so much grief.

He wrote to his sister and parents hoping to share his life with them. Occasionally he sent a note to his brothers in America, but that relationship weakened with the passage of time.

He was also lucky. Since his first days in Petach Tikva, Jewish and Arab farmers sought his services: fixing or installing water pumps. He was happy to oblige. He had to divide, unhappily, his time between field labor and mechanical duties. He dedicated his earnings to his family's future journey home. His travel gave him an opportunity to confirm what he thought to be the prevailing truth in *Eretz Israel*: Arab laborers were everywhere. *How do we build our life here where life is already present? Does our cause trump theirs? Is my promotion of Hebrew Labor not a veiled strategy to push the Arabs off the land? The reality is obvious,* he reflected, *as we buy land and dedicate it exclusively to Jewish Labor, the peasant has no other option but to leave.* That reality would trouble him for years.

The company of his friends, who were scattered throughout the settlement, was essential to his life. Together they sat at the workers' hall, sipping tea and discussing the issues of the day and those of the future. At times the conversation heated up. Especially when other Jewish workers joined the discussion. Twice a week he held Hebrew classes for anyone who wanted to learn.

On Friday nights they gathered to sing and dance. On Saturday, the day of rest, they broke rank and went alone or in a small group to explore the area surrounding Petach Tikva.

6 TENSION

Every now and then there was a flare-up between the Arabs and the Jews. Itzhak followed these carefully. In Rishon Le'zion the press reported an act of vandalism in the synagogue. Also in Rishon Le'zion a guard was brutally murdered. In Petach Tikva they witnessed occasional petty crimes. Yet all in all, and in spite of the unfriendly tone of the local Arabic language newspapers, the relationships with the Arabs were tense but non-threatening.

Then life took a sharp, frightening turn. Sorke confided in her diary: *October 22, 1912. Everyone was perturbed. We waited in the doctor's office, tense and sad. David came out on occasion to update us on Baruch's condition, which had worsened. He is a quiet man, a good man. His face is always glowing with happiness. I don't want him to die at the beginning of his life's journey.*

***

Shortly after Tova alerted the guard on duty, Gershon and he carried Baruch on a stretcher to the doctor's office. There he lay unconscious while his friends assembled at his bedside.

Later, Gershon described what they saw and heard: "Tova and I took a leisurely morning walk along the footpath outside the almond grove when we were startled by three Arab youths stampeding out of the trees, a short distance away from us. Each carried a large sack of almonds. In their haste, they did not see us. I was sure that they were stealing. I shouted and gave chase to the three thieves. Their panic increased. They dropped their load. Without it they outran me and quickly disappeared. I rejoined Tova and we backtracked to the footpath that bisected the plantation. There we saw Baruch on the ground bleeding from multiple knife wounds. Before he lost consciousness he told us that he'd unintentionally caught the youths stealing almonds. They panicked and rushed toward the path, where they collided with him. He fell to the ground. One young man with a large scar on his face lingered behind. He stabbed him and left him for dead on the side of the path. He then ran away to join his fleeing accomplices. I sent Tova to alert the guard on duty and sat near Baruch feeling totally helpless. Within minutes he lost consciousness."

Gershon was unable to hide his anger. "I am going to find those criminals and beat the hell out of them," he exclaimed angrily.

"I am with you Gershon," said Tova.

"Yes!" Yossel also was ready for action. "Let's find the bastards and punish them."

"You will do no such thing. That will start a blood feud that might ripple through Petach Tikva for many years. Capture them? Yes. But let the authorities deal with them," cautioned Moshe.

"I agree with Moshe. The dumbest thing you can do is to kill a member of an Arab family," proclaimed Itzhak.

"Sounds good to me," said Moshe. "I shall go to the head of the security committee to seek his help. I speak Arabic and that may come in handy in the search for the criminals. But," he looked sternly at Gershon, "I want you to promise me that there will be no retribution. We shall go with the security man and let him do the talking."

An hour later the five were on their way to the neighboring village. First, they visited the scene of the crime. From there they followed the footpath east. The footprints of the three escapees were etched in the sand. When they reached the village they noticed people trying to avoid them.

"Word of the crime must have reached everyone," declared Yossel with boiling anger.

"Calm down, Yossel. They should not think that we are here for revenge," advised Itzhak.

"I shall do my best," answered Yossel and took a deep breath.

The security man led the way. He knew the mukhta*r* (the head of the village). They stopped in front of a two-story stone house that rose above the dirt road, near the local souk (market in Arabic). They walked toward it. The door was wide open. The mukhtar stood at the doorsill as if he had expected their arrival. With customary Arab hospitality, he invited them into his large public room.

They sat on a carpet-covered stone bench that stretched around the perimeter of the room. A servant served tea. Then the mukhtar said calmly, "I know why you are here. I appreciate your peaceful approach. We want to prevent any long-running cycle of retaliations. I spoke with one of the young men. He confessed to stealing almonds and said that he had quarreled with someone who attempted to stop him. He and his friends will stand trial for stealing."

"Quarreled? Stealing?" retorted Yossel as he attempted to suppress his anger. "He stabbed our friend three times."

"I was the one who found him," added Gershon sternly. "He was alive but bleeding profusely. He gave me the description of one assailant, a young man with a long scar on his face."

The mukhtar assured them that he would deal with the crime and punish the three young men.

The security man was unconvinced. "We want the criminals punished by the police."

"For stealing almonds?" protested the mukhtar.

"No! For stabbing a man."

"That was in self-defense. Your friend threatened our young man."

"Our friend was surprised by your youth who attacked him just because he was there at the wrong time," protested Moshe.

"Please let me handle the conversation," demanded the security man.

"How is he?" asked the mukhtar with a hint of alarm.

The security man looked straight at his eyes and fired a short answer, "He may die"

Itzhak noticed an instant change in the mukhtar's disposition after that exchange. It was no longer a matter of petty crime punishable by a few months in jail that, probably with a nice bribe, could be reduced to a slap on the wrist. He was confronted with a possible murder for which the youths could spend a long jail term. One might even hang.

"We will punish them," repeated the mukhtar.

"That is unacceptable," argued the security man. "You must surrender them to the authorities."

"There is no need to resort to such an extreme solution. Your friend may recover."

"Whether or not he recovers has no bearing on the severity of the crime," responded the security man.

"You must consider the relationship between us when you involve the authorities in an uncertain crime."

They argued for a while until the security man realized that the mukhtar had no intention of cooperating. "He will do nothing," the security man told the four friends. "Let's go home and alert the police. Itzhak, I want you to go with me to the police in Jaffa."

"I will be glad to help."

The journey to Jaffa seemed endless. But it was not in vain. The police reacted unusually swiftly. They came to Petach Tikva, where Baruch struggled for his life. They spoke to Gershon and Tova, examined the wounds on Baruch's body, then left to visit the scene of the crime. Both Itzhak and the security man joined them. They searched the area. Gershon walked in an ever-expanding circle around the spot where Baruch fell. Ten meters or so away from that spot he found a bloody Arabic dagger. The police took it and were set to continue their pursuit of the criminals.

"The mukhtar knows who they are," Itzhak told the police before they parted company. "He wanted to settle things without your involvement. We refused."

The police continued to the village to arrest the criminals, but they had vanished. They arrested the mukhtar instead. "He will be released when you surrender the criminals," said the police commander in Turkish. No one understood his words but everyone understood his gesture. The mukhtar stayed in jail for a few hours. At sundown, the village elders arrived with the three escapees to secure the mukhtar's release.

For three days and nights, Baruch teetered between heaven and earth. His friends kept a continuous vigil in his chamber. Each person spent two hours at his bedside. The men stood near him. Some talked, others just kept silent while their heads spun with angry thoughts and helplessness. The women were freer with their emotions. Each woman, in her turn, held Baruch's hand, talking to him constantly with the hope that he would regain consciousness and live. But to no avail. On the fourth morning he died from his wounds, never regaining consciousness. Itzhak went to Jaffa to inform the Police about Baruch's death.

Eretz Israel had claimed its next victim. This time it was one of their friends.

The next day they buried him in the local cemetery. On his tombstone they wrote, "You glow with happiness forever."

Baruch's death provided a first-hand testimony to the hazards that threatened their project but made them more determined to succeed. Even Pinchas seemed more dedicated to their cause. Justice for the three young men was swift and harsh. The judge condemned the killer to death by hanging. He sentenced his accomplices to one year of hard labor.

7 GOOD NEIGHBORS

"The loyal Zionists have not yet dealt with the issue of what our attitude to the Arab should be when we come to buy land from them in Palestine to found settlements and, in general, to settle the country."

Dr. Y Epstein, The Hidden Question, lecture delivered at the Seventh Zionist Congress in Basel 1905.

The untimely death of Baruch did not dampen their enthusiasm. Moshe continued to lobby to promote *Gesher*'s readiness to settle its own land. He visited the *Eretz Israel* Office in Jaffa twice a month. His visits served one goal: to put *Gesher* in the front of any considerations for a new settlement.

From the outset he emphasized his friends' dedication and skill. "We have spent six months on a farm in Russia prior to coming here, and we have been working in Petach Tikva since our third week in *Eretz Israel*. We have an agronomist, an irrigation specialist, who can repair and install pumps. We have a culinary expert, a medical doctor and nine other members who are devoted to the Zionist cause and to Hebrew labor," he told the director and his assistant. "We want to settle the land and tie our future to it."

"I have heard about your pump expert. What he did in Petach Tikva was truly impressive."

"Thank you," Moshe replied. "He is also fluent in Hebrew and Arabic. He is an educated man of peace. And most important to us is his dedication to the Hebrew language. He teaches us Hebrew twice a week."

"Our director tries unsuccessfully to study the language. Do you think your man can teach him?"

"I have no doubt. He will consider that an honor. Although the logistics might be daunting if we settle far away from Jaffa."

"Study the manner of citrus cultivation, vegetable growing, poultry and dairy cows husbandry. These are important skills to have when you start a farm."

"We are and will continue to do so," replied Moshe.

"Oh yes, and see if you can expand your group. You will need approximately thirty to forty people to settle a new place. I also recommend that you send your agronomist to the Kinneret School to acquire relevant skills and knowledge to the agriculture of *Eretz Israel*."

The year 1913 replaced a bountiful 1912. Early colors of spring permeated the fields outside Petach Tikva when, one day in April, Moshe was summoned to the *Eretz Israel* Office in Jaffa.

Upon his return to Petach Tikva he called for an immediate meeting of the group. He could not hide his exuberance. When the noise subsided he outlined the possibility of settling a newly acquired land near Beit A'yan. "Does anyone object?"

"No!" was the only word they uttered. Song filled the hall. Exhilarating dance followed.

At the first opportunity, Sorke said, "Listen friends, I suggest that we call our kibbutz (a collective community with focus on agriculture) Hazohar in memory of Baruch. For those whose Hebrew is still weak let me translate. Hazohar means 'the glow.' Remember what we wrote on Baruch's tombstone? 'You glow with happiness forever.' Hazohar will forever remind us of our friend."

They voted unanimously to accept her suggestion. That night she wrote in her diary: *April 15, 1913 Halleluiah! Having nearly been consumed by the hardship of life we have seen a rebirth of our group. We have been in Eretz Israel for a year. Now we are ready to expand the redemption of our motherland. I am so excited I want to cry from happiness. I suggest moving Baruch's tomb to Hazohar as soon as possible.*

***

Around the same time, Itzhak read in an Arabic newspaper that the sentence of the three criminals was commuted. "After intense lobbying efforts by Arab dignitaries," wrote the crime correspondence, "the authorities commuted Mr. Farid, the killer of Baruch, to a five-year imprisonment. His accomplices were released to the custody of the mukhtar."

When Moshe heard about that decision he vowed to bring it to the attention of the *Eretz Israel* Office. In spite of their vehement protest, the Ottoman authorities remained adamant that their action was justified. Everyone in the *Yishuv* was furious at the authorities. Alas, justice under the Ottoman rule was unpredictable at best.

The excitement of the preparation to establish a new kibbutz took the edge off their anger. They channeled their energy to put their imprint on the redemption of the land and expanding the presence of the nascent Jewish nation in *Eretz Israel*. They were fully cognizant that one day a new Jewish State would be reborn, and its boundaries be demarcated not with barbed wire but with settlements like Hazohar and Petach Tikva.

Gershon was assigned the task of planning the move. Alexa was sent to Kinneret to upgrade her knowledge with specific agricultural issues relevant to *Eretz Israel*'s climate. Itzhak accompanied Yossel on a special tour of the designated area—four thousand *dunams* (about 988 acres) of land purchased recently from a rich Arab landowner who lived in Lebanon.

They left Petach Tikva early in the morning. A muddy road slowed their progress but not their enthusiasm. The rain fell incessantly. It was their sole companion. There was nothing to do but talk. "You were so young on the boat. Remember what I said to you then?" asked Yossel.

"I do. You asked me if I was on tour with my parents."

They laughed.

Yossel asked, "Tell me about your family. Mine did not understand why I wanted to leave Russia and go to *Eretz Israel*. I guess they belonged to the old generation who did not seek the redemption of our people."

"My parents did all they could to inculcate in me the love of Zion. They taught me the foundation of this love; they introduced me to the books and authors who gave this love a solid intellectual foundation. And when I left home at eighteen, I did that with their blessing.

"My sister Rachel worked in *Eretz Israel* until malaria nearly killed her. She had to return home, never to lose the desire to come back."

"How is she now?"

"She is healthy. In fact, I am planning to bring her and my parents to *Eretz Israel*. With Moshe's help I secured a teaching position for my father in Petach Tikva. A month ago I sent them a letter telling them of my intentions. A few days ago Rachel sent me a one-word reply. She wrote, "YES!"

"I am happy for you, Itzhak," said Yossel. "May I change the subject?"

"Sure."

"You spoke about the books and the writers. Could you share with me that intellectual foundation you acquired as a young man? I am sure it will make me a better Zionist."

"I would love to do that."

An hour later they reached their destination. Soaked and shivering they stood on top of a hill in a dream-like haze, imagining their future kibbutz; before their eyes stretched a beautiful rolling meadow surrounded by hills. Low hanging clouds provided nourishing rain that soaked the land, awakening thousands of spring flowers that covered the ground with a majestic and colorful carpet. Newly sprouted green grasses enticed herds of goats and sheep that roamed nonchalantly through the gently undulating terrain, moving steadily behind Arab shepherds.

A bubbling spring gave birth to a shallow brook, which divided the property from north to south, on its way to merge with the Yarkon River. Near the spring they could see two encampments of a local Bedouin tribe. Sounds of merriment filled the air. Children played in the spring: a few at the end of their water carrying chores, others at the beginning. They swam naked in the small pool, oblivious to the rain and the approaching visitors.

At the northern horizons, beyond the spring, rose from the land an arid amalgamation of stone and mud houses punctuated by the minarets of the village mosque.

Itzhak reflected aloud, "Remember the song 'When God returned us to Zion, we were like dreamers?' But now it is our free will that returned us to Zion." They burst into laughter.

The pastoral scene hid the seeds of strife from Yossel. But Itzhak saw them. The graffiti on the wall in Jaffa flashed alarm signs in his head. He looked at Yossel and said calmly, "Do not let this beauty obscure your vision. In this land, there are seeds of turmoil. These are slow germinating seeds that need the heat of fire to sprout. Sooner or later there will be that fire to give them life."

"And what are those?" asked a perplexed Yossel.

"I can count at least three perhaps four potential seeds of possible friction that may persist in the area awaiting the fire to give them life. When? I do not know. But we had better be cognizant of them and prepare a remedy for their germination."

"Please point them out. Name them."

"The grazing herds, the playful children, the two encampments and, possibly, that blob without shape that looks like a local Arab village." He replied in an even tone.

"Can you be less enigmatic?" Yossel was neither able to grasp the motives behind Itzhak's assessment nor to put cause and effect between turmoil and the four independent events Itzhak cited.

"Okay. Do we agree that the Arabs do not like our presence in *Eretz Israel*?"

"Yes."

"The reason for their animus toward us is multi-faceted. I have read much about it in the local Arabic newspapers. So let me build a case, using the limited knowledge I have."

"That will be helpful."

"Look at the issue this way. We have bought the land, registered it with the Ottoman's Land Office. What do we do with those encampments near the spring?"

"We evict them. Or better yet, we ask the Ottoman authorities to remove them. After all, this is our property and, as is practiced in any civilized country we have the right to use our land as we please, without the presence of trespassers."

"What about the shepherds?" persisted Itzhak.

"We treat them in a similar manner," said Yossel.

"Yes, but are they trespassers? Of course! In the eyes of the law, they are, but not in their eyes. Consider this. For as long as they remember they have used this land whenever they wanted. Mr. Ghali, the previous owner, was happy to receive rent from them and so they grazed these lush hills and beyond, where Miri land abuts this land. No one asked them to leave. Such was their ancient tradition. They all shared the bounty of nature. Do you think these Bedouins or shepherds understand the law of the Ottoman authorities? No. They are here by habit and will want to continue to do tomorrow what they have been doing for years."

"First what is Miri land?" asked Yossel who was up-to-date on the Zionist practices but clueless on matters of Ottoman laws.

"Miri refers to land in which the sole ownership is vested in the state."

"Thanks. By the way, regarding the tradition, we, unlike these nomads, have paid dearly for this land and we intend to work every inch of it to restore our tradition. What about land that is owned by individuals?" Yossel asked.

"First I understand and agree with your sentiments regarding private ownership. The Turkish authorities are in accord with us even though they object vehemently to the transfer of land to the Jews. Private land, in their language, is Milk, which has unrestricted private ownership," replied Itzhak. "But in the eyes of the Bedouins, we evict them from their land and rob them of their heritage. Consequently, we sow the seeds of trouble. But there is more. The spring is on our land. Everyone in the area uses it for drinking and playing: animal and human alike. I would not be surprised to see women of the village using this spring as a washbasin for the local laundry. Now it is our property. What should we do?"

Yossel hesitated for a brief moment then answered, "To begin with we shall prohibit playing, laundry and unfettered animal access in the spring. We must keep the water clean."

"I agree in principle, but once again we are facing the power of tradition. Furthermore, in both cases, we are also facing the issue of conflicting perceptions. To them, having goats and children in the water does not cause pollution. To us it does. Depending on our attitude regarding water usage we may be sowing another seed or two of malcontent. Moreover, if we look beyond the local realities, we must recognize the rise of Arab nationalism. We have already agreed that they do not like us inhabiting Palestine. Perhaps the poor local farmers are not engaged in the emerging nationalistic fervor, but I suspect that it is the fire that will set the conditions for these seeds to germinate here in our backyard. Oh yes, last but not least, we are for Jewish Labor. We will not employ them. "

"I hear you," declared Yossel. "What do you suggest?"

"First we must accept the wisdom of Ahad Ha'am, who recognized that the Arabs are no fools as some have said, 'a people akin to jackasses who do not understand what is going on around them.' He suggested that we treat them with respect. I also remember reading Dr. Epstein's thoughts that our national future depends on the way we treat the Arab question. And so, I think that we must meet the local mukhtar to discuss the water sharing and the grazing rights. We must provide them a way to draw water for domestic use and animal husbandry."

"Itzhak," said Yossel with a foreboding tone, "I believe you are a bit naïve. Don't you think that we have the right to redeem our ancient land? We do so with money, not with the sword."

"I have no doubt about our rights. But we need to live side by side with the Arabs. Soon they will be our neighbors."

"Neighbors?" interrupted Yossel. "With all the hardships we face we have nothing to worry about but their fate? We are talking about Jewish existence. This land is our home."

"It is their home also. They live here," responded Itzhak quietly.

"The Arabs have always disliked us. I see no possibility that they will change their attitude in the future. They never miss an opportunity to express their real feelings. Besides, Arab bandits endlessly harass our settlements throughout the *Yishuv*. They steal; they destroy our orchards, graze on our land in blatant violation of our rights and, on occasion, murder our people. You do remember Baruch!"

Itzhak felt ill at ease but did not abandon his argument. "I know and accept that Jewish existence is paramount. But it could also be true that there are other ways to ensure our presence in *Eretz Israel*. Could it be that we have ignored them, misunderstood their customs and traditions? Let's do a social experiment here. Let's approach them like good neighbors."

"I see your point, and we should bring the subject to discussion before we move here. If I were Moshe I would suggest that you and Avram take up this issue. Plan the cooperation parameters, how to approach the Arabs, how to create good neighborly conditions. Avram can design the facility around the spring, and you can implement it."

"Thanks, Yossel. I am a realist. I know that good thoughts alone do not necessarily blaze a trail to the desired results. But we lose nothing if we try."

By late afternoon they returned to Petach Tikva. After dinner, the members of Hazohar met with Yossel and Itzhak to hear about their visit. Yossel presented Itzhak's suggestion regarding the Good-Neighbor principle. An intense discussion followed. Gershon stressed their right to settle anywhere they wanted, and if they bought the property, they were entitled to use it unconditionally.

But in the end, they agreed to adopt Itzhak's approach on humanitarian grounds. "It makes no sense to prevent the locals from an orderly access to water If you will, we are building a bridge to the local Arabs," said Yossel, and the others agreed. As to the grazing pastures, they accepted Tova's compromise that stated, "Assuming good neighborly relationship, as long as we do not cultivate the hillside, they can graze there freely."

Everyone was pleased.

They set June 16 as the move day. Gershon managed the move, including the acquisition of the necessary building material. Sorke took it upon herself to expand further, in consultation with the members of *Gesher*, the membership in the group. Moshe coordinated the move with the *Eretz Israel* Office in Jaffa. Ribi was in charge of the kitchen. Alexa assumed the responsibility for formulating a plan for crops and animal husbandry. "The folks at the *Eretz Israel* Office in Jaffa are very experienced. They will be invaluable throughout the planning and execution processes," Moshe said. "Do not hesitate to call upon them for help."

The air inside the worker's hall filled with excitement. Anticipation was everywhere. One year after their arrival, they were ready to increase their contribution to the Zionist project. They had survived the physical hardship, the emotional toll of loneliness, of longing for a normal life, for contributing more to reviving the soul of their beloved country. Malaria did not hold them back. The untimely death of Baruch ignited in them a new fire to continue the march forward. United as ever, the members of *Gesher* stood at the gate of a new challenge to fulfill the original dream.

Itzhak and Avram worked on the good-neighbor aspect. They traveled to Beit A'yan to meet with the mukhtar. He received them in the best hospitality tradition of the Arabs. But the conversation was going nowhere. The old man protested vehemently the idea of a Zionist settlement on land that used to be in his family's possession until he was forced to sell it to Mr. Ghali. He was unhappy with the proposed change of the status quo at the spring while insisting that the issue was irrelevant because the spring belonged to him. Essentially, a good-neighbor relationship, according to him, was to leave things as they were before their visit.

Itzhak returned home dismayed and upset. Doubts assailed him. *Maybe Yossel was right after all,* he thought and immediately wrote to Rachel a long letter in which he poured out his emotions in long meandering paragraphs. Toward the end he regrouped his thoughts and told her to begin the process of coming home. "I have saved enough money to bring you, mother and father to *Eretz Israel*. I know that the high school in Petach Tikva would love to have Father teach there."

After that, he felt better and resolved to persevere.

The second meeting was worse than the first. The mukhtar accused Avram and Itzhak of using trickery to acquire the land. "The law forbids the Zionist from buying land in Palestine," he insisted. "I shall complain to the authorities." Upon returning to Petach Tikva, Itzhak reported the threat to the clerk at the *Eretz Israel* Office, who promised to deal with the matter swiftly.

The mukhtar was friendlier on their third visit. He accepted the notion of protecting the spring and the idea of free grazing on uncultivated land. He further promised to assist in the construction of the protective structure at the spring. Itzhak was amazed but somewhat pleased. He resolved to adopt Rabi Hillel's strategy of "Respect him and suspect him." *Time alone will tell if the mukhtar was genuinely conciliatory or if his obstinate persona will emerge*, he thought. On the surface at least the Good-Neighbor approach had worked.

Words about settling the area near Beit A'yan spread like wildfire. Volunteers contacted the *Eretz Israel* Office; offering assistance in every possible chore, from building to farm work. They came from everywhere. From cities and farm settlements. From the Galil mountains and the Yizrael Valley. When the caravan, loaded with their precious cargo, was ready to move, one hundred people joined on horses, by diligences and by foot. Moshe was overwhelmed but grateful.

Their first act was to bury Baruch on the hill before they transformed it into Hazohar. The ceremony was solemn. Gershon eulogized him. In the end, he said, "My friend, we brought you here so we can remain connected and grow old together. We love you." They sang Hatikva and began to erect their new home.

At night, in her new tent, sitting on a real bed covered with clean sheets, Sorke wrote: *June 16, 1913. A year and a few months have passed since we arrived in Jaffa. We have finally united with the land. Will Itzhak's Good-Neighbor policy work? Many think not. Gershon is very vocal expressing his disbelief. I believe he is right. The Arabs do not like us here.*

***

A week later, using only Jewish labor, the first building, the dining hall, rose proudly atop the hill overlooking the meadow. Not far from it were the tents to house the forty members of Hazohar. A community shower and toilet facility for men and women were built some distance away, near the new fence that surrounded the settlement.

Beit A'yan, gray and unappealing, was clearly visible beneath the northern horizons hugging the road that led from the spring, about two kilometers away. A garden fence surrounded the spring to protect it from human and animal traffic. Nearby, volunteers put the final touches on a cinderblock structure that housed two water pumps. The first supplied water to Hazohar. The other provided water to four troughs and two faucets for drinking water for Beit A'yan residents. No Arab assisted in the project. The Bedouin encampment had disappeared before the construction started. They moved some distance beyond the hills. Someone, probably the mukhtar, must have told them to leave.

Itzhak looked at his effort at the spring with mixed feelings, but he was pleased that Hazohar did all it could to promote the Good-Neighbor principle. Everything was ready to celebrate the newest settlement in the *Yishuv*. Folks from Rishon Le'zion brought their delicious wine. Farmers from Petach Tikva brought oranges and vegetables. The head of the *Eretz Israel* Office brought congratulatory words. People came from everywhere. They brought seeds for the vegetable garden, saplings for the new orange and olive groves, chickens for the new chicken coop. Everything was ready for the next day, a day that would begin the transformation of that neglected part of the motherland into the land of milk and honey that it used to be.

The mukhtar declined to come. He sent his apology by a messenger, who informed them that pressing family business required his presence in Jerusalem. But that did not impede the celebration. They ate and drank, listened to speeches, danced the Hora and sang. Hazohar illuminated the previously dark corner of *Eretz Israel* with a bright and vibrant light. A new energy burst with the whirlwind motion of the Hora and the explosive volume of the songs. Forty young souls rededicated their life to love and cherish the newly liberated part of the fatherland.

Quiet fell upon Hazohar after the volunteers left. Everyone retired to bed anticipating the activities of the next morning. Yossel was the first to rise. The day was still shrouded in a veil of darkness as he headed to the shower. His clothes came off swiftly. His mind readied his body for the shock of a cold shower. But nothing happened. No water touched his head. He dressed hurriedly and returned to the tent to look for Itzhak. When he approached his bed, he found Itzhak sitting agitated.

"I do not hear the pump," he declared with alarm. "Let's go to the spring. I sense trouble."

The two rushed down the hill toward the pump's shed. The light switch did not work. "Someone must have cut the wires," said Yossel. "Wait here, Itzhak, I shall fetch a flashlight."

"No need, there is a Kerosene lamp on the other side of the pumps. I wish I could find the matches in this darkness." After much feeling and moving hesitantly like a blind man, he made his way around the pumps where he found the box of matches. He lit the lamp and looked around. The two pumps were untouched. Whoever had visited the shed could have inflicted severe damage to the pumps but chose instead to cut the electrical connection. That, in itself, was an ominous message. It asserted without words "Be forewarned! I could have just as easily destroyed the pumps." Red graffiti in Arabic adorned the wall. "Go home, dogs."

Itzhak sank to the ground. He could see imaginary pieces of his Good-Neighbor principle falling from above, covering him with the remnants of his attempt to adhere to the wisdom of Ahad Ha'am.

"I do not do electricity," quipped Yossel.

"Same here. We'd better summon Avram."

Within minutes Avram repaired the damage and restarted the pump just in time for Ribi to prepare the morning coffee.

At breakfast, Moshe looked at Itzhak but said nothing. He just smiled an understanding smile. Later, the governing committee of Hazohar decided to assign round-the-clock guard duty at the pump's shed. To Itzhak's delight, they did not abolish the Good-Neighbor principle.

A few weeks went by with no incident. Itzhak's Respect and Suspect policy fit well with the Good-Neighbor principle.

Goats and sheep visited the troughs on their way to or from the grazing land at the edge of Hazohar's property. Women from the village, balancing large containers on their heads, came to the faucets to draw water from the spring. It seemed as if everyone enjoyed a good neighborly feeling.

During that time the folks collected a large amount of dung. They used it for planting a large vegetable garden. Beyond its perimeter, they added a citrus orchard and an olive grove. A large chicken coop was built at the far end of the garden. A fenced area provided for free-roaming chickens. They also increased their small milking herd and sent one of their women to Jaffa to learn the art of cheese making in the German colony. The members of Hazohar resolved to be self-sufficient and to rely on Hebrew labor exclusively.

Sorke noted and also speculated in her diary, *August 17, 1913. Hazohar is making incredible strides. Only a few weeks ago this was an uncultivated land. Look at it now! Itzhak is radiating happiness. I share his joy. Beit A'yan's folks seem to like the arrangement at the spring. Could*

Itzhak affect a breakthrough in the relationship with the Arabs? I am skeptical. I like the young man, but I think he reads too much of the wise men who had little practical experience with the Arabs. I shall hold on to my seat. I believe we are up for a wild ride.

***

The next night started routinely. After hours of endless walking in a circle, the guard rested a moment on the Hazohar side of the spring when two camouflaged men crawled to the fence, scaled it and rushed to the pump's shed. Once inside, they disconnected the electricity and swiftly proceeded to cut the belts.

The sudden silence from the shed alerted the guard, who approached the dark place cautiously. Unwittingly he stepped on a dry twig. The crackling sound alerted the two, who darted out the door just to be tackled by him. One of the prowlers carried the industrial scissors with which he cut the belt. Trying to push the guard out of his way, the intruder stabbed him. A sharp scream followed the guard's loss of balance. He fell to the ground but managed to fire a few shots at the escapees.

The sound of gunfire awakened a few folks, who ran in the direction of the gunshots. The intruders disappeared under cover of darkness, but the moans of the wounded guard drew them to his side.

"Fetch David!" shouted one man.

A second one ran to the compound and awakened David, screaming, "Hurry, David, the guard has been stabbed!"

David jumped out of bed, grabbed his first aid kit, and followed the man to the guard's side. Someone brought the Kerosene lamp. David examined the wound. He administered first aid and declared with a sense of relief, "He will live. The blade did not penetrate deeply. We must carry him to the infirmary where I will be able to treat him thoroughly. Our biggest fear is the onset of infection."

The next morning Avram repaired the electricity, Itzhak replaced the belt and Moshe left for Jaffa to alert the Turkish police.

When the police arrived, they traced the blood marks to Beit A'yan. They arrested the mukhtar, who quickly disclosed the whereabouts of the two suspects to regain his freedom.

Sorke wrote *August 19, 1913. The police arrested the two intruders. Itzhak is devastated. He feels guilty about the incident. I suspect the Good-Neighbor principle is dead. But what will replace it? Perhaps a hardline approach to Beit A'yan?*

***

That evening, Moshe chaired a raucous meeting. Many people presented their opinions. Some were extreme, others moderate. In the end, calm thoughts prevailed. They accepted the continuation of the

Good-Neighbor principle, provided the mukhtar would show tangible signs of cooperation. They also agreed to give him a stern warning and demand compensation for the repair cost.

Moshe asked Itzhak to accompany him to Beit A'yan. He walked silently behind him, carrying the burden of doubts. *Could Ahad Ha'am be so wrong? Could Dr. Epstein be inappropriate to the reality of Eretz Israel?* He wondered quietly. Moshe read his mind. "Relax Itzhak, we are not going to start a shooting war. Your idea is still valid."

"It is not my idea. I found it in Dr. Epstein's and Ehad Ha'am's writings. I just formulated their thoughts into the Good-Neighbor principle. My doubts about the applicability of the articles to everyday life grow continuously. Maybe I misunderstood them? I must reread the relevant sections. I think I have them in my library."

"I'd love to find out what they say. I have never heard of Dr. Epstein. I am not sure if I read the applicable Ehad Ha'am article. So, let's read them together."

"Thank you, Moshe."

The mukhtar received them cordially. Moshe thanked him for his kindness and immediately broke away with custom. He did not want to play any duplicitous game. Unceremoniously he came to the point. He spoke and Itzhak translated.

"Mr. Samir, we have tried to be good neighbors, but you stifled our effort from its inception. Your people sabotaged our pumps, which benefit your village also. You even acted violently against our friend who did you no harm. We are here to stay. So, the choice is yours: peace will give us both the opportunity to grow and learn from each other. Please note that I did not add friendship and cooperation to the word peace. Although, if you use these nouns you will find me very receptive."

The mukhtar promised to cooperate and invited them foral-salcha, a ceremonial meal to end a quarrel. They agreed and set the date.

After the meal Sorke wrote, *September 2, 1913. I am very troubled. I do not trust the mukhtar. I think he is a shifty, devious man. I see dark clouds over the horizons of Hazohar. I hope Itzhak will come to his senses and rethink the Good-Neighbor principle.*

***

Away from the belligerent welcome Beit A'yan gave Hazohar, the *Yishuv* was in a midst of a heated debate. An outsider reading the local press would fail to grasp the strength of the passion that swept the *Yishuv.* A person attending a public gathering would fail to comprehend the reasons for the high decibel it reached. The debate ensnared everyone, dragging the *Yishuv* Into a whirlpool of extreme rhetoric and, sometimes, blows. And it was all about language.

8 BATTLE OF THE LANGUAGES

On June 27, 1913, Sorke wrote in her diary: *I agree with Mr. L. who wrote in The Freedom "Hebrew is part of our bones, a flesh of our flesh." I shall add that our entire project is profoundly injured by the mere thought, however meek, doubting the supremacy of Hebrew in our national renaissance.*

***

For a few days Itzhak suspected that something was troubling Sorke. He had read the June and July editions of *The Freedom* in which the paper discussed at length the primacy of Hebrew and more explicitly the process of selecting the primary teaching language for the new institute of higher learning. Had she read those articles? Did she fear the coming of a cultural storm?

While working together at the chicken coop, he was perturbed to see her morose expression. "You know, Sorke, every now and then an event of an existential magnitude roils the *Yishuv*. Sometimes the event will persist for years and even decades. Such has been the struggle for free Jewish immigration and for unobstructed rights to purchase land.

"There are other types of existential events, those that persist for a short time. Once they disappear they leave the *Yishuv* in a healthier position. Such was the struggle against the Uganda proposal."

At first she did not reply. She fell into a deep silence, which reflected her feeling. It was as if Itzhak had peeled off many protective layers that surrounded her mind. "I think," she said at last, "I can sense a hint of such an event at the *Yishuv*'s doorstep. But everyone is sure that the issue will die in a whisper rather than explode in a threatening manner."

"What is it?" he asked.

"It has to do with educating our young men and women," she replied.

Itzhak observed a reluctance to talk and left her answer unchallenged.

A few weeks later he found himself seated at lunch with Gershon, Tova, Kalman and Sorke. The issue of the Hebrew language was constantly on people's minds, but the conversation meandered among many subjects.

At last, Kalman said to Itzhak, "Hebrew language is paramount on everyone's mind. While thinking about the controversy another linguistic thought flashed through my mind."

"Go on."

"Would you offer an Arabic course to those who wish to learn the language? After all, most of the people in *Eretz Israel* are Arabs. Knowing the language will foster better communication."

"Excellent thought. I second the motion," said Tova with a smile.

"I agree and I accept the challenge," replied Itzhak.

"It is a deal, " interjected Tova before Itzhak had a chance to change his mind. "I shall organize the Arabic language school."

"Great" said Sorke and immediately pivoted the discussion. "Today, Haifa is looking with pride at its newest possession: the Technikum (eventually renamed Technion) an institute for higher scientific and technical learning, the only one of its kind in the nascent Zionist project and, in fact, the only one in the Ottoman Empire."

Itzhak was hoping that Sorke was returning to their incomplete conversation at the chicken coop.

"Yes," said Gershon, "I have seen the photos of the completed building. It stands proudly on the middle slope of Mt. Carmel facing the Mediterranean, ready to embrace the first generation of students, who will become the scientists of tomorrow. We are leapfrogging into the future."

"Indeed," agreed Sorke, "but to assure a more glorious future the board of directors must select Hebrew as the language of instruction in the new school. Nothing else will do!" Then she asked a rhetorical question, "Will they? I am offended as I sense that they are debating the issue at length, in faraway Berlin. Will they err on the side of Diasporic Yiddish? Or perhaps German?"

So, that is what troubles Sorke, reflected Itzhak.

"The debate over the place of Hebrew in our national aspirations has been simmering for years," said Tova. "You must realize that the supremacy of the language and its inseparable connection to the Jewish awakening has been furiously discussed in literary circles of the late nineteenth century. So today's debate is simply a continuation."

"Call me a chauvinist. But I recall that my father never doubted the place of Hebrew in our national conscious," said Itzhak. "At that time his library in Gordov was full of books of the greatest Jewish writers of the time, like Shalom Aleikhem, Perutz, Mendele Moykher Sforim and others, who preferred Yiddish. Nevertheless he insisted that the renewed Jewish nation must speak with one tongue, Hebrew. He thought that Hebrew was the soul of the Jewish people and, like them, it had never lost its luster during thousands of years of darkness. In the Diaspora. I have never veered from his teaching."

"Moreover, I think that Yiddish is a symbol of the hated Diaspora. It, like German or Russian, has no place in the daily life of the awakening

Jewish nation. Hebrew is our national language, period," stated Tova emphatically.

"I think you did not mean to imply the complete rejection of these languages. Did you?" asked Gershon.

"No, not at all. I meant that our schools must teach in Hebrew. Our commerce must be executed in Hebrew, our culture, books, theaters and songs must be in Hebrew and so on. Hebrew for us must be as French to the Frenchman and English to the Englishman. Would anyone dare to contemplate the adaptation of German as the language of choice at the Sorbonne?"

"I agree," interjected Sorke. "Unlike the past rift between Hebrew and Yiddish, today the choice is most likely between German and Hebrew or French and Hebrew. The key difference is this: Then, we lived in the Diaspora and the redemption of the Jewish people was only a spark in the eyes of the few. Now, that spark has morphed into a volcanic fire that ignites the entire Jewish people. Now we have started the rejuvenation of our people, the forging of the new Jew. Now we must uncompromisingly adopt Hebrew as the language that expresses the antiquity of our people, the survivability of our people, the soul of our people and the rejection of the loathed diasporic life."

"Since *Ezra*, which supports much of the *Yishuv* educational enterprises and vigorously promotes the Hebrew language, manages the high learning institute they will stay true to form and declare Hebrew as the official language of the new Technikum," suggested Itzhak.

"Amen to that," said Tova.

"From your mouth to the board's ears," said Sorke in earnest.

"Itzhak, you seem to think that *Ezra* is crucial to the future of the Technikum. I hate to admit it but who are they?" asked Gershon.

"*Ezra* is a German-Jewish philanthropic organization," answered Sorke before Itzhak had a chance to reply. "In addition to what Itzhak has said it supports many schools on all levels and a huge work by Mr. Ben Yehuda to create the first Hebrew dictionary. They will decide on the primary language of teaching in the new Technikum."

"I am sure we'll find out soon," suggested Tova.

"Maybe yes, maybe no," said Sorke. "There is no definitive timetable to their decision. Meanwhile I can share with you one fact: there is an enormous public pressure on the group to do just that. Students, teachers and newspapers constantly remind the board that the *Yishuv* expects a decision in line with national sentiments."

The hour was late. It was time to return to work. They took their dishes to the designated cleaning place, emptied their trash and stepped into the yard, where they scattered to continue their respective unfinished projects.

A few weeks after that discussion, a simmering controversy burst onto the scene, shaking the entire *Yishuv*. It was not the Ottoman authorities that brought on the turmoil. It was not a new dispute with the local Arabs either. It was the Jewish foreign board of *Ezra* that forced the *Yishuv* into an unprecedented militant posture, one that pitted Jews against Jews. It was the board's decision to adopt German as the official language of teaching in the Technikum. Word about the decision, cast in Germany, reached *Eretz Israel* about ten days after it was made.

The local opinions were fierce in their condemnation. "A National Disgrace," shouted the headlines of one newspaper.

"The long history of the Hebrew language must remain alive in our hearts," screamed a poster from public bulletin boards.

"The soul of our people is its language and its bible," declared another poster.

"Resign!" demanded the headline of another paper of the Zionist members of the *Ezra*'s board. They did not need the paper's retroactive demand. They resigned in protest immediately after the decision was made.

The news opened emotional floodgates of protests and opposition. While Tel-Aviv and other urban centers exploded in demonstrations, and speeches of protest echoed from every public platform, Hazohar remained in the dark, as it was isolated from the news stream of *Eretz Israel*. It usually took a few days for the news to filter in.

When Gershon returned from a trip to Tel-Aviv he broke the news to Moshe. He was agitated and spoke in short, angry sentences. "Call for a special gathering tonight. I have important news. We must join the protest."

Moshe was perplexed. "What has happened, Gershon?" he asked in dismay.

Gershon did not elaborate. He replied tersely, "The board has voted to teach in German."

"No! How could they?" reacted Moshe indignantly.

"They could and they did, the donkeys! They should all be barred from the movement. They are like a malignant wound in the body of the *Yishuv*," responded Gershon.

Moshe said. "I shall compose a notice and hang it on the bulletin board at the dining hall."

"No need to compose anything. I brought you one. It is good enough for us." Gershon handed him the announcement and left abruptly.

Moshe looked askance at the back of his retreating friend. He feared Gershon was overreacting.

When the people returned from the field at lunchtime, they paused by the bulletin board and looked with dismay at the new announcement.

"Please read it before lunch. It is urgent," shouted Moshe from the sideline. "I know it was first issued elsewhere, but it is an excellent reflection of my sentiments."

Everyone crowded around but could see only fragments of the poster. There wasn't enough space in front the bulletin board.

"Let Itzhak read it," requested Sorke. "We read too slowly. We may not understand a word here and there and that will slow us even more. Itzhak can read, translate or explain misunderstood words."

"My thoughts exactly," echoed Pinchas, who barely spoke Hebrew and had difficulties in reading. Sorke remembered how he had reacted when Itzhak offered to teach the group Hebrew. It was astonishing. "Russian is good enough for Tolstoy, it is good enough for me," he'd declared. That day she formed an opinion about Pinchas' motives and dedication to the cause. In her mind he demonstrated total arrogance. He would not last long in the group.

Itzhak agreed to read. "As I read, please ask if you need for me to explain a word or a sentence," he declared.

A Call for Action

Brothers and sisters, the executive committee of Hazohar invites you to attend a protest meeting against the imposition of the German language as the language of choice in training our future scientists and engineers in the Technikum.

By doing so the board of the Technikum has denied our ancient national language the primary position it deserves for educating our children and redeeming our nation from the darkness of the Diaspora.

Brothers and sisters, you came to this land intending to forge a new Jewish nation. You have learned the language and abandoned, for the most part, all foreign tongues.

Now you must come to speak with one voice with the *Yishuv*; to support the students and the teachers across the land, who abandoned their study, their livelihood, in order to protest that shameful betrayal.

Come and unite in victory for our language: for the *Yishuv*.

Come and remind all foreign institutions that they must not abandon the Zionist path; that they must share the burden of implementing the Zionist projects not with money alone but with deeds. Hebrew is the soul of the rejuvenated nation. Protest its abandonment.

The meeting will be held tonight at 8 pm in the Hazohar dining hall.

***

There were a few questions, but all in all they understood. The more he read, the more agitated they became.

"What arrogance," someone said, referring to *Ezra*'s imposition of German.

"Distance breeds insensitivity," said another.

"I salute the students and the teachers who went on strike in protest," said a third voice.

"Save your comments for the gathering after dinner," proclaimed Moshe. "We still have a half a day of work before us."

Everyone chuckled. The rest of the day was more talk than work.

Itzhak was agitated. For the first time since he had joined them he sensed an opening chasm. He whispered to Moshe, "I think we are facing an issue that can divide us as did the Uganda proposal ten years ago."

Sorke protested in her diary: *November 10, 1913. How callous are the leaders of Ezra! Yes. They chose German and discarded Hebrew. How could any Jew tear up the soul of the nation? We are here sacrificing to build, to nurture the neglected Jewish soul and these heartless faraway Jews continue to injure it. When oh when will we speak and act in unity?*

***

A little after eight, Moshe gaveled the meeting to order. "I want us to hold a frank and open conversation regarding the language issue and then adopt a resolution that will be sent to the Young Worker newspaper. I want the *Yishuv* to know where Hazohar stands!" he declared with typical Moshe bravado. "I Invite Gershon to share with us whatever information he was able to gather in Tel-Aviv."

"Thank you, Moshe," said Gershon. "I was impressed by the combative mood of the people. Students boycotted schools. Teachers struck. The newspapers were replete with angry articles; 'Hebrew is first. It is worth fighting for.' Shouted the headlines. No one wanted to compromise. 'Hebrew is the language of the Jewish nation. It has been for two thousand years, and will remain so forever. It is non-negotiable,' the protestors shouted as they marched through the main street."

Itzhak rose to speak. "Was Hebrew dead? I asked my father, after hearing gossip at the Gordov synagogue. Everyone was talking about his attempt to teach me the language beyond what I needed for religious purposes. I was seven years old. He answered me that it might be anemic, but it had been alive for two thousand years and was not on its deathbed. He was uncompromising when he said 'Remember this, Itzhak, Hebrew is the heart of the Jewish nation.' He was right then, and what he said is appropriate to our time A nation without a common language is not a nation; we are a nation!"

Tova asked for the floor. Her voice quivered with controlled anger. "I agree with my friends. The language debate reminds me of the Uganda proposal. It failed because it was not an *Eretz Israel* centric proposal. So is any proposal to introduce a foreign language to our educational system. The Zionist movement is Hebraic—"

"I agree," interrupted Ribi, raising the anger decibel of Tova's incomplete thought. "It was Hebraic in its very soul. Why are we here? We could have gone to America and probably lived an easier life. I mean physically, socially, culturally and financially. Yet we chose to come here. We elected hardship over comfort. Loneliness over vast social possibilities; danger, that lurks on every corner from the Arabs, who dislike us, over the relative safety of life in America. Like those who came before us we insist on and will protect the Hebraic nature of the Zionist movement. There is no other language for us here."

Sorke continued her thoughts, "I agree and would like to add this: We abandoned the comfort of the Russian language, or even Yiddish. We vowed to speak Hebrew in spite of the incredible difficulties it presented us. We chose to add to our general discomfort the tension involved in speaking a new language. Think how much more comfortable we will be if we speak in a familiar tongue when we are in need of comfort or calm during the many stressful and sometimes despairing moments that we endure daily. Why do we subject ourselves to such additional hardship? Because we insist on the Hebraic destiny of our cause: the historical connection of our people with this land. A significant part of that history is our language.. Shame on those who reject such an idea. Hebrew is a core pillar of our national awakening. It is to us as water is to a wanderer in a parched land."

"I hate to cast a shadow on these eloquent thoughts," declared Pinchas. "In principle, I agree. But what are we talking about? Here is an institute of higher learning, the only school of its kind in *Eretz Israel*, a school that will train our engineers, physicists and other scientists.

Can the Hebrew language provide them with the necessary tools, such as Hebrew reference books? The necessary terminology? Of course not! Sure, Hebrew is the heart of the Jewish nation, but we can give her the time to grow, expand and develop to the proper technical level. We need to provide men and women with the necessary linguistic ability so they can translate the superb scientific literature that is available in German and other well-developed languages, so that our students can benefit in the same manner they do at MIT, Oxford or the Sorbonne. That will take much time and effort."

David interjected, "I know that there are people who have devoted their lives to expanding and enriching the Hebrew language. But their work is far from over. I agree with Pinchas. Hebrew can wait. And by waiting I do not push it into the corner of obscurity. I say it can wait to grow and mature."

Pinchas nodded in agreement. "That can take years. Meanwhile we let the well-developed and well-suited German or French educate our brightest. Hebrew can wait. Our future scientists cannot!"

There were rumblings of disagreement.

"Oh, let me say one more thing," said David who was aware of the growing hostility in the hall. "We did not know Hebrew and that did not prevent us from choosing this land. We have been working on it for more than a year and during this time we have acquired proficiency in Hebrew. Did the enterprise suffer from our initial lack of linguistic ability? No!"

The mood in the hall grew more acrimonious. Some people shouted "Shame, shame, David."

Ribi was not far behind "Boo, Pinchas! Boo, David!"

"There is no *Eretz Israel* without Hebrew as its crown!" shouted Tova.

Pinchas protested that a civilized society must allow for dissenting voices. "But obviously you are showing your true colors. Am I not a good Zionist because I see the merit of a different decision?"

The hall was a stage for uncontrolled anger. No one saw the merit of the two dissenting voices. Fanaticism ruled the evening.

At the end, emotions trumped reason. Moshe submitted a resolution that supported the demand for Hebrew as the primary language of learning and expressed solidarity with teachers' and students' protest and boycotts. Pinchas was present during the vote. He objected to the resolution. David left in anger earlier. Moshe also sought the approval of the members to appoint him as their representative in the forthcoming mass demonstration in Tel-Aviv.

The campaign for Hebrew was fast and furious. The *Yishuv* held massive protests. Newspapers published anti-*Ezra* articles. The land was flooded with posters in support of Hebrew. The entire campaign was defined in war-like terminology: The Battle of the Languages.

Three months later, the board rescinded its decision. Hebrew triumphed. Sorke smiled at Itzhak from the other side of the vegetable garden. "You were right. We are better off at the end of this existential crisis."

"Yes," replied Itzhak. "We, I mean the Jewish people everywhere, are more united. We acquired a common purpose and a unified view of our national priorities."

People throughout the *Yishuv* calmed down. Life returned to its daily routine. David and Pinchas, still unhappy about the reception their view received, left Hazohar. David went to Tel Aviv to practice medicine. Pinchas left for New York.

Sorke wrote: *February 27, 1914. Hebrew won, but we lost! Our behavior toward David and Pinchas was shameful. We must learn to live side by side with opposing views no matter how painful they may be. I wish I'd thought like this before I allowed my friends to be insulted. I am so sorry. It will never happen again. I shall keep in touch with David. Maybe the day will come that I will be able to apologize to him.*

***

But normalcy and the routine of struggling with their spartan existence did not last long. A brutal murder in Sarajevo blackened the horizons of Europe. Tension overflowed from the local papers. The *Yishuv* was on edge. In Hazohar, conversations at mealtime were speculative but focused on the implications of the murder on their daily life.

For days Moshe walked around in a daze, as if a heavy burden fell upon his shoulders, threatening his leadership of Hazohar. Anyone who listened to him heard more or less the same words. "The murder of the Archduke and his wife is a harbinger of troubles for the *Yishuv*. We are definitely facing the hardship-filled, lean years of the Pharaoh's dream.

"I thought Pharaoh's dream was about famine following abundance," said Tova jokingly.

"Yes, I have taken some liberty. But what I really fear is a war that will put an immeasurable hardship on the *Yishuv*."

9 THE LEAN YEARS

"The American Jews continued to remember us and sent more money. As the war went on and conditions in Palestine became worse, they continued to send more. Once they even sent an entire ship, the S.S. Vulcan, with provisions."

Arthur Ruppin, Memoirs, Diaries, Letters p. 151.

Before retiring for the night Sorke reflected on Moshe's words. She entered in her diary, *September 2, 1914. Moshe was right. Here is what I sense and fear:*

1. *The scent of gunpowder is in the air.*
2. *The atmosphere is growing tenser every day.*
3. *The Ottoman authorities are becoming more nervous, more suspicious and more unforgiving.*

The present portends a terrible future, I am afraid. What will become of me? Of us? Of our nascent Yishuv?

***

Fear of an ominous future hung over the people, seeping into and interfering with all aspects of their life. One by one, the local newspapers ceased publishing. Information became scarcer and scarcer. The one Hebrew paper left in circulation devoted pages to the unfolding madness in Europe. Everyone witnessed helplessly as the European governments raced toward the abyss, dragging innocent bystanders along an uncharted, deadly road to a future no one wanted. Surely the Ottoman Empire would follow.

As if to highlight the insanity of that race, the papers also carried advertisements that originated with European consuls instructing their citizens to report for army duty. Itzhak laughed at the advertisements. "We are not leaving Hazohar to go back to Russia."

The Ottoman government did not trail behind. It ordered a general mobilization throughout the empire. It further ordered all the residents of Palestine, who were not Ottoman citizens, to acquire citizenship or risk deportation.

The worries of economic collapse, and with it hunger and diseases, demoralized the *Yishuv* as well as the Arab population. The various banks appealed for calm. They published an advertisement on the main page of the paper in a desperate attempt to abate the storm that was blowing through the financial reality of *Eretz Israel*. The banks assured the public that there was plenty of liquidity and therefore citizens should not panic and rush to withdraw their funds.

But that was tantamount to crying in the wilderness: the sound traveled but no one listened. Indeed, within a few weeks the banks ceased operations. Only the Anglo Palestinian bank remained open for sporadic services. The financial squeeze touched upon every man and woman in the region.

In trying to salvage a portion of their money, Moshe collected all the Russian Rubles in Hazohar. He went to Jaffa to sell them. Alas, the value of the money plummeted faster than the arrival of potential buyers. Disheartened, he returned home with a pocketful of useless paper.

Signals of a pending financial calamity were visible everywhere. Gold and Turkish money supply dried up, and the ability of the poor and the rich alike to buy daily essentials evaporated.

Conversations heard in village coffee houses focused on existential questions. "Where do we find food to feed ourselves? Where do we find the kerosene to heat our homes? Where do we find work to provide us with money? Will the authority conscript our children and husbands to fight in a war that has nothing to do with our lives? If so, will they ever come back?"

The anticipation for war had other manifestations: forced expulsion of non-Ottoman citizens, imposition of restrictive edicts that forbade the display of Zionist emblems, collapse of international mail service, and more.

Army garrisons appeared overnight near towns and villages across the country. One camped at the outskirts of Beit A'yan. It brought along new images and sounds that overshadowed the familiar sights. The vegetable garden, the orchards of tree saplings, the fields of wheat, and the grazing meadows no longer looked the same. Their bucolic character was disrupted. New voices filled the air: the morning wake-up call of the bugle, soldiers marching endlessly through the empty fields, loud barks dispatching commands and sounds of rifle practice.

Hazohar, by its proximity to Beit A'yan, became a default second home to the Turkish garrison: a ragtag group of poorly dressed, ill-fed soldiers, mostly Arab recruits. They milled about everywhere, violating property rights and ignoring the rule of law. The law was a confusing abstract that had nothing to do with their daily survival needs. It benefited neither Hazohar nor Beit A'yan.

The new campsite was a boon to the miserable soldiers, a free source of bounty to be had at will. They took what they wanted, whenever they wanted, showing total disregard for the mess and destruction they invariably left behind. They trampled the young shoots in the vegetable garden to create a shortcut to the ripened tomatoes, snatched eggs so hastily that they invariably crushed the chickens that laid them. On occasion, they walked brazenly up to a flock of sheep, searching for the fattest lamb and ordered the shepherd to slaughter it right there and then.

Moshe and the local dignitaries of Beit A'yan overcame the tension between the two communities to reason with the officer on duty. "Please stop the pillage of food Your soldiers will be better off if we have an orderly distribution of foodstuff," they pleaded with him. Alas, the brute turned a deaf ear to their pleas. He accused them of rising up against the Sultan and dismissed them callously. Weeks of pillage and destruction continued unabated.

Lawlessness intensified throughout the land. Beit A'yan was no exception. One crisp autumn morning a unit of the garrison was marching toward Beit A'yan. The residents behaved in line with a newly acquired custom: when the Turks approached, the locals retreated behind closed doors.

Tova, who went shopping at Beit A'yan, noticed an eerie atmosphere when she approached the village. The streets were empty. Shops were locked. The usually bustling market was quiet and deserted as a graveyard on an off day. *The Turks must be coming,* she thought and turned toward home. It was too late. She could hear the approaching patrol ahead. Looking for shelter she noticed a few children playing on the street in front of a modest family dwelling. She tried to gesture to them to return home, but to no avail. She moved out of sight and waited in a nearby shed for the patrol to pass.

The commanding officer detected the children at play as soon as he cleared the ninety-degree angle of Main Street, just north of the main square. Among them was a young girl, about fifteen years old, exotically beautiful. Even though she wore a Hijab, he could see that her head was adorned with cascading silky black braids tied in a golden ribbon. He paused to examine her. His eyes flashed with unchecked lust. He ordered his soldiers to clear the street. "Just leave the girl on the side." They did as he commanded. No one saw Tova.

He walked directly toward the girl. She attempted to escape but failed. She sank to the ground and began to wail, quietly at first. He walked slowly, with determined steps. When he could almost touch her, he stopped to circle the girl and get a full look at his prey. She howled like a wounded animal. Neighbors and family members rushed to the scene but stopped at a safe distance from the offending officer. They watched helplessly. The officer's small army had a paralyzing effect on the bravest of men. No one moved.

He lifted the screaming girl off the ground, fondling her breasts as he threw her across his shoulders. The barrage of closed-fist punches she landed on his back only made him laugh uproariously.

Do something Tova implored herself. *Why should I? They are not friends of mine. They don't even like us.* Blood pounded in her veins. She could remain a coward no longer.

Tova rushed out of the shadows at the officer. She reached for the girl's hand, intending to pull her away, screaming at him in Hebrew and Russian. The amused officer responded in Turkish. Neither of them understood the other. The officer pushed Tova to the ground and commanded one of his soldiers to hold her at bay. She was bleeding profusely, but did not give up the fight to free herself and the girl.

The officer dropped the girl on the dirt road, grabbed her hand and dragged her like a farmer dragging a sack of potatoes to the market stall. His disheveled men followed. Tova trudged behind begging the officer to release the girl. He ordered one of his soldiers to escort her back to Hazohar. She was dragged against her will, screaming all the way. A few people in Hazohar, who were inside the settlement gate, rushed to her aid. As soon as she staggered into the dining hall, she told of the savagery of the scene she had witnessed.

Folks in Hazohar were furious. They resolved to come to the girl's aid. Moshe, Gershon and Itzhak went to the camp to try to buy her freedom. Moshe spoke in Hebrew, Itzhak translated his words into Arabic and someone at the camp translated his words into Turkish. But the officer was uninterested. He sent them home with a veiled threat. "Those who challenge an officer of the Sultan can be summarily jailed for sedition," he said angrily.

On their way out of the camp, the translator told Itzhak that his friend recognized the girl. She was his younger cousin.

For the next day and night the cousin, as well as everyone in the proximity of the camp, endured her screams as the officer repeatedly raped and beat her.

The next night the young soldier took his bayonet, walked stealthily to the officer's tent and stood by the flap. He glared in hatred at the snoring officer.

The girl lay naked beside him, tied to the center pole like a circus ape. She was awake but she uttered no sound and stared at a faraway space beyond the open flap. His eyes wandered between the officer and the girl, who looked haggard and disheveled. Finally, he made his move. He rushed toward his cousin and stabbed her repeatedly. She died silently. Subconsciously he knew that killing the officer was the right thing to do. But that could and probably would bring a major calamity on Beit A'yan.

Besides, according to custom, the girl's death was necessary to uphold the family honor.

He quickly fled the scene but was hunted by the commanding officer and his soldiers. They caught him, hungry and exhausted, in a cave a few kilometers from Beit A'yan. He was taken to Jerusalem, tried and sentenced to hang. The officer was promoted for his persistent dedication to justice within the Sultan's army.

The affair sent chills through the Hazohar community. A fierce debate ensued in which the men, without exception, suggested relocating the female residents to a safer place in Tel Aviv.

Gershon summarized the prevailing opinion. "War gives people guns. Guns breed power, which enables the powerful to impose upon those without guns any level of brutality, any arbitrary act with no ramifications. We love you, ladies. Because of our love we cannot afford to put you in harm's way, to keep you here."

A few men tried to convince the women to leave voluntarily.

"Soldiers always threaten women in order to affect men's behavior."

"They go beyond mere threat. They act. They rape women in front of their friends and kin. That causes a lifelong scar."

"I think we should not give the Turks such an opportunity."

Tova looked at them, incensed. "Do you think that this tactic will not be productive when applied to a man? Won't that induce a favorable behavior from the others?"

Alexa and Ribi nodded their heads in agreement.

Sorke added, "Women are as vulnerable as men when confronted with an arbitrary threat of atrocities. The nature of the evil may vary but it is still evil!"

Itzhak changed his mind. Now he supported the women. "We have struggled to eliminate the boundaries between a man's work and a woman's work. Women have been working beside us ever since we put our first spade in the ground of Petach Tikva. In doing so we have encountered many physical and mental obstacles but we persisted. Why should we change now?"

More people chimed in with repetitive arguments that added little to the merit of the case. All the women who were present objected vehemently to their departure. They were unanimous in their opinion that such a move would be a gross violation of their sense of equality, of their will to shoulder the burden of the coming lean time.

The discussion continued after dinner on the next day. The arguments lasted into the wee hours of the morning. At the end, the women prevailed. They remained in Hazohar to face an unknown future, determined to pull their weight in the battle for survival.

Sorke was thinking aloud in her diary after the heated discussion *September 20, 1914. Am I stupid? I know Gershon is right. The truth is that I am afraid for Ribi, Alexa, Tova and myself. That girl from Beit A'yan suffered unimaginable pain. But all the men there were cowards and did nothing. They were fearful of Turkish retributions. Only her cousin acted, albeit wrongly. And he was hunted like an animal and hung. Our men are brave. They will not stand idle. Are we putting our friends in danger by forcing them into unnecessary pain if we stay and are threatened? They will come to our aid and consequently suffer. Hazohar may even be destroyed. We must leave. On the other hand, I agree with Itzhak. Oy! I am so confused.*

***

War fever intensified. Itzhak, who persistently read the local paper, reported to his friends one evening, "For all of us foreign residents, I have bad news. The Ottoman government declared last week the cancellation of the Capitulation agreements with all foreign governments. That implies no more protection from the Russian consul. Furthermore, we are now subjected to conscription and payment of local taxes. I fear that the privileges of living where we want, which enabled us to build Hazohar and other settlements, to open schools and to establish public institutions, are now a thing of the past. Could it be that we are witnessing the beginning of the end of the nascent Zionist project?"

People were shocked. They were not used to seeing Itzhak in a gloomy, uncertain mood. "We shall defend Hazohar together. We shall prevail," said Tova without really internalizing the calamitous future that faced them.

"A war is coming and our main goal should be survival!" said Sorke. "And survive we will. We should multiply our food supply: increase our chicken brood and the size and variety of the vegetable garden. We must become self-sufficient."

"We have a bumper crop. Let's start a canning operation," suggested Alexa.

"Easier said than done," said Ribi. "Where do we get the cooking oil, the kerosene? The jars? Yesterday I went to the market at Beit A'yan. It was nearly empty."

"Yes, the Ottoman authorities recently announced a naval blockade. That means the end of import and export to and from the Yishov," observed Itzhak in a flat voice.

"All is not lost," said Moshe. "I like your idea. We should begin the planning process for food storage immediately. Alexa, will you recruit a few people to help in the planning?"

She nodded.

The next evening Alexa, Avram, and Ribi met to discuss the preservation project.

"We should heed the advice Joseph gave Pharaoh. You remember?" Avram, somewhat jokingly, asked Alexa.

She replied with a mischievous smile. "I do. He told him to build granaries to store the food from the good years so he could feed the population during the bad years. Now you are an engineer. Go design a granary that will allow us to save some of our predicted bounty for the upcoming lean years."

"We should build them underground," he said. "This way we hide them from marauding soldiers. It is also cooler underground. Furthermore, I am not an agronomist but, Alexa, could we use the soil we dig to expand the vegetable garden and thus avoid suspicion?"

"Yes, depending on the quality of the soil three meters underground," she replied. "I will recruit a few volunteers to start preparing for the expansion of the vegetable garden."

"You may also work on expanding the chicken coop," added Avram.

"Excellent idea," said Ribi and added, "since we will use canning for most of our preservation effort we need many glass jars with lids. The rest we have in the kitchen. I hope Moshe can find them in the market. Better yet, I shall go with him to Jaffa. Without jars, we have only limited preservation options."

The meeting was short and to the point. There was no need to linger. Everyone understood the needs and the urgency of the matter.

Ribi joined Moshe on his weekly trip to Jaffa. She scouted the market and the various shops on Bustros street but found only a few jars. Later, while waiting for Moshe at the *Eretz Israel* Office, she confided her disappointment to the office attendant. "I am afraid we've failed. Without jars we cannot accomplish our plans," she told him.

"What plans? What jars?" he asked.

She forced an apologetic smile and told him about Hazohar's food preservation plans.

His eyes lit. "I like your idea. It could help if all the farmers will do the same. Food preservation is a huge deal in America. It is necessary for the war effort. Maybe we can get the American consul in Jerusalem to help us. I shall go to Jerusalem tomorrow and promote this idea with him and few of our friends in town."

"Thank you," she said as they departed for Hazohar. "I am returning home happier and hopeful."

While Ribi waited for the promised actions, Avram designed the cellars, and work began post-haste to implement his design. Alexa dispatched a few men to collect manure for the expanded garden.

Within three weeks they had completed the expansion plan. All was in place except the jars. Disappointment crept in. The initial enthusiasm subsided and the cheerful atmosphere turned grim. They waited. There was nothing to be done.

After four tense weeks of waiting, Ribi was ready to leave for Jaffa when the diligence arrived with one thousand food preservation jars. The clerk on board was carried to the dining hall to join in a celebratory round of Hora. After they stopped to rest he told them that their initiative was being duplicated in many places. "You did well. Mazal Tov!" he declared proudly.

During the coming weeks, they worked steadfastly to preserve their Fall vegetables. Sacks of potatoes were moved from their temporary storage to one cellar. Soon the shelves of another were overflowing with preserved food and their hearts with optimism.

***

On November 7, 1914, Sorke wrote in her diary. *Sometime in the last week or so the Ottoman Empire has joined the war on the side of Germany. Itzhak was sad. When he is sad, I am sad. He was no longer able to communicate with his sister and parents. The war thwarted his plans to bring them to Eretz Israel.*

I think our paper kowtows to the Ottoman authorities. Every time I read it I sense that they stretch—as much as they can without being ridiculous—their support of the Ottoman's position. I guess that is one way to survive. Maybe they count on their readers' ability to read between the lines. Or, perhaps we'll have to do the same. After all, we live here. I am afraid that the entire Jewish world will adopt a split loyalty. German Jews will be loyal to Germany and may find themselves shooting at English Jews. What a nightmare!

***

A few weeks later, without warning, an Ottoman officer and a group of soldiers walked into the dining hall at Hazohar and ordered Avram and four other men to present themselves at an army recruiting station at the olive grove of Beit A'yan.

A Turkish doctor performed a rudimentary examination and pronounced them fit for service in the Sultan's army. The next day they were given dirty, ill-fitting uniforms and marched, along with twenty young Arabs from Beit A'yan, to Lydda.

Itzhak followed them in Hazohar's buggy. He approached the officer as soon as the group stopped to take a break. He was determined to secure his permission to assist Avram and friends. Even though the Ottomans' propensity for accepting bribes was common knowledge, Itzhak approached the commanding officer hesitantly. *A bucket full of rotten apples does not imply that all the apples are rotten. It would be my luck to meet with an honest man,* he reasoned as he continued his cautious advance. *I will end up in jail and my friends will suffer retributions.*

An overwhelming urge to retreat overtook him. Perspiration flowed from his temples. The palms of his hands were already moist. It took no special effort for him to hear the palpitation of his heart. He was sure that he looked like a man in distress rather than the confident person that he ought to be when attempting to bribe an Ottoman officer.

He focused his energy on his appearance. He had to look self-assured. "My name is Itzhak," he told the officer and handed him a dozen fresh eggs. "Please accept that as Hazohar's gratitude to you for protecting us." The officer smiled. Itzhak felt his breakfast rising from his stomach to his mouth. The officer reacted in Turkish but Itzhak understood that the eggs were a welcome gift that cleared the way for communication where gestures were more effective than words.

After some nonverbal negotiation and transfer of the customary bribe, Itzhak received a nod, the one that he interpreted as the permission to give his friends money to secure for themselves adequate food. He shook the officer's hands and walked backward in a gesture of respect. His stomach churned once again.

Outside, Avram and friends were happy to see him. "Do not come too close. Our uniforms stink to high heaven," joked Avram. But they hugged and were delighted in each other's company. "The money and fresh clothes are an affectionate reminder of home. It shows that our friends care," Avram said with tears in his eyes. "The Ottoman army is poor and malnourished. We are forced to fend for ourselves. Buy, confiscate or go hungry and dirty. Thank you, Itzhak."

They sat and talked for a while until the work gang was summoned back to the construction site. Itzhak promised to see them released as early as he could. They hugged again, and he left with a heavy heart. After his visit he resolved to study Turkish. He pursued his goal with much focus and tenacity. Within a few months he was able to carry on, albeit awkwardly, a conversation.

***

The conscription of Avram and the other four men was an unavoidable warning. Yossel saw the writing on the wall. He vowed never to fight on the side of the Turks. "They have never been on our side," he complained bitterly, "why should we be on theirs? I want no part of their citizenship or their army, which will ensnare me in its web as soon as it desires to do so. I will accept deportation. I am going to find a way to join the British army."

"I'll stay here," said Alexa in her quiet but firm voice. "I shall continue to expand and improve our agricultural fields. After all, what can I contribute as an agronomist to Great Britain's war effort?"

"The combined German-Ottoman army will soon be crawling all around," declared Gershon. "I side with Great Britain. But I am staying here. I will find a way to avoid the Turks' army. I will find a way to fight the Turks from within."

Moshe agreed with the "staying here" part of Gershon's statement. "We all must stay. We have invested too much energy and sweat in Hazohar to leave it behind. We must accept the Ottoman's citizenship. It is the only chance we have to keep our home, to realize the Zionist dream."

"While I shall stay," said Itzhak, "I support Yossel's decision to leave and fight from the outside. The future of our dream is in the hands of Great Britain. The Turks will never give us a thing. You, my friend," he spoke directly to Yossel, "are a different fighter than most of us. You have the warrior spirit: the one who will pursue the justice of our cause at any price. I feel that you have much energy to fight the Turks for all of us. I salute you. But we also need people who fight for the cause with the sweat of their brow and a will to sacrifice. I am with Alexa. We shall fight here to keep our home, your home, intact during the approaching turmoil."

Yossel was moved. He approached Itzhak and gave him a bear hug. "I shall return!" he said emphatically.

January 4, 1915, Sorke wrote in her diary, *War rages on. We begin to feel its cruel grip. If I was a religious person I would raise my fist and cry to the heavens, 'Why, why do you continue to stifle your children's aspirations?' Alas, I am not. So I pledge to my diary to look forward with hope; to work diligently for saving food; to survive in spite of the war, in spite of God.*

***

The Allied powers declared war on the Ottoman Empire. A new reality shook the *Yishuv* and overtook the spartan routine that dominated life in Hazohar. It was more austere, more helpless.

The Ottoman authorities pursued a policy of intimidation and harassment against the *Yishuv*. One morning, while everyone was at work, they arrived unannounced. Eight of them, loud, disheveled and in battle gear. Five soldiers took strategic positions around the inner perimeter of the kibbutz. They immediately assumed a menacing posture with guns aiming at the gate and at the few men who were scattered around the yard.

An officer accompanied by two soldiers strode across the yard toward Yigal, a new member of Hazohar, who was mending the door of the dining hall. He ordered the man to summon everyone. The worker did not react. He understood no Turkish. After the officer reiterated his command and failed to elicit a reaction, his mood grew more intense, more irate. When the angry officer raised his voice and shoved the muzzle into the Yigal's ribs the man assumed an urgent air. But he was still in the dark, sensing the gravity of the situation but understanding none of its meaning. The officer exasperated, showed him with a hand motion what he wanted.

"The bell. It is the bell that he wants me to ring," muttered Yigal to himself and sprinted across the yard to the bell post. He shook the rope swiftly, giving the bell's clang an obvious sense of panic. It was the first time the bell had tolled in Hazohar. Men and women responded from fields, from the vegetable garden, from the chicken coop and from the pasture. They rushed toward the yard, arriving there confused and frightened. Even in their befuddled state it was clear to most that the sound meant trouble.

"Surrender the munitions!" shouted the officer once the confusion subsided. No one understood. No one reacted. They looked around searching for Itzhak. Without him the encounter could escalate rapidly and cause unnecessary harm. Itzhak was nowhere to be seen.

"Ring the bell again," shouted Moshe. "Itzhak is missing."

The young man continued to ring with an added measure of vigor. At last Itzhak appeared. A chorus of frightened voices assailed his ears. "See what he wants, see why he is here."

Itzhak approached the agitated officer and asked him politely what he wanted.

"Surrender the munitions!" he screamed from the top of his voice.

"Hazohar has no munitions," answered Itzhak calmly.

The officer was enraged. He slapped Itzhak across his face, pushed him to the ground and yelled at him, "You are a liar. I treat liars with disdain. I'll give you one more chance to tell the truth!"

Itzhak repeated his reply. "It is the truth!"

The officer refused to accept that answer. He was sure that Itzhak was lying. After all, his sources had told him that Hazohar was awash with guns and had a large cache of bullets. He stood over Itzhak, raised his gun and smacked his face with the butt of his rifle. "See what I do to liars," he shouted.

They were confused. They saw the soldiers, the officer; they heard the exchange between the officer and Itzhak and witnessed the sudden aggression. Yet, no one had a clue what was going on.

A soldier pulled Itzhak off the ground. He staggered but quickly regained his balance. Blood was gushing from an open cut on his left cheek. From afar it looked menacing. Upon seeing his injury Sorke bolted forward to assist him. A bullet hit the ground a few feet ahead of her, stopping her abruptly. She dropped to her knees and begged the officer to let her help Itzhak. The officer raised his gun and was ready to fire again.

"Go back, Sorke," shouted Itzhak. "The wound is superficial. I will survive." Then he addressed the officer and repeated his assertion. "Sir," he said in a serious, confident voice, "We have no guns or ammunition in Hazohar."

"Arrest this son of a bitch. And bring that man over there," commanded the officer while pointing his gun at Gershon.

A soldier grabbed Gershon by his collar and dragged him closer to the officer. Another dragged Itzhak toward the gate. "Wait," shouted Itzhak "I am the only one here who speaks Turkish."

"Leave him here," shouted the officer. Meanwhile, the other soldier pushed Gershon to his knees and quickly retreated. There was chaos all around. The officer kept on repeating his command, "Surrender the munitions." Itzhak found himself in a peculiar position. Instantly he became the bridge between chaos and order, confusion and comprehension, and between a possible disaster and peace. He translated the barrage of commands as quickly as he could. He was in pain. His clothes were soaked with blood.

In a rare moment of calm the officer, fearing the loss of his translator, ordered a soldier to go and fetch the woman who had tried to help the detainee.

Sorke rushed to Itzhak's side, cleaned his face and treated his wound. "At least I stopped the bleeding," she whispered. Itzhak sat on the ground, leaning on Sorke.

Without warning the officer's mood reverted to his aggressive stance. He put his gun to Gershon's temple and shouted at Itzhak, "Tell your friends to bring the guns or I shoot him." His voice reached a high pitch. His face grew redder and his veins puffed and protruded across his neck. His bark was loud and it penetrated the ears of each and every person who stood at the yard. They moved nervously and emitted agitated sounds.

"Quiet! This is the last warning. Surrender the munitions or I kill this liar," shouted the officer.

Itzhak hastened to translate. "The officer wants all our munitions."

"There are no munitions in Hazohar," shouted Ribi.

"None," echoed Sorke.

"We grow food, not rifles," shouted a young man.

Itzhak observed that Tova was unusually quiet. But he continued to translate the barrage of denials. "Sir, we implore you. Search our place. We have no guns."

The officer pulled the lever of his rifle to load a fresh cartridge. Gershon was still on his knees. His entire body trembled violently.

"You are going to murder an innocent man! We have no guns in Hazohar. Whoever gave you this information is a liar. Bring that person here and let him show you where he saw our guns," pleaded Itzhak.

A tense moment followed. The folks in the yard hushed. The officer removed his gun from Gershon's head and fired at the ground next to him. "I shall keep this liar alive. We shall see how much information the two of you will give me after one night with my special interrogation unit."

Both Itzhak and Gershon knew that torture would follow. "With your permission, may I speak to my friend and see if he has heard of someone hiding munitions without my knowledge?" Itzhak pleaded.

"Be quick about it. Do not try my patience. I dislike liars," replied the officer.

"Listen, Gershon," Itzhak began, "sooner or later one of us will break under torture. Who knows what this lunatic can do. He can kill. He can even burn Hazohar to the ground. Is that what we want to exchange for a few guns?"

"I agree. It does not make sense to risk our entire enterprise for a commodity we can replace later."

"Then tell me where are the guns."

"Ask Tova, Itzhak. She hid a few guns for me."

The officer was fidgety. Itzhak turned to him and said, "My friend and I know nothing about guns in Hazohar. We want permission to talk to our friends. Maybe someone hid guns in Hazohar and we do not know."

The officer did not respond. Instead he ordered one of his soldiers to torch a small garden shed. "This is the first structure I'll burn, more will follow."

"Please allow me to remind you," said Itzhak in an excessively subservient voice, "we are all loyal Turkish citizens. We raise food for our beloved Turkish army. If you burn our place who will provide food for our brave fighting men near Beit A'yan?"

The officer signaled his soldier to wait.

"Please allow me to discuss the matter with our friends over there," Itzhak repeated.

"Go ahead, but hurry."

Itzhak rose and walked rapidly toward the people at the other end of the yard. "My friends," he addressed the Hazohar community, "we are facing evil in the eyes. Great calamity can befall upon us. This lunatic can torture one or many. He may kill without moral inhibition. He may even destroy Hazohar. And he may do all of that because someone hid a few guns and the Turks want them. Both Gershon and I agree that we must surrender the guns. I urge you for the good of our community to let me know the truth before this lunatic loses his patience."

Tova stepped forward. "I am sorry for being so blind and not revealing the truth earlier. I have hidden five rifles and some ammunition. You can find them in the garden shed buried about a foot underground."

Itzhak invited others to speak. "Come, say something so Tova will not be singled out to suffer in the hand of this brute."

A few men stepped out and spoke about the weather and the pending crops.

Afterwards Itzhak approached the officer and said, "One of our members who left Hazohar for America, before our just war, hid five rifles and some bullets. We will be glad to give them to you, sir. They are buried in the shed that you wanted to burn."

The officer ordered Itzhak to produce the munitions. He went toward the shed. A few people joined him carrying spades. Minutes later they unearthed the carefully protected munitions and carried them to the officer. His anger increased. He was convinced that both men lied to him. "You are under arrest for lying to an officer. You will be further interrogated and trialed by a military tribunal" He ordered one of his soldiers to shackle the two and march them out of Hazohar, leaving behind a stunned community.

A few days later Itzhak, bruised and exhausted, was released. He brought the news of Gershon's sentence. "When I spoke to him before his transfer to Accra prison to serve six months in jail, he was brave and relieved. He told me that his sentence was better than bearing witness to that brute burning down of Hazohar."

Later, after hearing of Gershon's fate, Sorke confided in her diary, *February 1, 1915. What a frightening event. Gershon will be rotting in prison and there is nothing we can do. I am convinced that because he suffers we have been spared. Years of sacrifices could have been erased from my life history in minutes and for what? For five lousy rifles! Tova must love Gershon so much that she revealed nothing until he told her to do so. I love her, she is a devout Zionist and a good friend, but she should have said something immediately.*

***

Every other week Tova visited Gershon in jail. She felt guilty for his incarceration. "It is my fault, Tova," he told her while he lovingly embraced her. "Thank you for not saying anything until I agreed. That was mighty brave of you."

A few months later Gershon was released. He was malnourished but otherwise in good spirits. "A Turkish jail is no fun," he told his friends. "Let me just say this, it is a boring, dirty, nauseating existence. I am happy to be home."

10 SERVING THE BRITISH ARMY

"At 11am on 25 April the men of the Zion Mule Corps aboard Dundrennon approached Cape Helles at the extreme southern tip of Gallipoli peninsula in the slowly clearing mist, hearing clearly the dull roar of the guns of allied ships and the Turkish shore batteries."

Jewish Virtual Library, The Zion Muleteers of Gallipoli, Gallipoli.

The Turkish authorities expanded their intimidation policy. They initiated a stringent implementation of the citizenship law. Thousands throughout the *Yishuv*, Yossel among them, refused the Ottoman's order. They were swiftly deported to Egypt. There, Yossel joined the many young Russian Jews, who were torn abruptly from their home, family and friends in *Eretz Israel* and thrown into a refugee camp in Alexandria. He did whatever was asked of him in the camp. The Jewish community of Alexandria took care of his daily bread. Three times a day they provided food for the refugees. It was a meager amount but it sustained the exiled.

No sooner had he arrived when he learned about a committee that was toiling to organize a Jewish unit in the British Army. "The Jews must take part in the liberation of *Eretz Israel* from the Ottoman's yoke," said one committee member.

Yossel felt that his destiny was unfolding before his eyes. There was no doubt in his mind. He recalled Itzhak's words before he left and volunteered to become a member of the proposed unit. To his dismay the British authorities would not allow the formation of any Jewish unit. But the leaders persisted. Later the military command relaxed its opposition but disallowed the formation of a combat unit. Unfortunately for the willing, the military command procrastinated and no Jewish recruit was allowed into the British army. Yossel was disappointed but not disheartened.

The leaders continued to petition the British command in Cairo. Eventually the Military authorities relented. They permitted the creation of a non-fighting Jewish unit. Its purpose would be serving the fighting men. Yossel and all the volunteers were very dissatisfied.

"We want to fight rather than serve the fighters," was the buzz at the first plenary meeting.

But Mr. Trumpeldor, one of the leaders of the proposed unit, stated emphatically, "We've got to smash the Turks. On which front you begin is a question of tactics; but for me, any front leads to Zion."

Yossel was impressed. The man's frankness and love of *Zion* touched him. "Who is this man?" he asked a fellow volunteer.

"He is one of the founders of our unit," was the answer "He was, like most of us, expelled from *Eretz Israel* when he refused to accept Ottoman citizenship."

"He lost his arm during the war between Russia and Japan," added a man who listened to the conversation.

"I like him! I will carry water if that's what it takes to clear *Eretz Israel* from the Ottomans," Yossel told the man who stood next to him.

The *Zion* Mule Corps (ZMC) was born that day. Its purpose would be to resupply the fighting men with munitions. After three weeks of training the ZMC boarded a transport ship for the short trip to the killing fields of Gallipoli, where thousands were killed, countless were wounded and many were captured without having an impact on the battle lines.

In spite of the bad reputation of Gallipoli, Yossel was exuberant. The mission ahead elevated his spirit to a new height. He was a soldier, fighting for *Eretz Israel* in a faraway land. He felt much like he did at the end of his voyage from Odessa to Jaffa. This time he kept his gaze fixed on the western horizon. Even though Gallipoli was his physical and immediate destination, *Eretz Israel* was his true long-term objective. Gallipoli, if he survived the war, would bring the *Eretz Israel* he first saw at the end of his voyage from Odessa, closer to the ultimate goal: a free, independent Jewish State.

But his cheerfulness was soon drowned in the brutal reality of war. The afternoon was misty when they disembarked. Faint sounds of explosions could be heard in the distance. They unloaded their cargo and their beasts of burden and quickly entered into a battle formation. Shortly thereafter they began the journey toward the front.

The excitement of the approaching battle lines was fleeting. Soon the din and fury of hell engulfed them. The ceaseless, deafening sounds of artillery shells buzzing overhead or exploding nearby, panicked the mules. They scattered to the four corners of the compass carrying their precious cargo that meant the difference between life and death to the soldiers at the front.

Yossel did not hesitate a moment. Under constant barrage of gunfire and artillery shells he ran after his mule. When he caught up with her in a small ravine he used all his skills to calm her down. Eventually he did. But the mule would not move. Yossel tied her to a tree stump and unloaded her cargo. Then he lifted onto his shoulder as much munitions as he could carry. The urgency of his mission turned him into a beast of burden. He trudged wearily toward the trenches, dodging bullets and shells, to deliver the munitions to the fighting men. He felt proud, like a true warrior. He was not alone. The rest of the soldiers in his unit did the same. After several hours of risking life and limb they regrouped, exhausted but satisfied. They prepared to return to base. The mules calmed down, having adapted to the deafening noise. Yossel thought that they, men and beasts, had learned their best lesson on the go. They became battle-hardened instantaneously.

At the assembly point the sergeant counted the soldiers. Two were unaccounted for. Immediately they scattered behind the front line searching for the missing ones. One was found wounded. The other was dead. Yossel had seen the first battle for *Eretz Israel* and grieved for its fatality.

***

Months had passed since Yossel was deported and their five friends were conscripted to the Ottoman army. During that time all foreign mail services in *Eretz Israel* were interrupted and eventually terminated. The Ottoman's inefficient mail was still working but news from individuals beyond the fighting lines did not reach *Eretz Israel*. Hazohar received no news of Yossel's whereabouts. Letters from Avram and their four friends arrived with irregularity.

After a few weeks of no communication a letter arrived from Avram informing them that, besides being hungry, dressed in rags, dirty, stinky, and perpetually tired, they were doing fine building roads not far from Hazohar. Everyone was overjoyed.

"*Eretz Israel*," Avram wrote "has been turned by the Ottomans into an enormous construction site and we have worked in many parts of it. We erect telephone poles; build roads, rail access to various army camps, and fortifications. Remember the song we sang on the ship from Odessa? 'We came to our land to build and be reformed by it.' I am smiling as I sing this song."

They speculated about Avram's smile. "He is a man of few smiles," said Ribi. "Why is he smiling?"

"I think I know why," said Alexa. "He knows that the Ottoman's censor reads every letter that is sent from the army. Perhaps he is smiling because the Turks are financing the construction for us. If they found out that the Jews are happy about that they might stop," she added with a smile of her own. Everyone laughed.

The next morning Itzhak set out to visit his friends at the construction site. He carried with him food and fresh clothes. He was determined to bribe his way to get his friends released. He was self-assured. No longer feeling paralyzed with fright as he had been months earlier.

Mid-afternoon he arrived at the campsite. From a distance he spotted a gang of workers building a new road. He steered his buggy in their direction, but a soldier blocked his path. Itzhak chose to ignore him. The soldier grew agitated. He raised his gun and aimed it at the intruder. This time Itzhak took no more chances. He followed the vexed soldier to a large tent at the edge of the road.

Doubts crept into his mind. *What if, this time, the commander is honest?* He began to sweat. His self-assured demeanor began to crumble. An officer met them at the tent flap demanding to know what was the source of the commotion. Itzhak recognized him immediately. This was the man who accepted the bribe at their first encounter. He breathed deeply. He wiped his brow with his sleeve and regained his composure. Upon recognizing Itzhak the officer invited him to his tent.

After they enjoyed the customary coffee, Itzhak spoke to him in a broken Turkish. He pleaded with him to release the five. His main argument was simple. "We need our men back at Hazohar so we can plant more and grow more and harvest more to support our government's war effort." His nausea returned. He took a sip of his coffee and, reassured, added, "and to feed you and your soldiers."

He repeated that line in multiple variations but the officer would not budge. Then Itzhak accompanied his plea with a dozen eggs and some money. The officer's eyes lit up but he remained recalcitrant. Itzhak was secure in his bribing attempt. He continued to plead for the release of his friends. Each plea was followed by more money. Eventually he gave enough. The man patted him on the shoulder and said, "Be sure to have food when we visit. Otherwise I shall take these five and a few more back with me."

Itzhak did not ask who the "we" were. He simply accepted the officer's words and promised, "We will do more." To ensure his friendly disposition, he added, "We shall plant a special area for you. We shall build a chicken coop for you and dedicate one of our milking cows to you. Daily, we shall send you eggs, milk and vegetables."

The officer was delighted. He commanded, "That is good. But I want cooked food!" For Itzhak, any price was a good exchange for his friends. "Of course. We shall send you cooked food for dinner. Alas, it will be cold by the time you receive it. Perhaps, Lieutenant, you can join us at Hazohar for a warm dinner?"

Itzhak had outfoxed him. *The walking chore is on the Turk. We can stay in Hazohar.* They shook hands. The lieutenant summoned the five and released them. They tried to control their happiness. One by one they hugged Itzhak, who whispered, "Save your jubilation for a later time."

They walked toward Itzhak's wagon as stoically as they could. Later in Hazohar when they were spotted at the gate everyone rushed to welcome them. There were hugs and shouts of "welcome home." Spontaneously people lifted the released ones on their shoulders. Then they moved together to the dining hall, singing and dancing the short distance from the gate.

It was destined to be a wild Hora evening when Ribi shouted, "They need to clean up, not to sweat more. They need to eat, not dance." She rushed to the kitchen to prepare food while the returnees told their jubilant friends of their trials and tribulations in the Ottoman's Labor Brigade.

The next evening, and every evening afterward, the lieutenant came to claim the prize for releasing the men. In Hazohar they quickly adjusted to his daily visits. One evening he failed to arrive. Later they found out that he had been transferred to the Negev in preparation for the second Suez campaign.

***

The punishing forces of war ravaged the cohesiveness of the social fabric of the Arabs but united the Zionists in a bond stronger than ever. Arab beggars became more visible on street corners in the major cities. Soldiers roamed the countryside and city streets. They provided a steady supply of money, which attracted a growing number of girls and women to street corners and bordellos. The authorities kept a blind eye to the disintegration of the social fabric in the countryside as well as in the cities. It was, after all, good for the soldiers, they reasoned. And if it was good for the soldiers it was good for the war effort.

Life in *Eretz Israel* moved forward slowly and agonizingly. Food supplies dwindled. Prices rose. Long lines appeared frequently in front of food stores. People's patience was stretched to the limit. Scuffles ensued often. Civility in the public place began to erode. Every town and every settlement witnessed panic. A murky future hung over the people.

Hunger persisted. Starvation and maladies killed thousands. Desperate actions multiplied across the land, and suicide was on the rise. There was an urgent call for action. American Jewry heeded the Zionists call. Everyone understood that the survival of the *Yishuv* was at stake. All across America, Jews donated money to buy food. A Food Distribution Committee (FDC) was pressed into dual action: managing the collection and the initial distribution of the food and lobbying the US Government for transportation support. One early aid collection reached a massive proportion. Nine hundred tons of food and related items were loaded on the battleship *Voulcan* for transport to Jaffa.

A simple distribution channel supported the process of handling the aid. The FDC in America shipped the aid to *Eretz Israel*, where a local FDC accepted the food and divided it. While the *Yishuv* was the major beneficiary of the aid, Palestinian Arabs, Christian and Muslim alike, enjoyed the generosity of the American aid as well. Two regional FDC branches divided the aid between the north and the central districts, where it was further distributed to local facilities for final distribution to the needy. Much flour was stored in the underground granaries at Hazohar, where Ribi baked bread for daily distribution. Volunteers staffed the entire process. Moshe was working with the central region committee. Itzhak and Sorke volunteered with one local distribution center in Jerusalem, a Tea & Bread facility where the hungry stood in lines to receive a daily meal.

For their first journey to Jerusalem, Ribi baked ten loaves of bread. They packed their wagon with kerosene, cooking pans, preserved fruits and vegetables, cheese, and fresh eggs and rode to Jerusalem with three young men as their protection. There they served a basic meal to the hungry and the destitute. On that day they fed four hundred. The bread was enough for only one hundred.

"I guess I must ask Ribi to quadruple the number of loaves she bakes," Sorke told Itzhak on the way back to Hazohar. "I feel so good I am euphoric."

"So am I," said an excited but tired Itzhak. "I tell you this, Sorke, today we began to enlarge the foundation of the *Yishuv*, to make it sturdier."

Sorke leaned her head on Itzhak's shoulder pressing her chest against his arm. They rode home mostly in silence. Each one was savoring the majesty of the day. There was no need for words to convey their happiness. Itzhak could feel Sorke's inner thoughts through her heartbeat, which was exploding rhythmically on his upper arm, much like the gales break on the sandy shore. He was happy and calm.

When they arrived home, people besieged them with questions. "There is only one answer to all your questions," Itzhak said. "The nation of Israel is alive!"

On subsequent visits they increased the bread supply. One day they fed six hundred people, one of whom was their friend David. He spent the war years working in a Turkish hospital in Jerusalem. It was serendipity that reconnected him with Hazohar. He was caring for a wounded soldier. The nurse, who normally fetched his food from the Tea & Bread facility down the street from the hospital, was ill and so David went out to receive the soldier's meal. To his astonishment he saw Itzhak and Sorke. They were busy and did not see him in the food line until he stood directly in front of them. They hugged each other with great affection and a great sense of relief.

Sorke cried, "I am so happy to see you David. I am so sorry. We behaved terribly. Please come to visit us." They made him swear to visit periodically. He did that with delight.

Later, Sorke reflected on the meeting with David and the American relief effort. *April 9, 1915. I am ever so relieved to have reconnected with David. We shall make amends for our stupid behavior during the language debate. David will remain our friend forever.* On the food relief program she wrote, *what would we do without America and its Jews? Without their persistent support the Yishuv would have been collapsed and annihilated by hunger and disease. A chain of brotherhood bridged distant and varying lifestyles to secure the everlasting bond among the children of Israel. This awesome chain spotlights the ancient dictate of the sages: "All Jews guarantee for each other." What a blissful day! This much-needed aid brought relief to the suffering and the needy. The Yishuv is forever connected to the world Jewry. I will be neglectful if I leave out Alexa's food preservation program. It is amazing! And to think that we got the idea from Joseph and Pharaoh.*

***

A few weeks earlier, Sorke had woken at dawn. She wanted to stroll in the fields to ease her mind of the ravages of war. When she set foot outside the door she was pulled back by an enormous inner power. A thick, dark cloud covered the sky, imprisoning the sun. It moved incessantly. It glided through the air in beautiful dance-like motions. It touched the ground freeing the sun for a moment or two and then rose again, only to descend elsewhere. But the seemingly elegant ballet was devastating.

Enormous swarms of locusts were attacking the verdant earth. Each time they rose from the ground they left behind a harsh and desolate landscape. A relentless ferocious enemy was at work. It mocked their effort to plan for the future. She fell to her knees and broke down sobbing uncontrollably She felt overpowered and helpless in the face of the invaders. Wave after wave rose and fell on a land already suffering the pain of war, inflicting additional wounds on the little that was not bleeding.

Her screams awakened everyone. They rushed out. Upon seeing the unwanted invaders, they retreated inside and returned with pots and pans from the kitchen. They swiftly spread across the vegetable gardens, the young orchards, and the pasture, opening a three-prong noise attack on the invaders.

The Ottoman authorities took note of the overpowering menace. The entire food supply of their army and the local population in Palestine was in jeopardy. Within days the authorities issued orders to every man, woman and child between the ages of fifteen and sixty to collect a quota of twenty kilograms of locust eggs. Residents of Hazohar complied with the edict rigorously. The actions of Beit A'yan's residence were lackadaisical. They looked upon the locust as God's army and saw no reason to fight it. They did, however, go to the field and collect many kilograms of locusts for their daily meals.

Later, on July 10, 1915, Sorke cried as she wrote in her diary, *The locust exacerbated the plague of war. We suffer so much. We grieve over the many victims of the southern campaign. People die by the hundreds from hunger, diseases and murderous instruments of war. And those of us who are still healthy, they break under the yoke of lawlessness, of wandering shell shocked, rag tag soldiers. When, oh when, will it be over?*

***

11 ESPIONAGE

Shortly after they issued the egg collection edict, the Ottoman authorities sought and received the active support of a famous Jewish agronomist from Zichron Yaakov. Alexa pointed out to the authorities the need to coordinate local and regional activities in "the war against the locust." Soon after, she was asked to meet with the scientist in his agricultural station at Atlit. She asked Gershon to accompany her and he agreed.

While she was discussing the ways to combat the locust, Gershon spent the time in conversation with the siblings of the scientist and one of their friends. "Call me B," said the friend who did most of the talking. The other two nodded frequently, agreeing with him. They talked about the youth of the settlement, who were first generation in *Eretz Israel.* They talked about their dedication, will to work for the good of the public, their practical affinity to the Ottoman Empire juxtaposed by their hidden loathing for the regime. Gershon felt an instant affinity to B.

Alexa's trips were frequent. Gershon always accompanied her. In a span of a few months he learned about B's service in the Ottoman army and his disillusionment that followed. He learned about Turkish brutality in their search for weaponry at Zichron Yaakov. He shared with them stories about the Turk's search for weapons in Hazohar and his subsequent jail sentence. He told them about his friends, their dedication, austere life and loneliness. He told them about Yossel, who opted to fight the Ottoman Empire from the outside. And yes, he hinted about his own feelings regarding the Ottoman authorities.

During those conversations he, the two young men and the woman, discovered common sentiments toward the Ottomans. Their bond grew stronger with each visit. On the last visit Gershon amassed all his inner strength to divulge his deepest secret. "I stayed in *Eretz Israel* to find a way to resist the oppressive Ottoman regime from within. I am still looking," he whispered in a serious tone. A few weeks passed; Gershon received a brief letter from B.

My friend,

I shall be in Beit A'yan on Wednesday to inspect their progress in the war against the locust. I will be very happy if we could meet there.

Your friend, B.

Gershon was delighted to meet him. They sat at the Café in Beit A'yan and talked about the war on the locust and the war of the nations. After a while B said, "Let's walk to Hazohar."

Gershon was puzzled. "We could have met in Hazohar. Why did I have to come to Beit A'yan?"

"We could, but it would have been impractical," he answered as they walked along the deserted trail that connected Beit A'yan and Hazohar. For some distance they walked in silence. It seemed to Gershon that something important was waiting to unfold. He was eager to understand but waited for B to choose his time.

After a long silence B said, "What I am about to tell you is top secret. You must vow never to reveal a syllable to anyone. Should you break your vow we will hunt you down and kill you."

Gershon felt a tremor shooting down his spine. His blood was pounding on his temples. "I promise!" he answered swiftly.

"I am," said B, "a member of a group that conducts espionage against the Turkish army in favor of the British army."

Gershon was shocked. In light of that revelation he understood the choice of venue for their meeting.

"You said that you were looking to act against the Ottomans. Here is your chance. Would you like to join us? We would be honored if you did."

Gershon regained his composure. "I would. Of course. I finally have found my path to resist the Turks."

"We have more than twenty members, but for safety's sake no one knows more than one person. You know me and I know you. Discipline is critical for our success and survival. To this end I will be your commander and set out your tasks."

"What should I do now?" asked Gershon. "I am eager to start."

"Nothing for the time being. Just prepare to leave your friends and Hazohar for a while. Neither reconnect nor communicate with them until the British army routs the Ottoman out of *Eretz Israel*. Go seek employment somewhere and never reveal to me your residence. I shall do the same so neither of us can betray the other under torture."

"I will do that."

"Occasionally we shall meet at a new place and at a different time. Our next meeting will be on Wednesday, two weeks from today, at 11 AM at Café Gedera in Gedera."

"I will be there. I want you to know that I have a phenomenal memory and thus have no need to write what I see. There will never be evidence to my clandestine work!"

"Great," said B and parted company with Gershon, who continued to Hazohar.

Gershon was alone, wrestling with his own thoughts. The first year of the war was coming to an end. The *Yishuv* was suffering from hunger and diseases; the population was declining rapidly. Many were deported. Thousands died. Rumors about an Armenian massacre persisted throughout the land foisting an unbearable fear on the citizenry. Everyone felt that unconditional loyalty to the Ottomans was critical to survival. Any act of sedition or slight disobedience could have had enormous negative consequences on the perpetrators and their kin and even on totally unrelated strangers. And now he had just committed an act of sedition that might endanger his friends at Hazohar, and perhaps other people whom he did not know.

For the next week and a half Gershon was restless. He disappeared from Hazohar for a day or two, searching for a new address. He went without leaving word of his whereabouts. When he came back he exuded happiness, and his new mood resulted in many questions.

"Have you met a woman?" Moshe asked in a very formal voice.

Gershon smiled.

"Well, if yes we shall excuse your absence. You do remember that we need you here with us?" he said reproachingly.

Itzhak was more philosophical. "Whatever it is you are doing, I know it is for the best. I just think that you must tell your friends what is going on so they will stop worrying about you."

"I am courting a woman in Zichron Yaakov," he answered mischievously.

Alexa was blunt. "Interesting. Now that you have mentioned it I can safely say, of course you met a woman. I remember every time we went to Atlit you visited with her and two other men."

Tova was alarmed when she heard Alexa's comment. She approached Gershon hesitantly, a bit shy but with a streak of jealousy in her voice. "Tell me, Gershon, is it really true that you have met a woman?"

Gershon smiled again, but this time it was an affectionate smile. He escorted her out. "No, Tova, I did not. My love for you is unbreakable. Let me tell you in confidence that I am involved but not romantically. I am planning to move out of Hazohar and smuggle myself to Egypt. I have reached the end of my patience. The hell with the Turks, I must join the Allies, as Yossel must have done. Please do not ask any more questions. At the right time I shall tell you. You must trust me," he said.

She looked at him with adoration and said, "Funny how things come out at the wrong time and the wrong place. Please be careful, my dearest friend." Then she whispered, "I love you, Gershon. I love you very much." Tears streamed down her cheeks.

Gershon hugged her lightly but immediately pulled her to his chest and covered her wet face with soft kisses. "I love you, too, Tova, you know that. Be strong and wait for me. I shall return."

On Monday, before his scheduled meeting, he announced his departure. When asked for the reason he restated what he had told Tova.

But his destination was Petach Tikva, not Egypt. He managed to arrange a job with an old farmer friend. He stayed in the barn with minimal possessions and minimal pay but was allowed to come and go as he pleased. Early on Wednesday morning he borrowed a horse and left for Gedera.

He was in Gedera on the appointed time to meet B. They had coffee and talked about this and that. After half an hour of friendly exchange B said, "Let's take a walk."

He paid for the coffee and the two friends went out for a friendly stroll. "These are your instructions," said B. "All you have to do is observe the Turkish garrisons near Rishon, Rehovot and Lydda. Record their size, appearance, weaponry and means of transport. Do they look haggard? Perky? Well-fed? And so on. In short, are they battle ready?"

Week after week Gershon wandered the countryside collecting information about the movements and strength of the Turkish garrisons that he encountered. He wrote nothing down. That came in handy when he was caught and interrogated. Since they found neither a written record nor writing instruments they wanted to know what he was doing in the area.

"I am looking for a friend who joined the Turkish army. I have heard no news from him for quite some time and wondered about his well-being."

"What is your friend's name?"

"Yossel Bora."

"Where does he come from?"

"Last I saw him he was in Jaffa."

They released him and told him that no one with that name had ever served in the garrison.

A few weeks passed routinely. Gershon collected information about the size of the Turkish garrisons at various places in the southern region. He committed the information to paper only when he came home. Each piece of paper was carefully crafted and stowed away in a small shoebox that he buried under his bed. Every month, he moved to another settlement and continued with his weekly routine: two days of work, three days of roaming the countryside, one day of rest and one day for meeting B. He was eager to know how the information was relayed to the British but for safety reasons he never broached the subject with him.

The war was entering its second year with no end in sight. Hunger and disease continued to thin the population. The toll of injured and dead in the southern front mounted. Fear and suffering engulfed *Eretz Israel.* The people were exhausted, yet Gershon continued to collect data with undiminished dedication, even though unproductive thoughts entered his mind every now and then. *What if I am caught again and they trace my residence to Hazohar. What will become of Tova? Of my friends? Moreover, what would the Turks do to the Yishuv if they uncover our spy ring? Given their brutality in past searches for weapons and their treatment of the Armenians, they may enter into a killing orgy where no one will be safe.* He fought those creepy thoughts by doubling his efforts. He was exhausted and losing weight, but he kept on collecting data.

During one routine meeting early in 1916, B avoided the usual chitchat. "Come, let's walk. I have something to tell you." Without naming names he spoke about the frustration caused by their inability to connect with the British authorities in Egypt; about the energy that had been spent in vain to secure British support in money and information sharing. "No one pays attention to our desire to revolt against the Ottomans. The few in the *Yishuv* leadership who know about us are skeptical about our work. They think that we endanger the future of the *Yishuv.* In short, things do not look as bright as we had hoped. Nevertheless, we are determined to continue. We will prevail. Are you with us?"

"Are you telling me that none of the information I have gathered, at a great risk to my safety and that of my friends, has reached British Intelligence?"

"I am afraid so. It is frustrating, I know."

"Thank you." He paused to digest the disappointing news. "I am staying with you. The struggle must go on!"

"Great. Take time out. Work. Save money. Rest and, by all means, gain some weight. We shall meet every other week until we make a connection with British Intelligence."

For the first time Gershon had free time to think of subjects other than his safety and information gathering. He spent sleepless nights feeling alone, lonely, homesick. His imagination carried him into the soft arms and tearful face of Tova. "I miss her," he whispered to his restless mind. "I miss her so much. When will we reunite in peace and joy? This accursed war must end. The Turks must go!"

His group's leader, who was in Port Said, Egypt, finally succeeded, in the spring of 1917, to establish a productive bridge between the mighty British Army and his little spy group in *Eretz Israel.*

In their next meeting B said, "We have agreed with British Intelligence to adopt NILI as our name. It is an acronym of a biblical phrase, 'The Eternal One of Israel will not lie.' NILI is our identification word. If at any time you find yourself in British hands, ask to speak to an intelligence officer and use this code name to identify yourself as a friend. The British intelligence requested specific information about Beersheba. They wanted information about Turkish army size, mobility, and disposition. They wanted information about the weather, water sources, road quality and type of road protection. They asked for a map of roads that leads into town from the four sides of the compass. They wanted to know the location of water sources near the town."

Gershon resumed their data gathering. He was back, meandering through the countryside, evading Turkish soldiers and gathering specific information to fulfill British requests.

He focused on Beersheba, a town in the northern Negev. He was certain, based on the data he collected, that the town was a pivotal place in the British plan to conquer Jerusalem and thus rout the Ottomans from Palestine.

On a cool September morning, in 1917, he went to meet B. He managed to evade the Turks. Perhaps luck protected him. In his memory he carried a storehouse of data. B seemed rushed, somewhat confused. He spoke fast, in short sentences. "The Turks discovered our network. People will be tortured. People will be threatened with unspeakable atrocities. The *Yishuv* survival may even be at stake. The captives will divulge the names of their comrades. Eventually I will be caught. They will break me. Torture and threats against innocents is their method. We must sever our connection. Go hide but remember, the *Yishuv* never accepted our work, as it was an act of sedition against the Ottoman authorities punishable by collective actions against guilty and innocent alike. Goodbye, my dear friend." He hugged Gershon and retreated behind the corner and disappeared. Gershon would never see him again.

Sensing a great danger to his beloved Hazohar if he sought refuge there, he decided to avoid the kibbutz. He would go to Egypt. He took his revolver with him, vowing to himself never to surrender, then turned south using all his skills to avoid contact with soldiers and civilians alike. Hungry, tired and disheveled he managed to cross the Turkish front where he was arrested by a British patrol. The code word NILI secured his quick release. He was allowed to join the British army. With his unit he marched across the Sinai and took El Arish. The information he supplied about fortification, troop movements, water sources and more was of great value. Soon they were knocking on the southern doors of Palestine.

They liberated Beersheba, the stepping-stone of the campaign to liberate Jerusalem. A month after the liberation of Jerusalem he stumbled upon a Jewish unit encamped north of Jerusalem. Within a few days he and Yossel exuberantly reunited.

December 1, 1917. The war is coming to an end, Sorke wrote in her diary. *General Sir Edmund Allenby is approaching Jerusalem. I spoke with Itzhak today about the future of the Zionist project. "Will Palestine be a part of Syria? Integrated into Egypt? Or be transformed into a Jewish state?"*

"The latter," he replied with no hesitation. "When? I do not know."

I just love his conviction. Secretly I can say that I love him, too.

***

Even though the north of *Eretz Israel* was still under Ottoman control, the *Yishuv*—or what was left of it—was breathing a sigh of relief. In spite of an enormous population decline, property destruction and loss of harvest and animals, those who survived the hunger, the diseases and ferocious war were ready to rebuild. In Hazohar, everyone was looking with hope to reunite with two of its members. Tova secretly longed for Gershon's return.

Sorke wrote, *December 7, 1917 A few days ago Itzhak shared with me the news. There were rumors in Beit A'yan emanating from the Egyptian press. Someone said the Jewish community in Egypt reacted jubilantly to a letter issued by the British Foreign Office. It was some declaration regarding the Jews and the Arabs in Palestine. Itzhak talked to me this morning at the vegetable garden and told me that he had seen a copy of the letter in a smuggled copy of Hazefira, a Polish weekly Hebrew newspaper. In it, in black and white for everyone to see, was the text of a declaration that he copied:*

Foreign Office
November 2nd, 1917

Dear Lord Rothschild,

I have much pleasure in conveying to you, on behalf of His Majesty's Government, the following declaration of sympathy with Jewish Zionist aspirations which has been submitted to, and approved by, the Cabinet. His Majesty's Government view with favour the establishment in Palestine of a national home for the Jewish people, and will use their best endeavors to facilitate the achievement of this object, it being clearly understood that nothing shall be done which may prejudice the civil and religious rights of existing non-Jewish communities in Palestine or the rights and political status enjoyed by Jews in any other country.

I should be grateful if you would bring this declaration to the knowledge of the Zionist Federation.

Yours,
Arthur James Balfour

Amazing. Sounds of jubilation must reverberate throughout the Jewish world. But what about the Arabs? I expect wails of mourning from them.

After two thousand years of yearning, our long journey is coming to an end. Eretz Israel is reborn in the eyes of the world.

We talked about the declaration. I pointed out to my friend that it was flawed. It set no boundaries to the homeland. One can think of it as a piece of real estate the size of a stamp. It uses the indefinite article 'a.' That means one of many homelands instead of the desired definite article 'the' that attributes exclusivity to the Homeland. And the Arab's 'civil and religious rights' clause probably precludes the transformation of the bland 'Jewish Home' into a Jewish state. But I think the declaration is a step in the right direction. I would love to read this entry in ten or twenty years from now and see what will have become of it.

***

It is January 1, 1918. A bright, cool day, wrote Sorke in her diary; *the war is not over, but we are free at last. I breathe deeply, rejoicing in the scent of freedom. While the war is still raging in the north, it is over for us. Many died from starvation and maladies. Many more fled. The Yishuv is a shadow of its prewar self. I have been in Eretz Israel for five and a half years. How am I feeling? I have lived under tremendous hardship while digging holes in Petach Tikva. I demonstrated and protested for Hebrew labor, free Immigration and the right to purchase land. I helped build Hazohar, participated in endless conversations about the future of the workers and danced the Hora so many times that I can close my eyes and not stumble as I dance. I survived the scourge of a brutal and senseless war. I suffered from loneliness; the antipathy of the Arabs and longings for more comfort. And with all that I am still unwavering in my pursuit of the cause. While others lead perhaps easier lives in the city or abroad, we sustain the renaissance of our people; we put down the mortar that holds the awakening nation together. There are many like me scattered throughout the* Yishuv. *Their lives mirror mine. Their dreams are my dreams but we rarely see each other. We are the builders. A builder possesses tenacity and dedication. A builder sacrifices much. Sadly, being a builder is a lonely task with a limited view. It is like being in an orchard and seeing only the tree that I harvest. One can easily lose sight of the mission. How do I feel? I am tired and lonely. How long can I endure? I hope forever. Itzhak is my shoulder to lean on.*

How long do I wait for him to return my love? He is my friend. I long to be in his arms. I crave his touch, his calm manners, his soothing voice. How long will I be alone, Itzhak???

***

Itzhak's fifth winter at Hazohar marked a frosty, somewhat suspicion-filled, and on occasion, belligerent year of non-existing relations between neighbors: Beit A'yan and Hazohar.

Much happened on that fabulous winter week, at the end of December of 1918. The war was over for Hazohar. Itzhak was hiking for the first time since the war started. By all accounts he should have been happy. Alas, he was not. He sat under the canopy of a tree that had survived the ax of the people of Beit A'yan, who, desperate for fuel, had left the hills barren. The Balfour Declaration was on his mind. Perhaps it triggered the pain of lingering doubts anew.

He thought back to the frosty relationship with Beit A'yan, before and during the war. His Good-Neighbor principle achieved, at best, a tense but incident-free relationship throughout the war.

What if we cannot reach a modus vivendi with the Arabs? Will the future of our enterprise in Eretz Israel grow bleaker? Am I, are we, sacrificing for a lost cause? He was alone, once again thinking about the Zionists and the Arabs.

Since his days in Odessa, he was intellectually aware of the possibility of conflict between Arabs and Jews. While many of the Jewish voices he heard ignored the Arabs, Ahad Ha'am brought them to the fore. Yet the lack of broader attention persisted.

As a young lad, while pursuing the Zionist path unwaveringly, he often wondered about the contradiction between Ahad Ha'am's assertions that the Arabs are people to be reckoned with and the muted Zionist reaction to them.

He remembered seeking intellectual solutions to his budding conflict, to no avail. After he stumbled upon Epstein's Hidden Question, he became more convinced that the realization of the Jewish national aspiration was intertwined with the Arabs' national aspirations. So profound was the discovery that it aggravated his earlier musings. He knew that thoughts like his were unpopular. He was leery to verbalize them. Instead he kept them active, yet virtually imprisoned deep inside his consciousness. One possible conclusion overwhelmed him: His Zionist march could undoubtedly become the Arabs' retreat. If it was possible, it could be perilous to his Zionist Journey. If it was true, it certainly deserved a search for solution.

Only a few isolated voices promoted one. It demanded sensitivity, mutual understanding and recognition that *Eretz Israel* was not a wild, empty space waiting for the Zionist to bring it to life. He remembered himself as a young teenager struggling with the two opposing viewpoints: the notion of an empty land and a cultivated one.

His conflicted mind meandered back to Jaffa on the day he arrived in *Eretz Israel*. The vibrancy of the town had taken him by surprise. He did not expect to see such a thriving city. That surprise and the incident that followed on the way out of the port injected a sense of realism into his intellectual worry. A faint doubt continued to chip away at his heretofore unshakable Zionist conviction. In *Eretz Israel*, he concluded after that confrontation, there were two people that coveted the same remote corner at the southern tip of the Fertile Crescent: the Arabs, who owned and cultivated some of it, and the Jews, who were slowly purchasing their way to taking a stake in it.

Still, he found little Zionist attention to the future relations with the Arabs. Later, he decided that addressing the issue had two sides. The first simply ignored it. The Hidden Question, which proclaimed unequivocally that solving the Arab–Jewish relationship was the preeminent challenge of the Zionist movement, was deemed as a misguided fantasy. The second was a continuous condescending attitude to the Arabs. Accordingly, the proponents of that line advanced the idea that the Arabs would welcome the Zionists with open arms as they stood to gain much from the Zionists' superiority in commerce, agriculture, industry, culture, and governance. Moshe was one proponent of that line of thinking. Itzhak was appalled to hear his reasoning.

Jewish attitudes were not the only contributor to his bubbling doubt. Arabs did much to aggravate it. His qualms grew stronger when he encountered, in Arab newspapers, plenty of reinforcement for his sense of the looming crisis. Both al Karmil and Filastin carried onslaughts of innuendos, rumors and outright criticism against the Zionists' aspirations and conduct in Palestine.

The papers were replete with blatant accusations that the Jews were grabbing up land or that the Jews were exclusive socially, commercially and intellectually. *Grabbing land? How? With an army they did not have? No one forced Arabs to sell their land!*

He did witness, indeed participated in, the Zionist effort to gain exclusive control over major Jewish aspects of daily life in *Eretz Israel*. They battled for Hebrew labor, Hebrew language, Hebrew watchmen of Hebrew properties, freedom from restriction on land purchases, and unrestricted Jewish immigration. All of which faced fierce opposition from Arabs, Muslims and Christians alike. In spite of his lingering doubts he vehemently supported that policy. And that caused him to further reflect, to no avail, on the need to find a solution to the emerging conflict.

As he mulled over the Balfour declaration he recalled the poem he read in Filastin. The poem called the Jews "weakest of all people and least of them." It accused the Jews of "haggling with us for our land." Later the poet admonished his readers when he said, referring to the Jews, "The danger is clear; can no one resist it?"

He was struck by the contemptuous references to the Jews. For him, the words he read evoked the same revulsion as the anti-Semitic diatribes that filled Russian newspapers in the *Pale*.

The emerging conflict between Jews and Arabs regarding the future ownership of *Eretz Israel*, or Palestine, as the Arabs called it, took center stage in his mind. Most of his friends, and for that matter, the local Hebrew papers, ignored it. He noticed that both Arabs and Jews used similar arguments to advance their agenda. Both claimed historical rights to the land. The Arabs also claimed ownership through working the land for generations. The irony with that argument, he observed, was the fact that the revered A.D. Gordon promoted among the Jews a philosophy that national redemption could only be achieved through working the land.

Quietly, Itzhak struggled to regain his unconditional conviction in *Zionism*, to eliminate his bubbling doubts. He shared his inner conflict with no one; actually, he made an effort to conceal his emotions. He carried his burden but searched for ways to abate its weight. His Good-Neighbor principle was the first time he gave voice to his struggle. But history did not shine a productive light on that effort. At best, it contributed to a tense, but incident-free, relationship with Beit A'yan throughout the war.

When he returned from his hike shortly before dinner he was "saved" by a rumor. Someone said something about a Mr. Samir in a tone of voice that carried a hint of malice. No one paid much attention to the rumor. Itzhak did. He asked the person to repeat what he had just said.

"I said that the water pump at Mr. Samir's farm ceased to perform, and that was good."

"Who is this Mr. Samir?" asked a person who stood nearby. He had just joined Hazohar a few weeks earlier.

"He is one of the wealthiest notables of Beit A'yan and the mukhtar (leader) of the village. Even though I sold him the pump and installed it, he is no friend of ours," replied Itzhak, who immediately recognized that Mr. Samir's misfortune had provided him with a gift. Itzhak felt as if a solution to his doubts was at hand. He wasted no time. There was his gift, his opportunity to reinvigorate the Good-Neighbor principle. He would make Mr. Samir a friend.

He packed his tools and rushed to Beit A'yan. On his way out he crossed Moshe's path. "I am on my way to Beit A'yan to fix Mr. Samir's water pump," he said without waiting for a reply. He heard it nevertheless.

Moshe shouted after him, "Good, let the donkey see how much he could gain from our presence here."

On the road, Itzhak decided to give cooperation with the local Arabs one more chance. This would tell him if it was the right antidote to their fear of the Zionists.

The parallel between his first day in Petach Tikva and what he expected to achieve on that winter day in Beit A'yan was striking. Then, his work established a friendly relationship between the belligerent Jewish farmers and his eager-to-work friends. He was hoping that by restoring the water flow to Mr. Samir's estate, he would resuscitate the good neighborly atmosphere that could foster routine friendly interactions between the two villages.

When he declared in Arabic his willingness to fix the newly acquired water pump, the dumbfounded Mr. Samir rejoiced. He followed Itzhak to the water pump, brought a chair and sat in front of the open shed, watching Itzhak at work. An hour later with dirty hands and a cheerful smile, Itzhak turned to Mr. Samir and pronounced, "Your water can flow into your beautiful gardens. Your flock may come to the trough."

When offered a payment Itzhak refused. "It is your friendship I seek, not your money," he told the old man, who insisted on having Itzhak as his guest at his dinner table. Itzhak agreed.

The two walked into a large guestroom full of carpets and pillows, took their shoes off, as the local custom dictated, and sat and talked. The old man expressed his gratitude over and over. They ate and drank and saluted friendship.

When the time came to leave, Itzhak felt relieved. He said, "Mr. Samir, throughout the war our water pump has served your village. We shared our food with your people, bought and sold at your market and cooperated with you to live peacefully with the Ottoman army. We respect your customs, as we want you to respect ours. We are eager to learn from you and share our knowledge with you as well. There is no reason for us to pursue any course but friendship."

Mr. Samir smiled, which Itzhak chose to interpret as a message of agreement. *There is hope for a friendly coexistence,* he thought as he walked merrily home. *My Good-Neighbor principle might still prove right.*

Itzhak returned home radiating happiness wrote Sorke on May 7, 1918. *He told me about his encounter with Mr. Samir. Does he think that the renewed flow of good deeds will foster friendship between Arabs and*

Jews? I doubt it. There is an irrevocable conflict here. Doing good deeds will not solve it.

***

The fall of Jerusalem did not bring the surrender of the Ottoman Army. To the contrary, the fighting continued. British units, including the Jewish contingent in which Yossel and Gershon served, moved slowly north, inflicting heavy casualties on the retreating army. Inch by inch, they liberated the land from the Ottoman's yoke. After eleven months of slow but steady advance, the Ottomans surrendered. The hostilities in *Eretz Israel* came to an end. A week or so later, Yossel and Gershon were free to visit home. It was an emotional reunion, in particular between Tova and Gershon.

A joyful routine took center stage after the fall of Jerusalem. The word 'routine' carried images of lackluster life. But that was far from the truth. The 'routine' in Hazohar included an early morning wake-up, breakfast with comrades and work until dinner, with a lunch break, most often in the fields.

Work was never just the act of planting, harvesting, milking the cows, or tending the vegetable garden. Work as a means to an end had never lost its luster or its essential characteristic. Six years after they arrived in Petach Tikva, work was still considered the path to redemption for the Jewish people.

They went to work cheerfully, with songs on their lips. Not once did anyone complain of the hardship. Quite the contrary, they delighted in the progress ushered in by the sweat of their brow.

Dinner, at the end of a hardship-filled workday, was always a welcome respite. It preceded a rich tapestry of evening activities. These covered cultural, social, intellectual, sporting, and political activities.

Monday night was school night. Itzhak had been running an Arabic language school since the Great Language Debate in 1913. He taught two classes—the first, Advanced Arabic, for his long-time students; the second, Beginning Arabic, for new students.

Wednesday was Politics Day. Moshe was always in charge. He determined the subjects, which addressed various topics, including the formal party's agenda—the majority of the folks in Hazohar were affiliated with the Workers of Zion Party. A small minority belonged to the Young Worker Party and a few were unaffiliated.

On occasion, he dedicated the evening to new developments in the *Yishuv*. Special presentations rounded up the discussion topics. Itzhak was often a guest speaker. He usually covered Palestinian topics; he called his sessions 'Of Interest to the Palestinian Arabs.' Ribi gave cooking instructions, which attracted men and women alike.

Fridays were devoted to merriment. Hazohar maintained the Jewish tradition of a festive *Shabbat* dinner followed by singing, dancing and performances by the locals, their guests or an occasional artist from the city.

Saturday night was one big dance party. During the day they often held sporting events with teams who came from far and near.

The rest of the week's nights were free, yet most folks gravitated to the worker's hall to engage in conversations, play chess or card games. Often, snacks provided an added enticement to join the informal chat.

Every corner of Hazohar saw a renewed energy, a reaffirmed dedication. The place burst with excitement, and love was in the air. Gershon and Tova were the first to declare their intension to be married. A few months later Moshe and Alexa tied the knot.

One Friday night, Itzhak left shortly after dinner. He walked to the gate on his way to the citrus path. He wandered, his mind engaged inward, when he hit a rock and nearly lost his balance. He sat down, his eyes darting from one dark spot to another. He looked to the skies. Millions of stars formed a tapestry of light that twinkled randomly above his head. The moon was invisible.

He was deep in thought. For months he had felt a growing tension inside his body. *What was I thinking all this time? Was I blind? Oblivious to my body's secretly calling, commanding me to yield to its demands? To look at Sorke, to want her in my arms?*

Apparently, yes. The cause has consumed my energy to a point where I ignore my recurring desire to hold her in my arms, kiss her and just savor the moment, standing together in a quiet embrace.

I am so out of touch with my feelings that I have no clue about her reaction if I reach for her shoulders and bring her closer to my heart. How do I interpret her gestures? Are they just signals of a friendly disposition? Or is she making an effort to awaken my suppressed emotions and draw them toward her? He was overwhelmed with questions. They rushed at him in an unstoppable pace. He sank his head between his hands. *What is happening to me? Should I dare approach her?*

He was restless. Sitting for a while, then standing, then walking aimlessly around the rock, then sitting again. The canopy above his head moved slowly westward when he noticed a glimmer of light on the summit of the Shomron Mountains to the east. *Oh, my. I have been struggling with my thoughts all night and I've reached no conclusion. What shall I do?*

He rose slowly and walked back to his place. Alas, he was still restless and could not fall asleep.

The next morning, at breakfast, he stood by the door of the dining hall waiting to catch a glimpse of Sorke. When he saw her, he pretended to enter as if he had just arrived. He walked slowly to an empty table and took his seat, hoping that she would sit beside him. Gershon and Tova appeared from nowhere and thwarted his plans. Yet, his thoughts of her, of kissing her lips, of being close to her, of rejoicing in her returned affection grew stronger, if unrealized.

He was unaware of his overt action to seek her company until Tova took his hand after dinner and pulled him to the side of the dining hall. "Itzhak," she whispered in his ears, "following Sorke into the dining hall will get you nowhere. Just ask her to join you for a stroll on the citrus lane. That is what Gershon did with me." She squeezed his hand and left him at the corner of the hall, lost in thought.

For weeks he failed to master his growing restlessness. In his mind's eye, Sorke was avoiding him. He was in pain, not knowing how to react. After a *Shabbat* dinner celebrating Gershon and Tova's marriage, Sorke approached him and said, "I'd love to go for a stroll. Will you join me?"

At that moment he felt the end of his unrequited love approaching. "I would be delighted to join you."

They slipped out of the whirlpool of the Hora dance and disappeared into the darkness. As soon as they were outside the gate and the lights of Hazohar dimmed after they took the curve, they fell into each other's arms in a powerful embrace. His lips searched for hers showing their inexperience. They kissed and confessed their love for each other. They melted in each other's arms. The night air was as restless as they. Cool wind blew through their hair.

"Let's walk and savor the moment," Sorke said.

He took her hand, and they strolled along the same path he had followed a few months earlier. When they came to the rock they sat down and Itzhak told her all about his first time there, when he was inundated by questions about his love. "I wondered then, and for months afterward, how to deal with unrequited love. Thank you, my dearest, for inviting me for a walk today."

In the coming weeks others strolled on the citrus lane cementing their love. Avram and Ribi were spotted on many occasions on the path that was dubbed Lovers' Lane.

12 WORDS, WORDS, AND MORE WORDS

"During the British Mandate, the political awareness of the Yishuv developed to create a rich map of parties and political societies."
Baruch Ben Avram, Political Parties, and associations during the National Home, Introduction, p. 7.

Sorke's diary had the following entry on February 10, 1919, *Life in Eretz Israel is full of amazing amount of words and politics. We talk and talk about the future of the workers and how to improve their present conditions. We send Moshe to every party's assembly and conference, and there are a few of those every year, where they talk more. When he returns, we hear more words.*

As far back as I remember we talked about the direction of our reawakening nation: Jewish labor, the primacy of the Hebrew language, demands for free immigration and unrestricted purchases of land. In short, our words moved us toward exclusivity or 'Jewish only' in all aspects of our life even though we are surrounded by Arabs.

Sometimes I think that our words rather than our deeds will reawaken the sleeping nation. Luckily there are only two parties today and the unaffiliated workers. Who knows what the picture will be ten years from now. I believe that all the workers must unite.

I have nothing against words. Words bring comfort to an aching body and solace to a lonesome soul. But sometimes I think that we utter so many of them that we move in a circle.

Moshe is going later to attend the Workers of Zion Assembly. Can't wait to hear if they have been discussing new issues?

An important note, Itzhak is elated. His family will be arriving home, to Eretz Israel, early this summer. I am looking forward to meeting them.

***

Moshe returned from the assembly of the Workers of Zion Party full of exuberance and renewed vigor. On Saturday he joined a few of Hazohar workers on a morning stroll along the citrus grove's path. They chatted about labor issues and their isolation from other Jewish settlements. A few minutes into the conversation, one of the men unexpectedly changed the topic and remarked, "I am drowning in words."

They stopped, looked at him astonished and almost in unison started to say something, the meaning of which was lost in the many parallel and different voices.

When the sound died down Moshe's voice rose over the silence to dominate the air space, "Really, do you care to give a few examples?"

"Sure," he said. "Hebrew Labor is debated ad nauseam. The moralists say that we displace the peasants when we buy land. The idealists chime in, 'we must work our land exclusively with Hebrew labor. It is through Jewish labor that we will redeem the Nation.' The finance people think that Arab labor is cheap, affordable and more experienced. The practical proclaims that we cannot continue to be a nation of small merchants. The bystanders speak without having a grasp of the issue. Our leaders talk and talk. Newspapers echo their debates with words and more words. All of that comes in addition to the current discussions about uniting the parties. Is that enough?"

"Yes." Replied Moshe. "I think you are right. But let me assure you that these words are good. They foster a debate in the *Yishuv* that will ultimately forge the best path to the destiny of our reawakened nation."

"I agree," said Yossel. "Those of us who have elected to come here are passionate people. We care, that is why we debate. Eventually, we'll trail blaze the path for redemption. Besides, when you speak of our leaders please remember that they have no herds to shepherd, no fields to plow; therefore, they tend to words instead. Then they inundate us with those words."

"That is okay," said the man, "I did not mean to be negative about it. I know that words count."

It was a tempest in a teapot. The storm subsided, and they continued their leisurely stroll, chatting about their work and praising Ribi's culinary talents.

Later that evening they joined all the workers of Hazohar, and many who came from nearby settlements, for a political discussion on the effort to unify the Jewish workers in *Eretz Israel* under one political umbrella.

The speaker, a leader of the Workers of Zion party, opened his remarks by saying, "My friends, there are many settlements scattered across the land. Their people, like you, toil in the fields, tend the vegetable gardens, pamper their orchards, and more. Their work demands dedication, incredible effort, and much sacrifice." He paused and switched to a more personal tone. "You work hard. You give no speeches, attend no Zionist Congress or lead any political party. Your garb is the ubiquitous khaki pants and a white shirt. You own no ties, no suits, no fancy clothing. You live a simple, frugal life, demanding little and giving much. No task is beyond your will, no challenge beneath your dignity. You are the worker bees of the Jewish people, the builders of our nation. You are the dreamers who signed on to the Zionist project to build a nation like all other nations for a People unlike any other People."

They loved his opening remarks and showed their appreciation with a standing ovation.

"Thank you," he said repeating his 'thank you' a few times before he could continue. "Our party's leadership appreciates your dedication and loyalty. Without you there would have been no forward strides toward the awakening of our people. Thank you.

"I know there are people among you who consider themselves unaffiliated. Also present are members of the Young Worker Party. To them I say, welcome.

"Our party has approached both groups with a proposal to unite. We all have the same objective in mind. We are all good Zionists. Unfortunately, the Young Worker declined."

A hiss in the hall interrupted him, but he ignored it.

"Let me begin by sharing with you two key elements that reflect our party's core belief. The labor movement in *Eretz Israel* is a branch of the International Socialist Labor movement. Furthermore, the labor movement in *Eretz Israel* is a branch of the Zionist movement which aspires to redeem our people from the Diaspora."

There was a murmur of disagreement in the audience, but he ignored it and continued.

"Now, let's examine the proposed program that will underlie the activities of our new party: The United Labor..."

"Before you do," said Yossel as he rose from his chair. "Am I correct in my understanding of your words, sir, that the United Labor Party stands on two pillars. The first accepts total allegiance to International Socialism, the second promotes Jewish nationalism?"

Yossel paused a moment to steady his voice. He was determined to restrain his agitation, to deliver his thoughts in a calm and civil manner.

The speaker attempted to reply, but Yossel spoke over him, "I am a member of the Young Worker Party, and I want to tell you unequivocally, I came to *Eretz Israel* as a Jewish nationalist. International Socialism means nothing to me. Because you give it primacy in your program, I, and I believe my party, reject the unity motion."

There was a hushed buzz of agreement.

"Thank you for your comment, Yossel. I appreciate the calm manner in which you delivered your thoughts. Now let's continue without further interruptions," pleaded Moshe.

The speaker continued. "I am proud to say that our Socialism is an International Socialism. As a branch of the world's Labor Socialist Party, we aspire to fully redeem man from the yoke of capitalist governments. Why? Because they impose capitalism on all aspects of national life: economic, cultural, scientific, and welfare. We reject governments that enable and encourage the few to acquire and control the national treasures and resources, as they deprive workers of their income, healthcare, and education."

Gershon jumped from his seat and protested indignantly, "What has all this to do with the Zionist project? These are words, words, and more words. I could easily say 'empty words.' Why are we spending resources on writing and promoting such policies when our people demand all our energy? That is an enormous challenge. Remember Vitkin? How selective was he outlining the character of the Zionists he invited to perform this task? We answered his call. Please do not burden us with a new call: the redemption of Human Kind is too big a job; it is also not a priority for us. We have no interest whatsoever in all the ills you have enumerated that afflict capitalist societies, nor are we interested in the state of affairs of the International Labor Socialist parties anywhere. May I remind you that these groups are no different than their predecessors? They have no interest in our dignity, human rights, or in our equality before the law.

"We must liberate ourselves of the various political strands that exist anywhere. In case you have forgotten, that is why we created the Zionist movement. That is why we came to *Eretz Israel* instead of going to America."

Once again, Moshe came to the defense of the speaker. "May we postpone comments to the end of the presentation?"

"I apologize, Moshe," Gershon said, and sat down irritated.

The party leader said, "Thank you," and doubled down on his earlier ideas. "Our party aims to establish a free society with human rights and equality for all. We intend to transfer control of the natural resources and the capital that has been accumulating for ages from private to public ownership..."

"Sounds like we are becoming communists" whispered Ribi into Avram's ear.

"It sure does," he whispered back.

"Furthermore," the speaker continued, "we proudly proclaim that our movement in *Eretz Israel* is a branch of the international Zionist movement that aspires to liberate the People of Israel from the Diaspora.

"Our party seeks the return of the Jewish masses to *Eretz Israel*; it wants to mold the life of our nation into a free society that lives on its labor, governs its affairs, organizes its life and develops its natural resources. Settling the land and working it, as you are doing, is the starting gate toward realizing the goals of the Zionist movement. We aim to achieve that with socialist workers. We are convinced that private capital alone will not accomplish the Zionist program, nor will it create enough opportunities to absorb the masses that we want to bring to the land."

Tova spoke, "I can safely say that we wholeheartedly agree with you on the assertion that the Labor Movement in *Eretz Israel* is a branch of the Zionist movement, and that it aspires to redeem the Jewish people from life in the Diaspora."

Itzhak rose and said, "Sir, we are not members of the same party. I am unaffiliated. However, I agree with my friend Gershon. I also appreciate the sentiments you bestowed upon us during your opening remarks. Indeed we do not ask for much. Why do you feel the necessity to offer us what we have not asked for?"

Sorke was recognized, "Please convey to the leadership—oh yes, I belong to your party—that I do not care about the well-being of Labor Socialist parties anywhere. What I seek is nationalism not the preparation for a class war. But I agree with the aspiration of the party about our people, as you articulated it."

Yossel spoke, "You identified obligatory actions. The first was the transfer of land in *Eretz Israel* along with all its natural treasures to the control of our people for all future time. Well, what do you propose to do with our Arab neighbors who have been cultivating the land we purchase? Allow me to acquaint you with critical Arab's sentiments. My friend Itzhak, who keeps track on Arabs' sentiments toward us, told me that they think we are exclusive, elite types and that translates to racism."

The party representative was unprepared for such a barrage. He was perplexed and lost for words.

Moshe rushed to his aid. "Yossel," he addressed his friend, "Your point is important. You know I have been thinking about it since we attempted, without success, to implement Itzhak's Good-Neighbor principle with Beit A'yan. I shall bring the issue to the attention of the Governing Board. I want to assure you that the resolution of the Arab question is at the front of our leaders' agenda. Please remember that the purpose of this meeting is just to get acquainted with the underlining framework of the new party and airing our comments. I shall do my best to raise your good comments during the final deliberations regarding the party's program."

They continued the conversation till a late hour. No one gave any ground. In the end, the members of the Young Worker Party proclaimed their opposition to the creation of the new party. Gershon, Tova, Itzhak, and Kalman who were unaffiliated also remained in the opposition. The speaker promised, as did Moshe, to bring the concern about the affiliation with the International, and the lack of clarity regarding the Arabs at the next plenary meeting.

A few hours after the meeting adjourned, life returned to its normal pace. Sorke updated her diary; *both Itzhak and I found a few things to agree on with the presenter. We are indeed the working bees of the Yishuv; we are Habonim (the builders).*

***

The aftermath of the formation of the United Labor Party was an acrimonious debate in the *Yishuv*. An avalanche of words in opposition to the idea came from the Young Workers' Party. The official voice of the opposition decried the notion of the dual framework of the party: the international Socialism and the nationalism. It adamantly rejected the first and with equal conviction defended the later.

The two opinions prevailed for years, causing upheaval in the settlements and among friends. Hazohar kept itself above the fray. The bond between Gershon, Tova, Kalman, and the rest of the folks remained unshakable. They united around local issues: love that expanded the marriages, new babies, expansion of their land holding, and increased absorption of new immigrants.

Itzhak was busy making last-minute adjustments to his plan to bring his family to Petach Tikva.

In mid-June he met them at the port of Jaffa for a tearful and emotional reunion. They travelled light, ready to restart their life in their real home. His mother kept touching his hands uttering, "My little Itzhak is gone. My baby is a man…I am so happy." She showered him with kisses; asked him a thousand questions, many of which were redundant. Itzhak was happy to reply.

His father was more reserved, but his excitement leaked through cracks of his controlled disposition. Whenever his wife paused to reflect on Itzhak's replies, or simply to regain control over her shaking body, he took over with questions of his own. On Bustros Street they found a quiet café. They sat there till closing and then continued to ask more questions as they strolled up and down the street.

Late that night, they retired to their rooms. In the morning, after a hardy breakfast interrupted with emotional outbreaks, they boarded the diligence and headed to Petach Tikva. Rachel marveled quietly on the many changes that had occurred since she was last in the area. His parents paid little attention to the unfolding scenery. Their minds focused on him. Their questions touched all aspects of his life. He was eager to tell them about Sorke, his work, the hardships and more. Only when they arrived at Petach Tikva did they begin to appreciate their surroundings.

"What a beautiful place. Alive. Full of blooming gardens," exclaimed his tearful mother.

"A thriving town. And there is a synagogue. I am finally home," rejoiced Reb Gershon.

They disembarked and strolled along the streets.

Itzhak stopped in front of a small house surrounded by an ornamental garden. A small citrus grove and a few farm animals were visible beyond the vegetable garden. "This is your home, Mother," he said, and led them through the white gate toward the door.

Later that day Itzhak took Reb Gershon and Rachel to the synagogue and introduced them to the rabbi. From there they walked to the high school to meet the principal. The kindergarten, where Rachel would work, was only a few blocks away. They went there for an introductory conversation.

A few days after they had settled down to a new routine, Itzhak left. He promised to return on the first Friday of the month for a *Shabbat* dinner.

Rachel walked with him to the gate. Before stepping into the street he paused, hugged his sister and said, "I will take you to Hazohar after my next visit. I want you to meet my friends. You belong with us. I want you to live in Hazohar."

She agreed. With more tears, and many kisses they parted company, and he returned to Hazohar.

Three weeks later he came to Petach Tikva. His parents' house was full with merriment. Many people sat around the dinner table. Itzhak felt it was like home at Gordov. "I am happy to see you among new friends. Welcome home!" he said as he raised the first glass. Dinner was in the best tradition of the Hacohen household. The food was his mother's best. The conversation flowed like the Rishon's wine. The day was lively and energetic. Itzhak was happy.

Early the next morning, he and Rachel walked to Hazohar. He told her about his love for Sorke, his friendships, especially with Yossel, whom he wanted her to meet. As they rounded the bend in the road, he spotted Yossel in a buggy riding toward them. *Serendipity* he thought. Yossel stopped when he saw them, raised his hand and waved a hearty hello. They climbed on the waiting buggy; Yossel and Rachel, perfect strangers a few minutes earlier, became instant friends. They talked nonstop for the rest of the way. Itzhak felt happily neglected.

At the end of Rachel's visit, Yossel volunteered to take her home. Itzhak smiled a happy smile and told Sorke, "I think Yossel is not me. He is not shy. He is not intimidated by love. He is ready for it."

It was love at first sight. Yossel went to Petach Tikva to be with Rachel every Friday night. He became a regular guest at Reb Gershon's table.

A few months later Rachel moved to Hazohar. From that day on, she and Yossel were inseparable.

13 A DOWNHILL SPIRAL

"Exactly what happened at Tel Hai on the morning of March 1, 1920, has never quite been understood... Tel Hai became a legend; like many national legends its potency far outstripped the strength of its heroes..."
Tom Segev, One Palestine Complete, p. 123-124.

Referring to the riots of Nebi Musa, Sakakini wrote "I went to the municipal garden, my soul disgusted and depressed by the madness of mankind."
Khalil al-Sakakini, Such Am I, O World, p. 137.

Yossel was a happy man. He was always willing to show his happiness, and his affection for Rachel. Wherever they went, their hands were gently connected. They were together at meals, at work and each Friday on their way to Petach Tikva. They spent most of Saturday with Rachel's parents or alone, strolling the flower garden.

"Is anything wrong?" asked Rachel one Saturday morning as they were strolling through the little orchard on their way to their favorite bench. "I noticed that your cheerfulness has lost its spark."

"Yes," he replied. "I have read that there is much nervousness in Tel Hai and neighboring villages. I am anxious to visit Mr. Trumpeldor, my commander from the *Zion* Mule Corps."

"Go in peace and do not forget to return. I want you calm and happy; I will miss you," Rachel said as she drew him to her with a loving hug. "I do not want to lose you to any of Tel Hai's women," she said with a smile.

"I will be back, my dearest," he reassured her, even though he knew she was joking.

A few days later he left for Tel Hai, a small agricultural settlement seated inside a frequently fluctuating border between the British Mandate of Palestine and the French Mandate of Syria. Arab villages dotted the area. They saw themselves as citizens of the Greater Syria ruled by Faisal Bin Hussein. United in their anti-French sentiments they sporadically harassed the French army. However, certain agitators pursued more than harassment of French troupes. They fermented and executed actions that often erupted into bloody hit-and-run battles. On occasion, Arab irregulars would stop at Tel Hai and other Jewish settlements in the area to search for French soldiers.

Once, in the vicinity of Tel Hai, Yossel heard a noise. Angry Arabic sounds punctured the calmness of the day. He moved carefully. Ahead, just as he rounded the sharp curve in the road a few hundred meters away, he could see a significant number of Arab irregulars advancing chaotically on Tel Hai. He could hear sporadic shouting, "Give us the French soldiers!" Instinctively, he veered off the road and took cover behind a small outcrop. The sound grew into a cacophony of shouts and the explosions of firearms.

There was great confusion in the courtyard of Tel Hai as the battle cries escalated. The gate was open but he couldn't decide whether it was a sign of welcome or one of belligerence. The disorganized mob stormed the open yard. It overpowered the small defense force. Members of the mob shot at anything that moved then withdrew as quickly as they arrived.

Yossel rushed to the open gate and found six fallen heroes. Among them was his beloved commander Mr. Trumpeldor. He did not linger over the bodies. "Get help! Get help!" he screamed. But no one came. Kfar Giladi was not too far away. Ignoring his own safety, he moved rapidly, losing all cautiousness. A few hundred meters away from the bloody courtyard he was gunned down by a lingering irregular who suspected the running man was planning to alert the authorities. He was left on the road to Kfar Giladi to bleed to death.

Yossel had a strong will to live and a good constitution to support it. He was also a lucky man. A wagon carrying refugees from Tel Hai stopped at his bleeding body. They managed to provide him with temporary first aid and took him to the doctor's house in Metula. There, he was given professional care to arrest his bleeding. After a day's rest, he was evacuated with the other farmers.

Everyone in Hazohar read the news of that incident and its aftermath. Rachel was overwhelmed with anxiety. The daily news that reached Hazohar increased her distress.

Newspapers' headlines proclaimed: "Threat Escalates near Tel Hai" and "Tension Persists in the upper Galilee."

Within days, additional incidents intensified the deteriorating situation; belligerence had reached a boiling point, causing the evacuation of three upper Galilee villages. No one knew Yossel's fate. Rachel was held prisoner by fear. Pessimism overtook her usual cheerful disposition. Itzhak and Sorke attempted in vain to console her.

When Yossel returned, at the end of Passover, Rachel attached herself to him crying with joy, and refused to release him or dry her tears for a long time.

After dinner, everyone stayed in the dining hall to listen to his story. While people lingered with Yossel, Itzhak pulled Moshe aside and said, "Moshe, I think we seriously need to prepare for possible aggressive actions from Beit A'yan. The festival of Nabi Musa is upon us. I can already detect the rising tempers and malcontent in the Arabic press. There is significant fear and anger in the air."

"Meaning?"

"The papers write provocatively about the British Civil Authorities. They feel betrayed, complaining about unfulfilled promises. They raise the specter of Jewish domination, increased immigration and Zionist demands for uninhibited land purchases. I tell you, Moshe, there is a swell of anti-Zionist rhetoric. At times I conclude that it is anti-Jewish in its core. Add to that the lethal events in the north and the Nabi Musa festival, which will be upon us in a few days, and you have the perfect situation for troubles. I brought a few papers with me. Let me share with you the extent of their anti-Zionist sentiments."

"Perhaps we should have this conversation with the entire community?"

"Good idea. Everyone needs to know what the word on the street is."

After everyone had arrived at the designated hour, Moshe raised his hand and asked for quiet. It took a few minutes for his request to reach everyone in the hall. When he had their attention, he said, "Following Yossel's travails, Itzhak wants to acquaint us with significant new information. Go ahead Itzhak."

"Arabic newspapers are overflowing with vitriol. Here are a few examples. One newspaper tells its readers that the 'Jews have a lot of cash and the immediate ability to raise as much money as they need. Soon they will buy many parcels of land, displace the farmers and rob them of their heritage. They tell us that they liberate the land. From us? We have never taken it from them. We have no debts to pay. Our ancestors conquered the land from the Byzantines. Let them go and argue with them and leave our country in peace.' Here is another, 'The Zionists are an exclusive society. They have their flag and sing their national anthem. They spread like the locust across the country devouring our land and displacing our farmers. The British Government, instead of stopping their incursion into our land gave them the Balfour Declaration, which welcomes them to our beloved Palestine. We must stop their torrential stream across the land.' These incendiary words surely will reach Beit A'yan. I sense trouble."

"Do we all hear him?" asked Moshe in a high-pitched voice.

"Yes!" responded the people in the hall.

"I, therefore, raise the level of alert to a high."

A few days later, during the Muslim celebration of the Festival of Nabi Musa, dignitaries spoke to the swelling crowd at the Jaffa Gate in Jerusalem about the evil of the Zionist expansionism. With incendiary oratory, they described the Balfour Declaration as a disguise for creating a Jewish state in Palestine. One notable even quoted President Wilson's statement to Jewish leaders in America: "I am moreover persuaded that the Allied nations, with the fullest concurrence of our government and people, are agreed that in Palestine shall be laid the foundations of a Jewish Commonwealth."

Whether or not it was a real quote did not matter. It achieved its purpose. The crowd shouted anti-Zionist slogans in high nationalistic fervor. Jerusalem exploded. Agitated revelers ran through alleys, ransacking every Jewish store they found. A few Arabs and Jews died and many more were wounded.

Gershon answered the call of his leader and rushed to Jerusalem to join his group who was ready to defend the Jewish neighborhoods. His intentions were cut short by a brutal attack that caused his evacuation to Rothschild Hospital with multiple knife wounds.

While he teetered between life and death, the streets of Jerusalem soaked up the blood of the victims, Arabs and Jews alike. The excited Arab revelers looted Jewish stores and ransacked schools, desecrating holy books in the mayhem.

A friend raced to Hazohar to inform Tova of the tragedy. She left immediately and spent the coming days and nights at Gershon's bedside holding his hand, caressing his brow and telling him stories or singing him songs. Not only did she refuse to leave her beloved, but she was also adamantly optimistic about his recovery chances. On the third day, his conditions worsened, but she would not give up. She kept her loving routine in spite of her fatigue.

When Gershon opened his eyes on the sixth day, she missed it. She was asleep in her chair by his bedside. Later, when the nurse told her what had happened, she sobbed uncontrollably.

He healed slowly. A week later, he held her hand and said, "I love you, Tova. When we return home, we must fulfill our promise to each other. We should get married."

"I was afraid you had forgotten that promise," she said and burst into tears. She raised his head gently off the pillow and covered his face with kisses and joyous tears.

The word of the clashes in Jerusalem reached Beit A'yan on the same day that Tova left. Hundreds gathered in the Main Square to hear nationalistic speeches. Words piled upon words, reaching a high pitch of incendiary sentences. Hateful slogans like "Death to the Jews" and "The land of Palestine is ours. The Jews are our dogs," reverberated through the air. People in Hazohar were on edge. Itzhak's head swirled in anger. In his mind, the Good-Neighbor principle had died during the Nabi Musa festival. He felt the darkness of tragedy creeping upon him. Fortunately, it was a false alarm. Tempers calmed down at Beit A'yan with the timely arrival of a British patrol.

"Too bad that good deeds have been forgotten so quickly, Itzhak," said Moshe.

Itzhak forced a smile but kept silent. Sorke thought that was the first time she'd ever seen Itzhak speechless. She wanted to tell him that Ahad Ha'am was wrong, but she knew how he felt. She could read his silence as if he wrote his thoughts on a piece of paper and laid it down upon the table. So she held her peace but put a loving hand on his.

Alexa liberated Sorke's unspoken words. "I think Ahad Ha'am was wrong. We can be friendly, helpful, you can use any positive sentiment you like, but at the end, it all boils down to their fierce opposition to our cause; and to us, for implementing the objectives of the Zionist movement in their backyard, on land they consider theirs."

Unspoken tension hung in the air. People limited their interaction with the Arabs of Beit A'yan to an absolute minimum.

On Hanukah (the holiday of lights) 1920, Sorke wrote a brief note in her diary. *Will Arab belligerence ever stop? Will we ever live in peace?*

***

A few months later Kalman went to Jaffa to meet his boyhood friend. The young man arrived from Odessa on Saturday morning and went directly to the Immigrant House. He was not alone. The facility, run by the Zionist Authorities, accommodated, at that time, about one hundred newly arrived immigrants, men and women.

After some directional confusion, Kalman found the compound and was able to reunite with his friend. It was as if they had just parted company; as if the nine years that had passed since their separation never happened.

They hugged and spoke of old memories and mutual friends.

"Let's take a walk, I shall show you the town, and we can have a good Arabic dinner," Kalman suggested.

"Great idea," replied his friend and the two began a slow and leisurely walk through the narrow alleyways, occasionally stopping to examine this or that store. "I never expected to see such a vibrant city in *Eretz Israel*," said the friend, as he scrutinized the food store in front of him. He marveled aloud at the diversity of the foodstuff, the colors, and the swarms of flies that persistently hovered over the open stalls.

"Yes," agreed Kalman, "There are many towns and villages in the interior. This is not an empty land. We, too, were surprised to see that when we arrived."

"I wonder how healthy is the population?"

"The natives have strong constitutions. They do not react as we do to poor hygiene."

They meandered for the best part of the morning, crossed a few side streets, and paused just before they reached Bustros street; the friend had to tie his shoelaces. At that moment four young Jewish men emerged from an alleyway. They said hastily, "Shalom," and shoved a bunch of papers into Kalman's hand before they rushed away. Kalman had a just a second or two to glance at the papers before a police unit swooped down on the fleeing young men and arrested them.

"What is that?" exclaimed the startled friend.

"These are, apparently, illegal leaflets. I am afraid we can be in trouble if caught with them," Kalman replied. As he tucked the papers inside his shirt, he added, "Move calmly forward."

The police were too busy with the four young men to pay any attention to Kalman and his friend, who melted into the crowd on Bustros Street. When Kalman felt safe, he led his friend into an empty alleyway where they stopped to read the papers. Kalman gave the Yiddish leaflet to his friend and kept the Arabic and Hebrew leaflets for himself. The more he read, the more anxious and agitated he became. A troubling cloud hung over him as he read a few more of the leaflets' declarations

'Down with the British and the French bayonets.'

'Long live the dictatorship of the Proletariat.'

'Down with the Arabs and Foreign capitalists.'

"This is subversive stuff," he said. "It is incendiary and inciting. Get rid of the papers," he instructed his friend.

They disposed of the leaflets in the alleyway and walked back to Bustros Street to search for a restaurant. After dinner, the pair walked to the Immigrant House. They agreed to meet the next day to walk to Tel Aviv and join in the May Day celebration.

The next day, after breakfast, they walked through the mixed neighborhood of Manshiyya on the way to Tel Aviv. Along the way, they encountered a small group of the Jewish Communist Party members getting ready to march in commemoration of May Day. They distributed flyers; the same flyers Kalman had received a day earlier. They shouted provocative slogans and raised the Zionist flags and the Communist red flags; they were heading north, to Tel Aviv.

Kalman pulled his friend to the side, away from the passionate group. But with no better route to Tel Aviv, the friends followed the marchers from a safe distance. A few kilometers to the North, in Tel Aviv, a group of the United Labor Party marchers was getting ready to start an authorized march celebrating May Day. They were planning to walk along the main street of Tel Aviv into Jaffa, via Manshiyya. At the edge of Manshiyya, the two Jewish groups collided. Shouts filled the air; some marchers were belligerent; blows were exchanged. The encounter deteriorated rapidly; pandemonium erupted. Agonizing screams of the wounded, loud curses and verbal threats alerted the police who rushed to the scene. Rumors spread across town: "the Jews are attacking the Arabs."

Neighbors streamed from all direction, screaming that the Jews had killed Arab bystanders. Waves of agitated Arabs infused with anger screamed as they assaulted the clashing Jewish groups. Words of the clash spread to all corners of the city, and the growing mob pushed toward the epicenter of the disturbance. Shots were heard. Someone fell. The Jewish groups disengaged with only a few injuries. The police dispersed the Arab mob. Kalman and his friend retreated from the scene and rushed to the Immigrant House, where Kalman chose, for safety reasons, to spend the night.

Tense silence drifted over the city; the town was abuzz with rumors. In the morning, before sunrise, people began to congregate at the gate of the Immigrant House. The crowd swelled quickly. Shouts were heard about shooting at the Arabs. Within minutes the excited crowd turned into a fuming, screaming mob that pushed against the gate.

Kalman and a few other men rushed to the gate in an attempt to secure it with their muscles, but to no avail. The gate was ripped off its hinges and fell to the ground. Hundreds of angry people wielding knives, wooden clubs, stones and shovels, poured in, trampling Kalman as they scattered through the yard on their way to the Immigrant House. A few residents panicked and ran outside but were beaten by the storming mob.

In distant streets, people who could not make their way into the yard ran amok, spreading false information about Jews shooting Arabs. Such stories contributed to the gathering of larger masses and increased the decibel of angry voices manifold.

Many residents escaped the yard and the first floor of the building and crowded into the second floor. The mob stopped short of pursuing them. Instead a saturnalia of pillage ensued. People ran out of the building with kitchen implements, bed sheets, bedspreads, pillows and blankets, some even balanced mattresses on their heads. Rioters pushed and shoved to reach more supplies. Within minutes the pulsating mob had stripped the place to its foundation. The police arrived before the crowd could turn the floors into firewood. The place looked like *Eretz Israel* in the days of the Locust, six years earlier.

After the police had cleared the area, they found four badly mangled bodies, Kalman's among them.

The riot in Jaffa spilled into neighboring villages and beyond. The turmoil lasted weeks and reached Gedera, Petach Tikva, and many other settlements.

In Hazohar they buried Kalman near Baruch and inscribed his tombstone, "May Day, 1921. Mayhem trampled on a gentle soul."

Sorke immortalized the events of the Jaffa disturbances in her diary. *May 15, 1921. Our relationships with the Arabs have reached their nadir. Itzhak told me that he was convinced the Arabs knew what we were planning. He said somberly, "They will never give up Palestine voluntarily. Why should they be different than any other people who dotted the historical canvas of civilization? They do not like our demands for free immigration, Hebrew labor, and uninhibited land purchase. They will continue to harass us. But at the end, our cause is just. We'll prevail.*

Without changing his demeanor, he changed the subject. "Sorke," he said, "I think we should get married." No hugs preceded his extraordinary statement, which was uttered in a casual manner. I smiled at the dear fellow and said, in the same manner he proposed, "Of course, Itzhak, I love you, too." Then I hugged him with uncontrolled happiness. I wanted to shout but held myself. I did not want to embarrass him. So I whispered, "I have waited for this for years."

***

Waves of immigrants streamed to *Eretz Israel* after the Great War. Cities expanded, and so did the agricultural settlements. A few people left Hazohar in search of a different lifestyle in the city or abroad while many others came to set roots.

A nurse, her name was Dina, was among the newcomers. She successfully lobbied the Management Committee to build a modern medical facility, which would extend medical services to the Jewish residents of the area.

Sorke was thinking about David. Ever since she and Itzhak reunited with him during the war, at the Tea and Bread distribution center, they had kept in touch. He was a frequent visitor to Hazohar.

"It is time to act, Itzhak," she said.

"Yes. I agree. The old arguments about the Hebrew language primacy have withdrawn into the far recesses of memory."

"I shall invite David to work in our new clinic."

"Excellent idea," agreed Itzhak.

Once the Medical Center was completed, Sorke invited David to work in Hazohar one day a week. He was happy to oblige.

In spite of recent tension with Beit A'yan and the other Arab villages in the area, Moshe, still accepting the value of Itzhak's Good-Neighbor principle, visited Mr. Samir at Beit A'yan. He extended him and his folks an invitation to use the new medical facility in Hazohar. Within weeks of its inauguration, the little clinic became a critical feature of the life fabric of the area. David was visibly happy. He soon requested the Management Committee to allow him to work in the clinic two to three days a week. He built himself a modest home and began to divide his time between Hazohar and Jerusalem. Three months later, he confided in Sorke, "I love Dina."

"She smiled. Take her out on Saturday. Stroll our Lovers' Lane. When you reach the oak tree, go behind it, give her a soft hug and plant a delicate kiss on her lips. If she returns the kiss, propose to her. Then the four of us will have a grand wedding party."

On Saturday Sorke's gaze followed David and Dina as they walked side by side beyond the gate, toward Lovers' Lane. Their hands brushed against each other but did not lock. When they disappeared behind the oak tree she held her breadth, closed her eyes, and counted till thirty. Almost gasping for air, she took a deep breath and opened one eye. "Oh my," she exclaimed loudly. "They are still behind the tree. I can hear the sweet sounds of the wedding march."

Three months later the two couples invited family and friends to attend their wedding. It was a modest but warm and energetic party. Sorke and Itzhak finally tied the knot. David and Dina did the same.

Sorke wrote, *I have loved Itzhak since the time I met him on the ship, on our voyage to Jaffa in 1912. I am happy!*

14 MORE WORDS

One cold November night in 1925, folks filled the dining hall to participate in an unusual Wednesday's political meeting. The format was a roundtable discussion, and the subject was, "The Arab Question—the Zionists' relations with the Arabs." There was enough buzz leading up to the day of the meeting to draw scores of guests from nearby settlements.

Itzhak opened the meeting. "I will come directly to the point. I have concluded that the focus of the Zionist leadership heretofore has been on solving the Jewish problem. Consequently, it has been directing its energy and resources to land purchases, immigration issues, the primacy of Hebrew, and the conquest of labor. In short, they tenaciously advanced the Zionist agenda, which promotes, but does not proclaim, a Jewish State in *Eretz Israel*. They spent much time and money on political assemblies, meetings, discussions here and abroad. They even set institutions to act as shadow governmental bodies. Once we become a state, we'll have the required governmental departments in place.

"We, of course, have done our share performing the necessary legwork to liberate our nation through working the land. We were faithful disciples of A.D Gordon, who told us 'if we do not work the soil with our hands the land will not be ours not only from the social and national perspectives but most importantly from the political aspect: the country will not be ours, and our people won't be hers.'

"Our leaders have, for the most part, neglected a critical side of our national agenda, or at best have given it many words but little action. The Arab question festers on without a genuine effort to solve it.

"Earlier warnings by Ahad Ha'am and Dr. Epstein remain largely unheeded. Listen to this portion of an article I read in Doar Ha'yom last week, I paraphrase Mr. Ussishkin. 'The more we talk about peace with the Arabs the more we complicate matters. The majority of the Arabs do not object to either our presence or our work.' I ask you to think back to our first day in Jaffa, then to the death of Baruch, Kalman, and beyond. I ask Mr. Ussishkin from what planet is he observing such a skewed reality? Anyway, he continues. 'Those who object to us are a small minority of Christian Arabs: the elite, the newspaper editors. They demand that we end land purchases, immigration, and forgo the Balfour declaration. I tell you that on the day we become the majority, regarding political, economic and cultural power, the Arab question will resolve by itself. We will always live in peace with the Muslim Arab world. But as long as we are weak (the minority) there will be no peace but capitulation.' Such thoughts permeate our leadership. I have scanned the Young Worker's newspaper just around the time of the 12th Zionist Congress, in September. It does not even mention the Arabs who live among us."

Ribi said, "I recall Itzhak discussing with us Epstein's 'The Hidden Question.' Somehow I cannot forget these words: 'In general we have made a crude psychological blunder in our relationship with a large, if assertive and passionate people.' At a time when we are feeling the love of the homeland with all our might, the land of our forefathers, we are forgetting that the people who live there now also have a sensitive heart and a loving soul."

Yossel took the floor, "Wait, Ribi. Have we? I remind you of our first days in Hazohar. Since we cordoned access to the spring, we have adopted Itzhak's Good-Neighbor principle; we built troughs for their herds and faucets for their domestic water consumption. We allowed their shepherds to lead their herds in uncultivated areas. Itzhak's principle was the dominant tone that guided our dealing with the people of Beit A'yan. But the return on our investment has been nil. Their frosty attitude brought us dangerously close to the brink of a bloody dispute when they viciously attacked our guard at the pump's shed. There has never been a thaw in the belligerence they harbor toward us.

"Arab villages in *Eretz Israel* mirror Beit A'yan's behavior. The Arabs are no fools. They are politically savvy people, who understand exactly our undeclared plan: build a Jewish state with a Jewish majority in *Eretz Israel* or, as they call it, Palestine. They are, for the most part, Muslims, and we are Jews. The bridge between us is shaky at best.

"They know, let me emphasize this thought, *that our success will be their defeat.* So they resist us in any way they can. Do I suggest abandoning the principle? No! We must strengthen it. We must explore additional ideas to allay their fear of our intentions."

"Yes, I agree with you, Yossel, when you speak of our behavior. But what about the leadership of the *Yishuv*?" Ribi asked.

Sorke rose to comment, "Maybe we have to urge all our schools to teach Arabic. If we speak the language, we can communicate better with the Arabs who live around us. This will eliminate many potential misunderstandings."

Gershon, who was a member of the panel, replied with a hint of sarcasm, "We all speak Arabic. We communicate well with the people of Beit A'yan. They understand what we say, and we understand them. Does this create a welcoming attitude toward us? I think not; just look at the latest atrocities during the Nebi Musa festival and the Jaffa riots. The reality is simple, no matter what we say about welcoming Arab workers, they do not want us. Palestine, as their newspapers proclaim over and over, is their motherland. We are unwanted intruders; we are threatening their conviction."

Tova was recognized, "Allow me to add a few thoughts," she said. "A dangerous wind is blowing over the Zionist enterprise. It originates among German Zionists, more specifically with the elite of German-Jewish intellectuals."

"Do you mean the Brit Shalom (Covenant of Peace)?" asked Moshe.

"Exactly."

"Well, it has roots here, in *Eretz Israel*. I agree. It is a threatening idea," repeated Moshe.

"Could you stop talking enigmatically and tell us what that ominous wind is?" demanded Ribi.

"In a nutshell, this elite group of intellectuals suggests that the only way to deal with the Arab Question in *Eretz Israel* is to abandon the core aspiration of *Zionism*," explained Tova.

"Do you mean reach a Jewish majority in *Eretz Israel*, so we can have a Jewish State," declared someone from the back of the hall.

"Yes, but in line with Balfour, it will bestow dignity and human rights on the Arab minority."

"Okay, and what do they suggest to put in its stead?" asked Ribi.

"A bi-national state within the Mandatory umbrella, in which Jews and Arabs will have equal status regardless of the numerical reality," replied Tova.

"Interesting," interjected Itzhak. "Let me quote you Rumi, one of the most prominent voices in Islam. He said,

'To the Egyptian, the Nile looks bloody,
To the Israelite, clear.
What is a highway to one is a disaster to the other.'

Does anyone believe that the Arabs will see any reality other than Arab majority rule in Palestine? Would the Zionists?"

Gershon suggested that the Brit Shalom idea "nullified our lifelong struggle and commitment in *Eretz Israel*. There is no Arab Question. There is a Jewish Question, which means the redemption of the land and the creation of a Jewish state with a numerical majority of free Jews. Let me tell you about another idea, which is more realistic. It is rooted in the conviction that the Arabs will never leave the land voluntarily and we will never push them out. Mr. Jabotinsky formally published the idea of the Iron Wall a few years ago. Here is the essence of it. We have a choice, fold our tents and withdraw from the Zionist project or vigorously continue it under the protection of the British Mandatory Authorities."

A heated discussion followed. In the end, Moshe suggested that "we keep on building, keep on investing our energy and stamina in the Zionist project. But, in spite of all the setbacks of the early twenties, we should continue to pursue Itzhak's Good-Neighbor principle."

Everyone agreed.

***

One morning, early in 1927, Rachel suddenly fell ill. For days, she was in constant pain. Her unusually high fever persisted. The medications David prescribed for her neither controlled her pain nor brought her fever down. He was puzzled.

After a few days of inexplicably high fever David decided to send her to Rothschild Hospital in Jerusalem. Yossel left hurriedly to Petach Tikva to bring her parents to Hazohar.

In his absence, Rachel asked David for a pen and a paper. She scribbled something, put two notes in envelopes and said with a forced smile, "I know I may never come back. Please give one note to my brother and the other to my husband. Tell Itzhak to deposit my note in the *Kotel* (the Wailing Wall, or the Western Wall). Please tell Yossel that I have loved him very much. I am ready to go to the Hospital."

In Petach Tikva, Mrs. Hacohen collapsed upon hearing the news. Her wailing rose to heaven, knocking on the Lord's chamber, wanting to deliver her plea for help. She was in no condition to travel to Jerusalem. Yossel had to return alone. He rushed to the hospital and stayed at his wife's bedside, refusing to leave.

His recurring interactions with the doctors exposed their puzzlement and helplessness to either explain or provide an effective treatment to improve Rachel's rapidly deteriorating health.

She ate less, wheezed when she breathed; she lost weight and energy, and when she attempted to speak, words came out of her mouth incoherently.

"Why?" demanded Yossel. "What is afflicting her so viciously?"

No one could offer an explanation. He kept a vigil near her bed watching her withdraw further and further. He could see the light of her life flicker. "I love you, Rachel, please do not leave me," he repeated tearfully, but she was far away and could not hear his request. At three PM on Tuesday, before Passover of 1927, Rachel attempted a painful gasp for air. It was her last.

Yossel sank into deep melancholy. He locked himself in their room, refusing to go anywhere. Grief overcame him. He mourned for weeks, barely touching the food that Sorke brought him.

Sorke wrote in her diary, *Rachel was taken from us in the cruelest of ways. A painful silence descended on us who loved her. Yossel is grieving. He is inconsolable. He looks like a shadow of himself. Itzhak is stunned.*

Mrs. Hacohen never recovered. She had lost her will to live. She died a month later. They buried her near Baruch, Kalman and Rachel.

Slowly, with the constant support of his friends, Yossel regained his composure: he reentered the life rhythm of Hazohar, lost the ghostly pallor from his face, and gained weight. *Life must go on. You must remarry, have children, and continue the struggle* he recalled Rachel's whispers before she died.

***

Early Sunday morning, Itzhak and Sorke took the train to Jerusalem. They arrived in town on the eve of the holiest day on the Jewish religious calendar: *Yom Kippur*. It was September 23, 1928. Sorke and Itzhak came to honor his sister's request. They had a few hours to spare before the eve of the holy day shortly after sunset. Yossel was sick and could not join them.

To the Muslim, it was a day to guard against Jewish violations of the status quo at the Wailing Wall—Al-Buraq to them and the *Kotel* to the Jews. History had witnessed countless disputes between Muslim and Jews. Muslims who owned the area imposed restrictions on the manner of praying at the Al-Buraq, and the Jews struggled to gain unfettered access to the *Kotel.*

"You know, Itzhak, I always wanted to attend the *Yom Kippur* service, especially the famous *Kol Nidre* service at the *Kotel*. Let's stay till tomorrow?"

He felt mischievous. He knew that Sorke came from a home that had little to do with religion. So, before he replied, he decided to see how much she knew about that critical prayer and day.

"What is *Yom Kippur*?" he asked with a serious air.

"You must be joking."

"No! I am serious.'

"Okay. Since I love you even though you give me a little credit, I shall answer this condescending question. It is the Day of Atonement. It comes ten days after the Jewish New Year, and it culminates a period of ten intensive days of prayer to atone for our infringements and transgressions, and to seek forgiveness from men and God." She paused briefly, looked at him sternly and added, "Ah Yes! Let's not forget the women!"

Itzhak felt embarrassed for posing that question. "So with such a concise and clear explanation maybe I should withdraw my second question?"

"No, now that you are on the path of insulting me, you might as well continue. I still love you." She looked at him with a forgiving smile while touching his hand lovingly. She was amazed, as always, to see how poorly he read her feelings. He behaved as if he took her love for granted although she knew what a devoted and loving husband he was. She was happy to be with him, to be in his thoughts, to be his buddy, his lover, and his wife. "Could I get a hug?" she asked mischievously. He complied with a loving, tender, long lasting hug. She smiled.

"Do you know what *Kol Nidre* means?" he asked apologetically.

"It is the opening prayer of the *Yom Kippur* Service."

"Yes and no."

"Stop joking, Itzhak!"

"I am not joking. Yes, it is the opening prayer. But what does it mean?"

"Funny that you ask. I don't know, it is written in Hebrew. As a child, I neither went to synagogue nor studied Hebrew," she answered with a hint of embarrassment.

"You speak Hebrew better than most," he said to atone for his previous insult. "*Kol Nidre* is written in Aramaic, not Hebrew. It seeks to annul personal vows to enable the congregation to devote the holy day to seeking forgiveness of past infractions. I must tell you, in all seriousness, that *Kol Nidre*, while rooted in Jewish history, has been surrounded by controversy throughout the ages."

"Why?"

"It is actually not a prayer. It is a one-sided legalistic declaration that annuls many types of vows. That action was a cause of major conflicts. Throughout its long history it had to endure a tenacious and continuous opposition from eminent rabbis and many Muslim and Christian adversaries and anti-Semites. Notwithstanding the antagonism, *Kol Nidre* has persisted to become a centerpiece of Jewish liturgy. It is the Jewish soul."

She looked surprised. "I did not know that. Thank you for the lesson. You tempt me to research the topic. Now, will you respond to my request?"

"I shall be happy to stay," he replied. "I think it is an excellent idea. I must confess that I had the same interest. My father always said to me, 'Itzhak my boy, one day you will stand before the *Kotel* and see for yourself a mighty testimony to our national endurance.' So, I am delighted to stay. Last time we were here, we worked at the Tea & Bread outlet. Remember? We had no time to explore the town. Let's go out and see the old city."

"Let's do that. You can be my guide." She moved close to him and without words, invited another hug. As always he was happy to oblige.

15 THE *KOTEL*

"During the 1920s the status quo at the Wall was increasingly challenged, with the Jews demanding possession of the Wall and the surrounding areas. The Palestinians were suspicious of the Jewish intentions and resisted their demands. By the late 1920s, the two communities were heading for a showdown"

Philip Mattar, The Mufti of Jerusalem Al-Hajj Amin Al-Husayni and the Palestinian National Movement, p. 35.

Itzhak and Sorke meandered through the narrow streets of the old city, sampled sweets at the market and lingered near the entrance to the Haram Al-Sharif.

"This is the third holiest site in Sunni Islam," commented Itzhak as they stood and looked at the bright golden dome that adorned the mosque. "To us, it is the desecrated holiest site of Judaism."

"Do you mean the ruins of the Second Temple from the Roman period?"

"Yes, but the Muslims added insult to injury."

"I think I know what you mean, but tell me anyway."

"Caliph Umar conquered Jerusalem, cleared the site and built a mosque over it. Just imagine the outcry in the Muslim world if we had conquered Mecca and built something over the Ka'aba. I mean, at any future time after that; one year, hundred years, a thousand years..."

"They will forever try to regain possession of it no matter how many years have passed."

"Right, but having experienced, in theory, the same emotion as we had, they begrudge us the use of the *Kotel* (the Wailing Wall), a sliver of the original Temple area. Is this the height of hypocrisy?"

It was early afternoon. They continued to walk along Via Dolorosa. "You know, Sorke, we are now walking in the footsteps of Christ's last journey to the cross. Here he carried the burden of humanity's sinful ways to Golgotha where he would be crucified. There, about six hundred meters from here is The Holy Sepulcher Church. To the Christians, the entire path and the church are holy grounds. They believe that the church was erected on the site of both Jesus's crucifixion and his grave," he explained as Sorke's tour guide.

The small plaza in front of the church was crowded with pilgrims.

"Everyone wants Jerusalem," said Sorke as they entered the square. "Everyone says, 'this land is mine!' At the end, who is going to get it?"

"We will! I'll say this, unlike our Bible that is replete with adorations of the city; Jerusalem is not mentioned in the Quran at all. The Quran uses the term 'the Far Mosque.' The Muslims say it was here on Temple Mount. But I found a better interpretation to the notion of a physical place."

"Please tell," she said.

He pulled a piece of paper from his pocket and read, "Rumi said,

'The place that Solomon made to worship in,
Called the Far Mosque, is not built of earth
And water and stone, but of intention and wisdom and mystical conversation and compassionate action.'

"In other words, it could be anywhere."

"Do you think we'll ever build the third Temple?"

"I doubt it very much. We'll be lucky if we manage to buy the *Kotel*. The Zionists' leadership has tried numerous times but failed. I am sure they'll continue their effort. Eventually, it will be ours. The other two sites will remain in the hands of the Muslims and the Christians."

The sun was rushing toward the western horizon. "It is time for us to head to the *Kotel*," he told Sorke, who had immersed herself in the site of the holy church.

For a while, they lost their way in a maze of narrow streets. After receiving directions from local merchants, they arrived in the vicinity of the *Kotel*. From afar they saw it rising along a narrow alleyway in the Maghribi neighborhood of Jerusalem. A dark, unwelcoming lane stretched before their eyes. Discarded scraps of paper, rotten fruits and vegetables covered the path alongside piles of animal dung. The space between human dwellings and God's abode looked like a cesspool. A sharp stench of urine rose from the ground. Putrid air hung over the earth where the scent of perfumes used to delight God's nostrils two millennia ago.

"Pee-yew," said Sorke. "Arabs do not care much for cleanliness."

"Nothing has changed. Remember Jaffa on the day we arrived?"

"Yes. It was awful."

They walked silently, observing the colors, listening to the sounds and looking at the *Kotel* that stood one hundred meters in front of them.

As he and Sorke jostled for a clear path forward, he thought about Rachel. She was not a religious woman, yet in her last days she'd felt the extraordinary pull of the ancient shrine. From her deathbed, she had charged Itzhak with her last words. She wanted him to merge her thoughts with those of the many who preceded her. Itzhak reached for Sorke's hand and squeezed it without words.

The alley was alive with the sounds of commerce, clatter of cooking pans, mundane conversation and prayers. Arabs and Jews mingled without communication. Old men seated on donkeys moved effortlessly through the crowded street. A few Jewish men were bowing in front of the *Kotel*, occasionally putting their lips to the stone in an act of devotion. No one seemed to mind the dirt and the noxious air.

Itzhak and Sorke approached the formidable but solemn remnant of the Second Temple. Sorke said, "Think, my love, Jews of generations before us came here to pray, to send their petitions to God. You can see that every nook and cranny is stuffed with notes, letters and pleas. I imagine they contain dreams, hopes, words of thanksgiving and simple requests and prayers. What an amazing national shrine this is."

"And now we join the chain of our brothers and sisters who, seeking solace, gravitated to this holy place throughout the dark days of the Diaspora."

"Amazing," said Sorke. "Here, not far from the *Kotel*, I feel that we are finally at the end of our long quest for national redemption."

Itzhak reached into his pocket and pulled the envelope containing Rachel's note. His face grew somber. Sorke looked at him with anticipation. She knew that he would share his sister's final thoughts with her.

He opened the envelope and read silently. When he finished, grief overcame him. Tears streamed down his cheeks. Sorke stood silently by his side. She put her arms around Itzhak's shoulders and hugged him gently.

He looked at her and began to read in a shaky, broken voice:

> *My dearest husband, brother and Sorke, I am leaving you at the beginning of my journey. We have spent a short but a loving time together. Even though I will not be a witness to the conclusion of our work I trust that you and the Yishuv will live to realize the goals of our long march. I am joyous and secure in our love for each other. I know that, as Papa would have said, God will be with you and protect you and our friends on the arduous journey ahead. Am Israel Chai! (The Jewish nation is alive!)*
>
> *I thank you for the care and love you bestowed upon me throughout my struggle. Do not lament my departure. Continue the fight to redeem our people. Please put this note at the Kotel. Perhaps God reads these notes after all.*

Your loving wife, sister, and friend,
Rachel

Sorke rested her head on Itzhak's shoulder and began to cry. After a while, Itzhak lifted his head and smiled. "Sorke," he whispered in her ear, "thank you. You are my best friend. I am happy you came along with me." He moved away. "Wait for me here," he told her. "I shall be back shortly."

He moved forward to the men-only section of the *Kotel* looking for an eye-level crack in the wall to deposit Rachel's message. A flood of memories filled his consciousness. He could vividly recall how she led him to the *Habonim* meetings in Odessa. How she discovered his crush on Estie and kept it as their secret. He had always looked up to her.

The Mourner's Prayer surfaced on his lips. He began to pray. When he finished, he wiped his eyes and held the note with his damp hand. He inserted it in a crack that was deep and relatively empty. "Goodbye, my dear. May your message reach its destination and find there an attentive ear," he said and kissed the stone.

Sorke observed him from afar. When they reunited, he told her, "As my lips lingered on the cold stone an image flashed through my mind. All those kisses from the lips of hundreds of thousands of Jews throughout our Diaspora fused together in a long chain. My kiss added the latest link. This unbroken chain binds us, wherever we may be, to the *Kotel* and through it, to *Zion—Eretz Israel*."

"What a lovely sentiment," said Sorke with a warm smile.

"I was thinking of Rachel before the *Kotel* that leads to heaven. I loved her."

"I did too," said Sorke. "She was a fine woman. I shall remember her with joy, the way she wanted everyone to remember her."

Itzhak smiled tenderly. "Me, too."

"It is time for us to separate," said Itzhak. "Let's meet here in half an hour."

Sorke touched his hands lightly then turned to the right and walked to the designated area for women. She knew that Itzhak paid full attention to her gesture.

Itzhak joined a small jubilant group of religious Jews who followed an aging beadle to the *Kotel*. They moved in ecstasy, singing and dancing with reverence and prayers of thanksgiving. They carried brooms, a large ark to hold the *Torah* scrolls, a table, a few mats, lamps and a screen to create a divide between men and women worshippers in preparation for that evening's *Yom Kippur* services.

They lay down their accessories before the *Kotel*, and together they cleaned a wide area for the service later that night. Afterward, they began to erect a screen connecting the *Kotel* with an old nail attached to a wall of a house across the alley.

Suddenly, British police carrying guns rushed into the area, ignoring its sanctity. They quickly surrounded the group. A high-ranking officer approached the beadle and ordered him to remove all the items they had brought with them "You are violating existing rules of access and worship."

The astonished beadle and his small congregation protested meekly but to no avail.

"You are forbidden to introduce new items to the area. The ark is too big and therefore new. The table is new. And this screen disturbs the locals, who use this alley to walk to and from their homes and shops. Take the screen down!"

"But sir," protested the old man "our religious custom demands a separation between men and women at prayer. This is why we erect the screen as we did last year and the years before it."

"Take the screen down," repeated the officer "or I shall have my men do it for you."

"We will. We will," capitulated the beadle, who had no intention of obeying the order immediately. In his mind he was prepared to take down the screen after the service of the entire holiday was completed. That meant on Monday after sundown.

The officer, satisfied with the beadle's promise, did not wait for his actions. He ordered his men to leave.

Itzhak was horrified. "Wait one minute," he called after the departing troops, "we have a legal right to pray at the *Kotel* and to bring with us whatever accessories our worship requires. You, sir, have the legal obligation to protect our presence here."

"I also have a duty to protect the public safety, free passage in the street, and to rid our city from public nuisances like you. This screen blocks the narrow road that leads to people's homes. Now you keep your peace, and I shall guarantee your freedom of religion," said the officer with a sardonic laugh.

Itzhak did not budge. "The Mandate for Palestine commands the authorities to respect all worshipers, Jews included, and guarantee their religious freedom. Your actions here violate the Mandate stipulations! Besides, the locals can use another street one day a year. They always have. Please note that no Jewish synagogue allows the mixing of men and women during prayer."

The officer, clearly agitated, laughed at Itzhak. "Show me where this is stated in the Mandate Agreement, and I shall withdraw."

Itzhak was angry. "This is a dirty trick, officer. You know I do not carry the agreement on me. But you, sir, are violating our right to pray unmolested. You are mocking centuries of customs. You are degrading our Holy day. You are a disgrace to the Mandatory Authorities."

Sorke, who could hear the angry exchange, rushed toward Itzhak and pulled him away. "Please, Itzhak, the police are leaving, and they have done nothing beyond warning the beadle. You have made your point. Now let's wait without anger for the service to begin."

"Yes. You are right. But I must tell you that this incident is not over yet."

She put her arm around his waist in an affectionate display of support. He did not object. He needed a little help to enable him to calm down. Her face lit up with a satisfied expression. She was grateful for his tacit permission to assist him.

"I wonder who alerted the police to the *Kotel*," muttered Sorke.

"No doubt it was the Arabs in their bid to assert control over the *Kotel*. They have been doing so for years. The *Kotel* is a *Waqf* property. And the Arabs are always on the alert. They are afraid of any change in the status quo."

"What do you mean?" asked Sorke.

Itzhak did not reply. He was pensive. He wanted to give her an objective answer. He knew that the *Kotel* was the Western Wall of the Haram Al-Sharif, which was Sunni Islam's holy place. The Arabs owned the *Kotel*. They feared the Jewish ambition to rebuild the Temple and thus destroy the Haram Al-Sharif. For that reason, they used every excuse to harass the Jewish worshipers.

"You know, Sorke," he said, breaking his long silence, "The *Waqf* status of the land is only a part of the story. According to the Quran, Mohammad took an overnight journey through the air on the back of Al-Buraq, his magic horse. When they arrived at their destiny, the Quran does not mention the exact geographical location, the Prophet tied his horse to the *Kotel* then ascended to heaven. Since that time the Muslims call the *Kotel* Al-Buraq and consider it a holy place for Islam."

"And this is the way they keep Holy sites, littered with garbage?" interrupted Sorke.

"I suspect that they claim holiness just as a ploy against the Jewish claim."

"It makes sense." You know, Itzhak," she said, "I think it is the height of hypocrisy that the Muslims claim the area as their holy site when they usurp our rights and have the temerity to desecrate the remnants of our holiest temple with their mosque."

Itzhak was amazed. "Incredible observation, Sorke. So you see," he continued, "it is not a simple matter. They use their holy scripture to define their aspirations and actions, but they protest when we use ours to support our claims. What we hold holy, they hold holy."

"My dear," said Sorke with a clear hint of admiration, "you do have command over Islamic history. But what is the *Waqf*? I believe you've mentioned it before."

"Mr. Aziz, my friend from Odessa, was a good teacher. *Waqf* is an Islamic endowment of an inalienable property held in trust for religious purpose."

Darkness crept over the *Kotel*. One by one the congregants arrived dressed in their finest. Men took their place on the left of the screen and women on the right.

"Let's join the congregation and partake in the evening service."

"I remember hearing *Kol Nidre* only once, in Odessa. I have always wanted to hear it again, especially here, at the *Kotel*," she said and moved toward the women's section.

The congregation sat silently waiting for the rabbi to take his place behind the table. At last he arrived, and the service was on its way. The rabbi opened the Ark. He took the *Torah* scroll and placed it gently in the hands of one congregant. Then the sound of *Kol Nidre* rose to the heavens. Solemn. Devotional. Euphonious. It ushered the beginning of an intense period of prayer and fast. The service was sublime. For Itzhak and Sorke it was full of emotional connection but light on the religious relevancy. Contrary to Itzhak's anticipation, the service concluded with no incidents.

On Monday morning, *Yom Kippur*, Sorke said, "We are here, so let's attend at least the morning part of the *Yom Kippur* service."

Itzhak agreed. They returned to the *Kotel*. The service started and progressed without incident. But just then, at the height of devotion, as the congregants affirmed its loving bond with God, British troops stormed the *Kotel* area, disturbing the holiest day on the Jewish calendar, breaking the sound of an important prayer in the Jewish liturgy, and desecrating the holiest place in the Jewish consciousness.

Itzhak was convinced that Muslim religious leaders, following a long-standing tradition of limiting Jewish access to the *Kotel*, had summoned the police. He was livid.

The police sergeant, unmoved by the solemnity of the moment, ordered the removal of the screen. Silence fell on the astonished congregation. At last, the beadle found a few words that returned them to the reality of the moment.

"This is a holy day. Our holiest. We must continue to pray. Please leave."

"Take down the screen, and we'll leave you in peace!" retorted the officer.

"We are forbidden from mixing men and women during our prayers," countered the beadle.

"I give you permission to mix," said the sergeant with obvious scorn.

"We can't take down the screen!" shouted an old woman who stood behind the screen.

"You will rot in hell for such blasphemy!" shouted one congregant who was hidden from view.

"Sergeant, please leave us in peace and may God be with you," begged the beadle.

"The Lord is with me but not with you! Now I am in no mood to continue this argument. I give you three minutes before I order my men to clear the alley."

"We are forbidden to work on *Yom Kippur*," said the beadle adamantly. He refused to move. No one moved. The rabbi resumed the interrupted prayer. They all turned their focus from the sergeant to God. No one paid any more attention to the continuous desecration of the holy day.

The sergeant was furious. Swiftly he commanded his soldiers to remove the screens.

Itzhak moved to confront the soldiers. It seemed to him a return to a bygone day, a visit to that distant inn near Gordov, where David met Goliath. "What do you think you are doing?" he demanded. "Have you lost your mind, sergeant? Your behavior is shameful, devoid of compassion and understanding. Is there only darkness in your cold heart? Would you accept a behavior such as yours in the middle of your communion?"

The sergeant hesitated then moved forward. He ordered his soldiers to take down the screen. Itzhak moved passively toward the screen and called for the congregants to follow him. "Move with me but do not resist. Remember, a threat to the soul (and body) postpones the prohibitions imposed by the sacred."

The congregants followed him to block the soldier's access with their bodies.

Itzhak stepped forward again and said, "You must remove us first because we intend to defend a long tradition of prayers: a tradition that reaches back to history, when England was still a barbaric place. We pray here every year. And every year we put a divide between men and women. Since when is this activity disallowed?"

One of the policemen pointed at Itzhak. "Sergeant, this is the bloody pest who interfered yesterday with official duties. Our officer threatened to arrest him if he did that again."

By the time the sergeant reacted, Itzhak had melted away within the agitated congregants. He shouted at the sergeant, "Go back before the situation deteriorates. Maybe we should all march on The Holy Sepulcher and desecrate it? Or better yet, how about a march up the hill to the Haram Al-Sharif?"

A few police officers moved forward to obey the command. They tore down the screen and began to retreat. A scuffle erupted. British police pushed a crowd of elderly men and women, who had offered no resistance. A number of women fell to the ground and were slightly injured.

The sergeant rushed to separate his troops from the crowd. While running forward he yelled a clear command, "Arrest this man!" Another scuffle erupted near the torn screen. Someone tried to shelter Itzhak from the advancing police but to no avail. Itzhak was handcuffed and dragged forward with the retreating police unit like a lifeless corpse.

"Get in touch with Mr. Israeli. He is a lawyer who lives in Rehavia. Tell him what has happened!" Itzhak shouted urgently at Sorke.

"I will!" she shouted back. For a moment she was alone, confused, not knowing what to do Then she bolted forward and rushed to Rehavia in search of Mr. Israeli.

Words about the incident spread faster than Sorke's frenzied run. Rumors of unspeakable behavior abounded. Everywhere, she saw agitated people rushing toward the *Kotel*. A rabbi from a nearby synagogue led his young students, wrapped in prayer shawls, to the wounded *Kotel*. They moved in unison, an impregnable mass. Tempers mixed with wailing rose to the heaven on that holiest of days.

The *Kotel* towered above the filthy alley as if it was no longer a collection of neatly arrayed stones. As if it had taken a human form. As if it morphed into the essence of the *Jewish nation,* that was steeped in mourning.

The Day of Atonement was shoved aside to make room for British vulgarity: an irreverent conduct of insensitive men contaminated the crown jewel of the people. Words about the desecration at the *Kotel* spread like lightning. People deferred the holiness of *Yom Kippur* to defend the soul of the nation. A constant stream of men, women and children flowed from every corner of town toward the *Kotel*. Thousands of livid marchers protested vociferously against the British Police, pushing forward and shoving Sorke against her will. One minute they shouted in anger, calling the Police 'Brutes,' 'Savages,' ' anti-Semites,' ' Puppets of the Mufti,' and in the next moment they stood solemnly and sang Hatikva, the Zionist's national anthem. Their voices swept over the streets like a mighty wave that rose in size and ferocity as it approached the shore. A sea of Zionist's flags fluttered proudly in the morning breeze. Hastily drawn placards were raised above heads. Some were calling for the resignation of the police chief and for the urgent inquiry into their atrocious behavior. Others accused the British police of the abominable act of desecrating *Yom Kippur*.

Even though writing and marching were unspeakable offences on *Yom Kippur*, the police assault on the Jewish heart was in itself a powerful argument for suspending, even violating the prohibitions of the holy day. The streets of Jerusalem roiled with anger.

Sorke pushed against the swelling human tide flowing toward the *Kotel*. Time seemed to stretch out and press upon her stressful soul, adding pain and discomfort to her effort. When she finally arrived in Rehavia she searched for Mr. Israeli. After receiving conflicting information as to his whereabouts, she managed to locate him at the steps of the synagogue. She approached him with urgency and stood directly in front of him.

"Pardon my abrupt interference," she gasped.

He looked surprised and attempted to back away from her but to no avail. She had left him no room to withdraw. She felt exhausted and emotionally drained, unable to conceal her alarm. "I came as fast as I could, but the *Kotel* is far from here."

"Please calm down and tell me why you are so perturbed."

"We were praying at the *Kotel*. The British police interrupted. They attacked the worshipers, tore the screen. Some have been hurt. Itzhak tried to stop them. They arrested him." She managed to convey parts of the message in a few short and rushed sentences.

"Who is Itzhak?"

"Itzhak is my husband. We are from the Hazohar, west of Jerusalem. He told me to contact you."

Mr. Israeli took her arm and led her to a nearby bench. "I know what happened at the *Kotel*," he said. "Please tell me what happened to your husband, Itzhak."

Sorke tried to control her excitement. She breathed deeply and slowly. After a few minutes she managed to deliver an account of Itzhak's involvement in the events of Sunday night and of Monday *Yom Kippur* morning.

Mr. Israeli listened attentively. When she finished he spoke to her with admiration, "You should be proud of your husband. Itzhak is a brave man. His spirit and his deeds are what give the *Yishuv* its ability to redeem the land and its returning children. I am joining a protest delegation to the governor's office later on today and I will demand the release of Itzhak. Meanwhile," he added, "you should return to the hotel and rest. Come back and see me here this afternoon at five."

She meandered back to the hotel, wondering if the entire incident could have been prevented. She thought about Itzhak's explanation of the *Waqf.* She realized how unfair it was for the Haram to belong to the Muslim and the Church of the Holy Sepulcher to belong to the Christian, yet the *Kotel* was not owned and managed by the Jews.

A person carrying the Zionist's flag wrapped in black crossed her path. "The whole shameful act could have been prevented if the Jews owned the *Kotel,*" she remarked with tears streaming down her cheeks.

"Yes. So why don't they buy it?" lamented the stranger and moved on shaking his head in disbelief.

Sorke knew that someone at the National Committee had tried without success to buy the *Kotel* in the past. She felt drained and hopeless. She kept on moving not realizing that each stride took her farther away from the hotel.

She thought about her train ride thirty hours earlier, on Sunday morning. It was a normal day. A day like all other days. The sun looked down on the holiest of holidays marching into the Jewish consciousness in the same manner as it did on any other day. She remembered reading the daily paper, Davar. There was nothing ominous on its pages; nothing that gave the slightest of hints about the events that would unfold over the next twenty-four hours. The paper said nothing about the status quo, about what was allowed and disallowed in the service nor did it contain a word regarding Muslims' attitudes toward Jewish prayers at the *Kotel.*

On the same day, the eve of *Yom Kippur,* she could sense tension in the air. Late morning of Monday, *Yom Kippur,* the city seemed like a boiling kettle, which was tightly covered yet ready to blow its top.

More and more people crossed her path speeding toward the *Kotel.* They carried flags; some even carried black flags to convey their enraged sense of mourning. She ignored the passersby. Itzhak's fate was on her mind: his welfare, his suffering, his isolation and lack of knowledge of the outside world. She felt the urge to confide in her diary, which she had left in the hotel. She wrote on a piece of paper, *Yom Kippur, September 24, 1928. I am distraught. Today I have lost my husband to the cruel reality of Eretz Israel. When will I see him again?*

***

Itzhak paced incessantly. Darkness blanketed his eyes. He moved carefully. His hands stretched before his body, searching for his cell's walls. He could smell the musty air. *They have no right to hold me here. All I did was protest their insensitive, shameful behavior. They should be embarrassed for what they did. For their blatant anti-Semitic act.* His head was full of disorganized thoughts. *Have the people heard about the incident? Has the governor apologized? How has the National Committee acted? Are they aware that I am in jail?* He was tired. His aching body pulled him down. He dropped to the floor.

I can see the headlines in Doar Hayom and Davar tomorrow morning. 'Shame, Great Britain!' Or maybe, 'Insensitivity Trampled on Religious Freedom."

Hoping to clear his head, he closed his eyes, eager to fall asleep. Alas, his mind would not yield. Instead he was overcome with fear. *How many days, months will they keep me away from my friends; locked in an isolated cell away from the light and sounds of everyday life? Will they send me to the notorious prison in Acre? No. The governor is a smart man. He will not want to drag on the Kotel incident. He will see the wisdom in quickly apologizing and cutting his losses before the incident is exploited. The Mufti will not be the only one to take advantage of the situation. There are plenty of extremists on our side also. Together they can fan this ember into a dangerous conflagration.*

He wanted the governor to apologize so that hot tempers would cool down. *But will the governor weigh the stupidity of the act against the potential national and international outcry and apologize? I do not expect the Christian world to rise in vociferous protest. Maybe there will be a mute reaction. But the Jewish world? It will scream to high heaven. Imagine such behavior during the Friday prayer at the Haram or any prayer at the Church of the Sepulcher. But will the Christian governor be persuaded by Jewish public outcry?*

He was thinking of Gershon. His friend was always on the front line when it came to protecting the cause. *The redemption of the Jewish people in their ancestral land requires sacrifice. I know Gershon would have done the same as I did. He, too, will assume responsibility for our future. There was no other way to behave.* Itzhak was proud. He did well. His fatigue finally overcame him and he fell asleep.

Sorke had been walking for hours, since mid-morning. First, from the *Kotel* to Rehavia then again after Mr. Israeli sent her back to the hotel. A little before five in the afternoon she returned to the synagogue in Rehavia. She waited apprehensively at the door. Shortly after five she spotted Mr. Israeli approaching with a group of men. Itzhak was not among them.

She could hear her heart palpitating against her chest. She rushed toward them. "Where is my Itzhak?" she asked with an air of resignation, fearing she already knew the answer.

"Unfortunately, the police decided to keep him in jail," said Mr. Israeli. "We visited with him. There were numerous witnesses that joined us in our protest to the deputy commissioner. They all recounted Itzhak's selfless deeds at the *Kotel*. He is a hero. *Am Israel* needs people like him, so we are not going to let him stay in his jail cell. I shall do all I can to secure his speedy release. In case it comes to a trial, I shall defend him with the support of the National Committee."

Sorke was devastated. "Should I stay here and visit him in jail?" she sobbed uncontrollably.

"No. You should return to Hazohar and tell your friends all that has happened," replied Mr. Israeli in a fatherly voice.

16 THE *KOTEL* COMMITTEE

"Ye Jews, and national Jews in all parts of the world! Wake up and unite! Do not keep silent or rest in peace until the entire Wall has been restored to us!"

Pro Kotel Committee's Appeal as published in Doar Hayom August 12, 1929.

At night, still crying and feeling emotionally drained; Sorke reread her earlier entry into her diary dated September 24, 1928. She added, *within three days, if Itzhak is not released, I shall go on a hunger strike in front of the British police to protest their stupidity, the injustice of the Arabs' behavior at the Kotel, and to demand the release of my hero.*

***

The next morning Sorke returned to Hazohar. Everyone was eager to hear the news. "We did read *Davar* this morning," said Moshe, "but we are anxious to hear a detailed report on the incident as you saw it. We are most interested in Itzhak's fate. I have already contacted members of the National Committee. They assured me that a first-class lawyer will be by his side and that the Committee has launched a serious complaint about his arrest. The whole country will go on strike if those bastards do not release our man."

Sorke could sense the bureaucratic flavor in Moshe's statement. She thought that his exaggeration was true to form, but he was caring. "Thank you. Your help is important to me, Moshe. I have met Mr. Israeli, the lawyer. He seems like a good, caring man."

Itzhak's arrest caught the attention of everyone. At dinner Moshe circulated a petition. It read,

In these turbulent days when British police violate the sanctity of our national shrine and flagrantly hinder our religious freedom, and, in light of the provocative arrest of a man of honor who rose to defend that freedom, we, the people of Hazohar, demand the immediate release of Mr. Itzhak Hacohen from British custody and the swift resignation and punishment of the perpetrators of that shameful act.

Moshe asked everyone to sign the petition. "I shall send it immediately to the National Committee. In addition" he said, "we have already read in the papers the authorities' rational for their disgraceful behavior. Their unacceptable explanation that the worshippers have exceeded a long-standing agreement regarding permitted accessories at the *Kotel*, makes no sense if examined on historical background. I think the danger is that the Mufti's influence with the authorities is taking on ominous proportions. That must raise a red flag. What is next? What else will the Arabs do in the coming weeks?"

On Thursday morning, three days after his arrest, a nameless British police officer summoned Mr. Israeli and unceremoniously remanded Itzhak to his care. There were no comments, no explanations and no documents following his release. The entire affair was treated as if it had never taken place. Mr. Israeli asked no questions. He had no reason to douse a simmering fire with oil. After all, the authorities were desperately trying to extinguish it. Perhaps they realized the stupidity of their act. Perhaps the swift international Jewish reaction pushed them back into the safety of their British sensibility. He was convinced that no matter what the motives were, the Brits were embarrassed. With a clandestine smile barely visible on his face he accepted the prisoner. He foresaw future benefits for the cause if he allowed the matter to evaporate into thin air.

"Freedom is good," Itzhak told Mr. Israeli as he accepted an invitation for lunch. After a good meal he went to the hotel, cleaned up and changed his clothes. He was tired but eager to get home. With a few minutes to spare he reached the afternoon train to Jaffa and was able to secure a window seat. Itzhak loved the unfolding view from the window of the slow-moving train. The hills of Judea intoxicated his sense of beauty.

He arrived on Thursday evening just in time for dessert. Sorke spotted him at the door and rushed forward to fall into his arms. They stood close to each other for a long time. Everyone waited patiently for the two to complete their merry reunion. Then they cheered him and pressed him for details of his ordeal.

Late in the evening, after Itzhak had shared his experience with his friends he concluded with a comment that seemed ominous to everyone. "I think," he said, "we have not heard the last word on the *Kotel* issue. We must brace ourselves for progressively deteriorating relations between the Arab and the Jewish communities, emanating from Muslim fears of our intentions toward the *Kotel* and the Haram."

Moshe, whose connection with the National Committee exposed him to relevant details, held similar views. "I strongly suggest that we must become more vigilant from here on."

Itzhak agreed. "Perhaps we should assign information-gathering actions then meet periodically to review the situation. We must not be caught by surprise as the *Yishuv* was with the Nebi Musa riots. We should meet as Moshe suggested and reevaluate the situation."

Moshe quickly reclaimed the initiative. "I'd like to ask Sorke and Itzhak to work together to prepare for the next meeting. He should have his pulse on the Arabic press and Sorke on the Jewish press. I shall maintain contacts with the National Committee. We will gather here on Friday, November 23, after dinner to discuss any repercussions of this incident. The November date will give us time to assess the situation.

"Oh, one more thing. On Thursday, for one hour starting at five, there will be a general protest against the Mandatory Authorities. Gershon, will you please ring the bell a few minutes before five pm?"

"Of course."

"Thank you. We will meet at the yard in front of the main gate. I shall send a telegram with our petition to the High Commissionaire in Jerusalem. We'll sing Hatikva and then disperse. Let the people of Beit A'yan see and hear us."

Everyone agreed.

Words held a critical role in the *Yishuv*. Hazohar was no exception. Ever since Itzhak could remember, public discourse, especially political conversations, offered a good distraction from everyday hardship. Everything was political. Even mundane things, such as dress code, the aesthetics of the living quarters, inside and out, took on a political overtone. Nothing was excluded from public debate.

Hazohar had many voices that wanted—better yet, needed—to be heard. No person had ever missed an opportunity to express an opinion. They talked about the Arabs, about the Arabs and the Zionists. They talked about the value of the Hebrew language and the merit of Jewish work to the exclusion of the Arabs. They examined the value of work and its impact on the redemption of the people; the relationship between land and work, the ways to organize the labor movement. They discussed ways to feed the workers, to care for their health. Every subject had proponents and opponents. And no discussion had ever been devoid of tempers. But in the end, the voices of Hazohar always united around the cause.

Many of those discussions throughout *Eretz Israel* had led to unique solutions to festering problems. Debates and arguments brought the Hebrew language back from the brink and made it once again the vibrant and cherished language of the Jewish people. Challenging conversations led to the establishment of the workers' union, workers' kitchens and more.

The *Yom Kippur* affair was also a major topic of conversation. It was particularly relevant to Hazohar as it involved two of its members. On Friday, the day of the meeting, Gershon, Ribi and Sorke engaged in a heated discussion on the cart that took them and five of their friends to the vegetable garden.

"The *Yishuv* is too weak to provoke the Arabs over the *Kotel* issue. We should negotiate with the Mandatory government and reach an accommodation with it," suggested Ribi.

"We have tried and failed many a time. The *Kotel* is the property of the *Waqf* and the government will not force the Mufti to allow us free access," said Sorke in her typical mild-mannered voice.

"No way!" Gershon protested in a slightly louder voice. "The *Kotel* may be the property of the *Waqf*, the Mufti may live in the neighborhood, but it is ours, plain and simple. It has been ours and it will remain ours forever. Let me remind you that we were not in Jerusalem to prevent Omar's army from desecrating our holy shrine by building his shrine atop ours. Take note, Mufti, we are here now to prevent further desecration of our holy site."

Sorke declared, "I agree with Gershon one hundred percent. We should buy it. And if they do not want to sell, we should form a worshiper's brigade that will be at the *Kote*l every day to protect our right for free access!"

Everyone was astounded to hear such militant thoughts from Sorke. Gershon thought that her *Yom Kippur* experience had made her position more adamant.

"Brava, Sorke!" he exclaimed. "What a superb idea."

The conversation ended abruptly when they reached the tomato patch where work required a new focus.

Later, during the *Shabbat* dinner, Gershon reignited the discussion. He continued his militant line, "I wonder how the Christian world would react if we habitually disturbed their religious ceremonies at the Church of the Sepulcher? Better yet, how will the Muslim world respond to a Jewish demonstration at the Haram during the Friday prayers? I assure you they will not be peaceful about it, nor will they seek accommodations. I am convinced that we should adopt an eye-for-an-eye strategy. If they harass us at the *Kotel* we should harass them at the entrance to their Holy places."

Everyone was stunned, even Sorke, who had earlier offered her own provocative idea for dealing with the evolving crisis.

Avram shook his head in disagreement. "Eye for an eye? Are we back in Biblical times? Even the rabbis discounted that Biblical adage by introducing the supremacy of the law. Eye for an eye, they said, should be a monetary fine. We must let the government deal with the issue. They are obligated to secure our freedom of access."

Alexa agreed. "Even though I view the event on *Yom Kippur* as an important incident in the history of the *Yishuv*, I see no room for an eye-for-an-eye strategy. Violence begets violence, and such an approach will undoubtedly create a vicious cycle that, knowing the Arabs' proclivity for long memory, could continue for many years. We must reach an accommodation with them. After all, they live here, too."

Gershon was indignant. "Who called the police to the *Kotel*? Do we call the police when they loudly call to pray numerous times a day at Beit A'yan? No. It is their custom, and we respect it. Why, since we live here, too, don't they respect our need to put a screen separating men and women?"

"They do not respect our needs, Gershon, because they do not respect us. They think we are intruders, a bunch of colonialists who have no right to settle on their land," answered Ribi.

Gershon was in no mood for such a sentiment, even though he knew that Ribi was right. "Well, Ribi, in that case we really have two options, fold our tent and leave, or defend our rights and stay. I am convinced that we have a full right to the land. I am ready to cohabitate peacefully with the Arabs. However, should they continue to prefer the sword to deny me my rights I shall be ready to defend them, even if I have to pursue an eye-for-an-eye strategy to the end of time. By the way, our continuous presence here is a proof that you believe in our right to the land. Don't you, Ribi?"

His question remained unanswered. Moshe, unaware of the discussion, interrupted their conversation. He requested help in rearranging the room for the pending meeting. Everyone pitched in. They moved the tables to the sides, arranged the chairs in five rows and put a table facing the chairs for the speakers.

Moshe, Sorke and Itzhak took their place. Moshe wasted no time. He rose with his usual flair for bureaucratic relevance and said, "Friends, two months ago a seemingly small, and what could have been a local friction at the *Kotel*, became the epicenter of a controversy that has shaken the entire *Yishuv*. It seems that every day brings with it an escalation of rhetoric that raises the tension. Itzhak, Sorke and I accepted the task of gathering information about the public reactions and the leadership's action. Sorke will report on the reaction of the Jewish public. Itzhak will report on the Arab's reaction and I shall discuss the National Committee actions. Please start, Sorke."

"I shall remain seated, " she said. "Hope no one objects." She looked around and smiled broadly. No one objected. "The facts are simple, but the consequences are complex and far reaching. By now everyone is familiar with the *Kotel* Incident of *Yom Kippur*. So I shall not describe it again. The protest was swift and vocal. There were mass demonstrations across the country: In Tel Aviv, Haifa, Jerusalem and even here. Our various local communities inundated the Mandatory Authorities with telegrams and petitions. World Jewish leaders did not tarry. They flooded the British Government with letters of protest. After many local and national gatherings, our leadership formally protested to the highest levels of the Mandatory Authorities.

"But beyond the protest lies a festering problem: we insist on an unencumbered access to the *Kotel*. But it belongs to the *Waqf*. I shall yield the floor to Itzhak."

"Muslim leaders who fear the broader implications of our repeated attempts to buy the property will continue to attack and erode our fundamental demand. They fear that we want to take over the entire complex, including the Haram. They reject all assurances by our leadership that we categorically negate such allegations."

"Perhaps I should interject," said Moshe. "A few days ago the National Committee addressed the Muslim fear head on. It published an open letter assuring the Muslim community that the Zionists had no intention to encroach upon Muslim ownership and rights to their Holy Places."

"I am afraid that did not do much to assuage Muslims' mistrust of our intentions." Itzhak continued, "It certainly did not abate their fear of our ability to mobilize international money and power in support of our cause in *Eretz Israel*. I know that those of you who read *Davar* or *Doar Hayom* have an idea about the reaction of the Palestinian leadership. But I submit that much of it is slanted to the Jewish editor's point of view. I intend to give you an unbiased summary of what I have read in the Arabic press.

"They describe the Al-Buraq campaign, yes! As you know they call the *Kotel* 'Al-Buraq.' As part of that campaign, according to the papers, the Mufti insists that because Al-Buraq is an integral part of the Haram any changes to it or its surroundings impacts the integrity of the most holy shrine.

"Arab newspapers echo the Mufti's assertion that Al-Buraq is a *Waqf* property and a holy site. Although they acknowledge that if Al-Buraq was a standalone structure its value as a holy site would be tertiary at best.

"They faithfully report on the Mufti's campaign to retain Al-Buraq under full Muslim control and to limit to an absolute minimum the Jewish freedom of access to it. They claim that, in light of previous attempts to buy Al-Buraq, the Mufti is right to be suspicious of the Zionist intents.

"The Mufti initiated extensive lobbying efforts in Arab capitals. His delegates promote unity among Arabs in support of the Mufti's struggle, on behalf of all the world's Muslim communities, to protect the integrity of the Holy Places in Palestine. A local incident that occurred many times in the past is fast taking on an international flavor.

"We also must pay close attention to the Mufti's political ambitions. Please note that this is my own conclusion based on what I have read in *Al Karmil* and *Filastin*. The Mufti wants to consolidate his power as the supreme leader of the Muslim community in Palestine. To do so he rallies his constituents against what he believes are the nefarious intentions of the Zionists. He does what many before him did. In the process he ignores the Zionists' assertion regarding their intent not to interfere in the Muslims' affairs at the Haram. He also lets his own imagination run freely. He inflames the public against a common threat and shows his prowess as a leader who stands up to the all-powerful international Zionist forces. Thus he gains the public adoration and support.

"Let me continue with a review of the main Palestinian press. The papers report a large gathering of Arab leaders from neighboring countries as well as from local communities. They met in Jerusalem to review the threat that the Zionists pose to the Holy sites in Palestine. The meeting produced a set of resolutions, among them the creation of an international committee for the protection of the Holy sites with special attention to Al-Buraq and an appeal to the League of Nations and the British Government to safeguard the integrity of the Muslim Holy Shrine.

"My conclusion is inescapable. The Muslims continue and intensify their campaign against the Zionists' enterprise in Palestine. The problem of access to Al-Buraq in not going away at any time soon. On the contrary, the rhetoric takes on a more pernicious, more ominous tone."

Moshe took the floor. "I just want to emphasize two points. One, the Governing Board of the International Zionist movement has petitioned the League of Nations regarding our demands for unfettered access to the *Kotel*. Two, we have formed a defense committee with two objectives. The first is to follow up on the evolving belligerence of the local Arab populations, specifically that of Beit A'yan. And second, to prepare a comprehensive defense plan for Hazohar, just in case the *Kotel* problem continues to escalate."

A lively discussion ensued. They resolved to meet periodically to update the members on the *Kotel* state of affairs.

Time was a poor healer of angry sentiments. With the flow of days and months, the *Yom Kippur* incident remained high on the public mind. Demonstrations of Jews were as frequent as those of the Arabs; each group claimed full ownership of the truth.

An ominous specter hung over the *Yishuv*. Tension grew steadily and reached a boiling point in August 1929, with the approach of the *Tish'ah Be'Av*—the annual fast that commemorated the destruction of the two Holy Temples in Jerusalem. Everyone was on edge.

The strain was very real in Hazohar where members engaged in heated debates about the ongoing threats to the *Yishuv*. They met twice to discuss the escalating tension and to review the defense plan for Hazohar.

After dinner, two days before the *Tish'ah Be'Av* holiday, Gershon rose and declared that he was summoned to Jerusalem. "The heart of the *Yishuv* is in danger. I am joining my friends at the Pro *Kotel* Committee."

"Committee? What are you talking about?" Sorke asked with an obvious hint of discomfort. "I have never heard of them." She was embarrassed to show her ignorance.

"Do not feel bad," said a young man, who had recently joined Hazohar. "I have no idea what he is talking about either."

"Neither do I," echoed Avram.

Gershon looked at Sorke with a smile. "Remember what you said after the *Kotel* disturbances?"

"Vaguely."

"You advocated the formation of a worshiper's brigade."

"Ah. Yes, I did."

"Well, that was ingenious. Indeed your idea has materialized. After the *Yom Kippur* incident, I attended a demonstration against the Mufti's provocations. The demonstrators were bold, determined, and ready to meet might with might, aggression with aggression. It was a no-nonsense group. I liked what they did. One member told me, 'After all, we are in our home. This is not the *Pale*.' We marched to the *Kotel* with flags, patriotic songs and placards."

"You refuse to let go of the eye-for-an-eye idea," Avram chided him gently.

Gershon ignored him and continued, "Some time ago, I went to Jerusalem again to attended a meeting in which professor Joseph Klausner formed the Pro-*Kotel* Committee. He teaches at the Hebrew University. The committee members are dedicated to aggressively protecting our access rights at the *Kotel*.

"Yesterday I received an urgent message mobilizing the committee members to Jerusalem, ahead of the holiday. There are real fears of a major disturbance at the *Kotel* and throughout the *Yishuv* during the coming holiday. So, I shall be going to defend our right to be and to pray at the *Kotel*. The *Kotel* is ours! Here," he pulled a copy of *Doar Hayom* from an earlier day, "read our leader's plea." He laid down the paper for everyone to read. "No maybe I should read a few lines." He picked up the paper and read, "*On Friday evening, announcements of the committee were affixed to all public bulletin boards. They urge the public to rise to the defense of the remnant of our Temple.*'"

Sorke reacted instinctively, "Never mind the committee. We need you at home."

"My dear, Sorke—" he looked at her sternly "—we must remain vigilant everywhere at all times. Now duty calls me away from home, from wife and friends."

Sorke thought it was a noble idea, but its timing was bad. "If things escalate we must have everyone here to defend Hazohar! Who knows what the people of Beit A'yan plan," she scolded him.

"Not so," he replied indignantly. "We must think in line with our priorities. I know that Hazohar is where we shed our sweat and tears. Yes, Hazohar is my home. It is important, but it pales before the *Kotel*. The *Kotel* is the home of the nation. It is critical to our national survival in *Eretz Israel*. It is, after all, the essence of *Zion*, and thus our national symbol. It is the gathering place for generations of Jews. The article puts it well. Listen to what it says. '*If we accumulated all the tears of the generations before us that were shed at the Kotel's stones, we'd have a mighty ocean that would drown all our enemies*'.

"The article ends with an appeal to the youth: '*Come help by taking part in our just war for the Kotel. The victory is near.*'

"The *Kotel* is one of the key rationales for our being here, in *Eretz Israel* rather than in Uganda." He knew that everyone was familiar with the Uganda debate in the seventh Zionist Congress, some twenty-five years earlier; nevertheless, he decided to appeal to an Eretz-Israel centric thinking. "Uganda directly relates to my point," he added. "You remember that the Congress considered numerous lands, including Uganda, on which to settle the Jewish people. But the Jews saw *Eretz Israel* as their historic homeland. After many challenging debates they resolved to accept nothing less. Their goal was to end two millennia of continuous yearning and waiting. Theirs was a homecoming voyage. They believed *Eretz Israel* was waiting to be reclaimed by her returning children: waiting to be freed from the people who occupied it. They thought that Jerusalem was the center of *Eretz Israel* and the *Kotel* was its crown. Now the Mufti dictates to us how to use our Holy place. Never!"

"That is true," said Sorke, who was not ready to yield. "To paraphrase the words of Bialik, our National Poet, we remember that *Eretz Israel* is rising from the ashes of neglect one little settlement at a time. And, in my opinion, if we do not protect the little things on the land, we will not have its center."

Tova looked at Gershon with admiration. "I salute you for being active and assuming responsibility for the *Kotel*'s fate. I am your wife. I am also with you. I think I shall go with you to Jerusalem."

"Yes. Just remember," said Avram "You must assume a defensive posture. We must leave room for a dialogue, for an agreement. Remember eye for an eye belongs to a remote corner of history."

Itzhak spoke quietly, "Avram, while I have always accepted the notion that reaching an accommodation with the Arabs is preferable, I sense that the likelihood for that has heretofore eluded us and probably will continue to be unattainable. We are facing the classic Gordian Knot dilemma. The problem is—who is right? We state that we are right. They claim that they are right. When adversaries assert exclusive ownership of the truth, accommodation is difficult if not impossible.

"I remind you that there is no absolute moral code anywhere that guides us to determine who is right in the case of the *Kotel*. At the end he whose survival needs are stronger and more lasting will be right. That is the way of the world from time immemorial. So I say, go Gershon. The *Kotel* is not a bunch of stones. It is our national symbol; it is at the heart of our survival wishes. It has been alive in our consciousness for two millennia. Go protect it from death."

"Let me add a few thoughts, Itzhak," said Ribi. "You know that the Arabs of Palestine do not like us being here. I suspect they do not like Jews period. Why do I say that? Read the Quran and see for yourself. Early in his life in Medina, Mohamed was favorably disposed to the two Jewish tribes who lived there. But when they refused to convert to his new religion he became progressively angry and treated them with disdain.

"The Quran reflects that attitude. It calls the Jews haters of Muslims, violators of the Covenant with God, falsifiers of Scripture, and more. It claims that Jews will have disgrace in this world. It accuses the Jews of striving to make mischief in the land, and so on. Indeed, one should not be surprised to find that Muslims are generally ill disposed toward us." Ribi minced no words.

She looked at Itzhak and said, "But let me return to the locals' sentiments toward us. The Arab leadership cannot prevent their greedy notables and merchants from selling land to us. So what do they do? In a cowardly manner they pass the responsibility to the Mandatory Authorities. They want the Brits to act on their behalf. They also want them to renege on the Balfour Declaration and the League of Nation's mandate and limit or cease Jewish immigration, but not Arab immigration to Palestine. So, I agree with you Itzhak. We must move forward without them if necessary.

"If they want to build with us we shall welcome them, as we did in the past with your Good-Neighbor principle. But, let them know in no uncertain terms, they can burn our crops, they can ambush our settlements and kill innocent people, they can whine and protest but we are here to stay, work the land that we buy and build the Jewish Homeland. Go, Gershon. Go, Tova. We shall defend our little place and you shall defend the center."

Quiet descended on the hall after she finished. At last Moshe broke the silence. He secretly objected to the evolving militant tendencies in the group. He wanted to prevent Gershon from going and felt that the majority of the group supported the accommodation strategy. He said, "Those of us who wish to support Gershon's mission might be right. But there is an overriding issue at the heart of this discussion. Are we a group that moves forward in line with a decision of the majority, or are we a bunch of independent people acting on our own whims? I think the decision to go to Jerusalem must be our decision. We should vote to see if the group authorizes Gershon to go."

Itzhak viewed Moshe's infatuation with collective thinking as irrelevant to the larger point at hand. He thought it was a display of bureaucratic and narrow-minded thinking.

He rose in support of Gershon. He said, "I see your point Moshe. I even agree with you if the issue at hand was not so critical. But the *Kotel*? What can be more critical? The *Kotel* is our life. It is in danger. So we must act. Bureaucratic procedure must be deferred. I also want to remind everyone of the eternal vow 'if I forget thee O Jerusalem, may my right hand forget her cunning.' That vow has never been forgotten during a long and dark Diaspora. That vow is what Gershon wants to defend. By that I mean only respond to an act of aggression, not cause one. I say he should go with or without our blessing. Of course I prefer that we all support his plan."

Ribi agreed. "Do not forget that, in spite of rampant anti-Semitism throughout the many years of our Diaspora, the Jewish people's cry at the end of the Passover meal 'Next year in Jerusalem' has never vanished from their lips. We know that Jerusalem without the *Kotel* is like a man without his heart. I agree with Itzhak, Gershon should go to defend it, and I mean defend our right for unfettered access. He should have our unanimous blessings. We will be able to defend both Hazohar and the *Kotel* at the same time.

Itzhak thought of Saadia and of his own experience at the *Kotel*. Gershon was ready to assume responsibility. He deserved support. "Since we bring historic rationales for Gershon's move, allow me to add another one. When the Israelites returned from their exile in Babylonia they rebuilt the temple and sang a song of thanks,

'When the Lord restored the fortunes of Zion
We were like those who dream.'

"This song still reverberates to the present days in Jewish homes and synagogues throughout the world. It attests to the primacy of Jerusalem and the Temple at its center in the psychic of the Jewish people. I say Gershon's wish is a noble wish. Let him go with our blessings."

Moshe's initial intent to block Gershon's move faded away. He rose in support of Gershon's and Tova's departure. The group approved their wish unanimously.

Itzhak thought that Moshe was a good politician after all. Moshe had managed to secure the principle of collective decision-making, and that was a critical theme that buttressed the strength of the Hazohar group.

The holiday was two days away.

During that time, messengers from the Mufti scattered across the countryside bringing inflated news and rumors about the Zionists' intent to take over the Haram al Sharif. The messages were delivered with an urgent sense of a pending calamity. It had a clear meaning: "Arm yourself and come to the defense of the holy site."

Militant leaders inflamed the masses' anger at public gatherings after the prayer, accusing the Jews of killing Arabs and of wanting to take control over the Haram Al-Sharif. An angry mood settled over the villages and towns of Palestine. Agitated peasants armed with sticks, knives and a few guns streamed into Jerusalem, where they heard more provocative oratory about the nefarious plans of the Zionists.

Two days after Gershon and Tova left, *Eretz Israel* exploded in violence. The *kotel* was at the core of the calamitous events. At issue were two conflicting realities: the Jewish demand for complete and free access to worship at the *Kotel* and the Muslims' old fears regarding the Zionists' secret plans to take over the Al-Buraq and the Haram Al-Sharif. Once again, Jewish blood spilled in the streets, sending tremors of rage throughout every household of the Jewish community.

It is Kishinev revisited, but at least this time we fought back. I am proud of Gershon, Sorke reflected in her diary with a mixture of pride and anger. As an afterthought, she dated her entry a few days later: *August 17, 1929.*

The newspapers reported daily about the bloodshed. Arab mobs massacred defenseless Jews in Hebron, Safed, Jerusalem and many other towns. Over a hundred Jews died and many more were injured in the disturbances. The Jews, who were well-organized, inflicted many casualties among the marauding bands of Arab militants. The British police inflicted most of the Arab casualties during their attempt to halt the violence.

Tova returned after a week of intense violence and deadly clashes. She was alone. Everyone braced for the bad news.

"We demonstrated against the Arab interference in the prayers at the *Kotel*. We were unyielding in our demands. We carried flags and banners but we were unarmed. There was a scuffle between the local Arabs and us. Three people died. Gershon was stabbed. He is in the hospital for a few days."

From afar they could hear frantic sounds emanating from Beit A'yan mosque. The village was not spared the agitations and the inflated rumors. There was unusual rhetoric during the Friday prayers that incited roaring shouts. "These are not normal. They portend trouble. We'd better be ready for anything," Avram, head of Hazohar defense committee, warned everyone as the funeral abruptly ended.

Everyone feared an imminent attack by the neighboring villagers. Avram ordered an evacuation of the normal sleeping quarters and asked everyone to move to the dining hall. By evening the place had become their temporary living quarters. People were anxious. No one knew what the night would bring. They went to bed in a high state of alert. No one bothered to change clothes. They slept with their shoes on, their guns by their sides. They were ready to act on the first sound of an alarm.

At the end of a shift, the guard on duty entered the dining hall. He went directly to Yossel's bed. He shook him gently and whispered, "Wake up, Yossel."

"What time is it?" mumbled the sleepy man in an unsteady, tenuous voice.

17 HAZOHAR UNDER SIEGE

"Suddenly, just one hour before candle lighting, pandemonium broke loose. Window panes were smashed on all sides. In our building, they broke every window and began throwing large stones inside. We hid ourselves. They were breaking windows in all the Jewish homes. Now we were in deathly fear. As we were blessing the Shabbes candles, we heard that in the Yeshiva one young man had been killed. It was bitter, the beginning of a slaughter."

Aharon Reuven Bernzwei, Megilat Hebron September 1929.

"The Violence spread across the country; Arabs even tried to penetrate Tel Aviv. The British Authorities called in reinforcements from Egypt and Transjordan, but despite the additional forces the atrocities continued."

Tom Segev, One Palestine complete, p. 326.

"It is two a.m. It is time for your shift. Get up, man!" the words rang in Yossel's troubled ears. They carried a sense of impatience, of urgency. The guard shook him a bit more forcefully. "Time to go," he whispered as he held Yossel's shoulder in an effort to steady his friend.

The sleepy man rose from his bed, a little unstable, unsure of his place. His eyes still closed, Yossel searched for his gun, staggering to his right toward the door. The guard slipped into the warm bed. Within minutes he was snoring gently.

Outside, a sudden warm breeze swept the last traces of sleep from his eyes. He was fully awake. He walked briskly to the guard station to meet Alexa.

"Good morning, Yossel." She welcomed him with a friendly smile. The watchdog was happy to see him as well. His arrival signaled the last two hours of her watch. She was tired and scared. "I do not like the total darkness beyond the fence's light. I suspect that the local peasants are lurking there."

"We are well-protected. We shall defend ourselves against any of their nefarious plans," he said in a soothing voice. "Let's make our first round."

They began a slow march around the inner perimeter of the settlement's fence. They walked silently. *I have never been so fearful for the cause as I am now,* he thought. "You know Alexa," he broke the silence, "our dream may be unrealistic for there is no exclusive, contiguous Jewish land. We are spread all over the land of *Eretz Israel,* and so are they. Near every Jewish settlement there is at least one Arab village. Our security is threatened as we are always outnumbered and outgunned. That is an open invitation for conflict and violence. How can we ever form a cohesive and secure homeland? By winning armed conflicts?"

"Do you think they will attack us tonight?" she asked with a shaky voice, ignoring his philosophical musing.

"I do not know, but the events of the last week or so do not give me a sense of security. Are we prepared for a possible attack? Do we have enough ammunition? Enough people to defend our home? Or will we make our last stand much like Trumpeldor did in Tel Hai? We must fend them off, no matter what!"

"Are you afraid Yossel?" she asked.

"I am. But not for my life. I am more troubled by the precarious position of our enterprise, starting with Hazohar and including all the places where the Jews live. Look at the massacre of the innocents in Hebron. And those people were Jews who had nothing in common with *Zionism*!"

Their discussion was cut prematurely when the dog began to bark. He looked at his watch. It was three o'clock. He stopped and peered through the darkness beyond the fence.

"Do you see anything?" he asked Alexa.

"Nothing," she replied.

They continued to walk. A sudden gust of wind brought a new scent to their nostrils.

"How delightful is the scent of oranges," said Alexa, who reveled in the unexpected pleasure.

"Yes. But take a deep breath. You may discover another smell mixed with the scent of oranges. That is the smell of the Arabs' domestic animals. Could it be that they sent their cows and donkeys to divert our attention from their plans?" he wondered aloud. "Yes. I think the wind saved us. You see, Alexa, they sent animals, which will make noise. And once we spot them, the Arabs hope, we will let down our guard. Tricky thinking."

The dog barked again. This time his bark turned into an incessant growl. He moved nervously along the fence: a little forward, then, after a sharp turn, backtracked his steps to reach beyond his starting point and back again. Thick darkness swallowed the grove and the fields beyond the fence. The night was warm, the air stagnant. No breeze disturbed the sleepy branches of the fruit trees. Yossel strained his eyes but could neither see motion nor hear a sound. But the dog kept growling and moving to and fro along the fence in an alarming speed. Yossel sensed that something menacing was hiding deep inside the darkness.

"Take cover in the trench," he commanded Alexa, "I need to get a better view. I am going to the roof." They parted company. She crawled rapidly toward the defensive trench. He tied the dog to the light post and proceeded carefully zigzagging to the ladder that led to roof of the Mess Hall.

Once on top he strained to cut through the darkness. Nothing moved. He was overcome with a sense of discomfort. He felt threatened and looked for a better observation point. With a few quick steps he retreated to the water tower and climbed to the roof for protection and the better view afforded from that height. From his safety behind the sandbag fortifications he aimed his binoculars beyond the reach of the night-light and surveyed the darkness in a sweeping, slow 360-degree motion.

He noted motion in the trees but could not discern whether it was a domestic animal or stealthily moving humans. He remained alert, ready to sound the alarm. Three cows strolled freely into the vegetable patch and began to munch on the free food. *So, not only are they trying to destroy our home, they also attack us economically just in case their first plan fails,* he reasoned as he observed more cows, donkeys and goats invading Hazohar's sprawling vegetable garden. There was nothing he could do to scare the unwanted invaders. He could not make noise of any kind, as he knew how tired everyone was. He doubled his alert but could see nothing.

Beit A'yan has won the first round. He was disappointed for being so helpless.

Thirty-nine adults were in Hazohar on that day. Each one knew his designated defense positions. Sixteen people were assigned to the outer perimeter: four to each side of the rectangular yard. A one-meter deep trench dug along the outside fence that surrounded the settlement. Sandbags that piled on the outside edge extended the protective barrier by an additional half a meter, enough to provide a reasonable cover. It also enabled the sixteen men to spread around the entire perimeter.

Six people were assigned to the roof of the water tank, the tallest structure in the settlement. Two persons manned each of the four towers at the inner fence. One woman stayed at the nursery. The remaining seven men and the one woman were responsible for re-supply and evacuation of the injured.

Sometime later, Yossel felt confident that there were no people behind the herd. He decided to rejoin Alexa and continue to circle the internal perimeter. Minutes into their walk the dog began to bark, a loud, menacing bark. Both Yossel and Alexa peered into the darkness. At last Yossel was able to detect movements in the trees. Soon, the entire grove swayed in front of his eyes. Branches collided with unseen objects. The silence of night was broken abruptly.

He told Alexa to take cover and rushed to the ladder. He climbed two steps at a time. On the roof he moved quickly to the northern side of the building to survey the area. His instincts, sharp and focused, forced his gaze toward the orange grove. Then he saw them. Dozens of people were moving aggressively inside the grove.

He sensed that those moving around Hazohar greatly outnumbered and outgunned the settlement defense force. He recalled the severity of the disturbances in Jerusalem and Hebron. The thought that this night might be their last stand crept into his consciousness again. He breathed heavily as he focused the binoculars on the suspicious area ahead. More shadows moved through the grove. The trees danced in front of his eyes as the dog's growl gained vigor. There was no time to waste. He reached for the bell and sounded the alarm just as the first shot hit the wall behind him. Pandemonium erupted.

Within minutes the entire adult population of Hazohar took their designated positions. They waited for the attackers to approach the fence. Gunfire, followed by continuous wails of Arab women and a steady accompaniment of banging on pots, assaulted their ears.

A hail of bullets from close range welcomed the first wave of fighters who reached the outer fence. A number of attackers fell by the fence and the rest retreated to the grove, regrouped and resumed their attack. Wave after wave assailed the outer perimeter. Wails and banging on pots accelerated. Livestock was hit in and out of the defense line. Two defenders were slightly wounded. But Hazohar remained secure behind its fortifications. The battle raged for hours. The retreating mob left behind their casualties. Inside Hazohar, the wounded were given first aid in the dining hall.

Eerie silence fell on the battlefield. The attackers regrouped beyond an outcrop on the northern side of the defense line. From a safe distance they continued to fire intermittently at the settlement. There was a stalemate, but no time to relax. The attackers, hidden behind rocks scattered at the edge of the cultivated fields, some four hundred and fifty meters from the fence, made no attempt to cross the open space. Neither did they abandon their intent to resume the battle. Every now and then someone fired a shot at the water tower.

Secure in the status quo, half the defenders returned to the dining hall to rest. Sorke alerted the men. "The bullet supply is dwindling fast. We need to call for reinforcements." Since the telephone line was cut, Moshe asked for a volunteer to communicate with the British police. Dina volunteered. Ribi objected. "You are a nurse. We need you here. I'll go."

She left Hazohar through the southern gate and quickly vanished in the receding darkness. The two people who escorted her outside returned. No shot was fired. After waiting at the gate for twenty tense minutes the people returned to their post. Ribi's chances of reaching the British police seemed much better.

"She will make it," said one man.

"Yes, she will. She is a good athlete. She can run pretty fast. By now she must have covered a considerable distance to the police station," said another man with an obvious sense of relief.

"I hope she will not fall into an ambush," said the first man. "If she does, Hazohar could be destroyed."

"Let's not proclaim defeat. Ribi is a careful woman. I am sure she took a circuitous route. No one will set an ambush in the fields, off the road," replied the second man. "Let's hope for the best."

Both men went to their designated post with heavy thoughts on their mind. For the next thirty minutes they listened for sounds on the southern plank of Hazohar.

Yossel, still positioned on the water tower, was ready to leave his post when he noticed a movement in the vegetable patch some twenty meters from the outer fence. He trained his binoculars and scanned the open area.

"What the hell. ." he exclaimed when he saw a young child lying in the middle of the tomato patch. "Why would anyone bring a child to the danger zone?"

He rushed down and told Avram, the first defender he encountered, that he needed his help. He took his white undershirt off, tied it to a stick and gave it to Avram. "Please raise a white flag on the side of the orchard. Let them think that we want to surrender. I am going to the vegetable patch," he told Avram, who looked dismayed as Yossel turned to his right. "I shall go out through the southern gate and make my way undetected to the vegetable garden to retrieve the boy before someone shoots him."

"What boy?" asked Avram.

"Never mind I shall explain when I return. Just cover me." Yossel asked and moved around the corner of the dining hall. He slipped into the trench and moved under cover to the southern gate. It was a circuitous path but a relatively safe one.

Once outside the fence, he crawled as close to the ground as he could. He moved undetected until he reached the vegetable patch. There he entered the field of vision of the shadows that lurked inside the orange grove. He continued until he came within a few meters from the child. The sun was climbing behind the mountains. It flooded the field with light. Yossel looked back. The white flag was clearly visible above the trench.

Someone spotted him. The shout "Kill the Jew" vibrated through the air. No one heeded the white flag. They were there to force Hazohar out and reclaim the land that was once available for their grazing needs.

A barrage of gunfire followed. The boy was hit. Yossel shouted in Arabic "Stop shooting. There is a little boy in the field! I want to rescue him before he gets killed." More shots were fired. Yossel pushed against the ground in a vain attempt to dodge the bullets. He moved cautiously, as fast as he could. At last he reached the boy, who was bleeding from his left arm. He turned him on his back and crawled backward to the gate, dragging the boy behind him. The attackers continued to fire at the direction of the moving figures. Yossel was hit in the chest. He summoned the rest of his energy and pulled the boy backward. A few meters from the fence he lost consciousness. Avram rushed toward him. He dragged the two into the trench and closed the gate.

18 FORBIDDEN LOVE

When Yossel regained consciousness, he was in a hospital. The little boy slept calmly in a bed next to him. Dina stood between them, smiling. "You are a lucky man, Yossel. Both bullets missed your vital organs. You shall live to a good old age. But you must stay with us for a week."

"What happened in Hazohar?"

"The British police arrived in time to fend off the attackers."

"When did they bring me here?"

"Yesterday morning."

"How is the boy?"

"He is alive and well. He suffered a serious wound to his arm, but he, too, will recover."

He dozed off as soon as Dina left. When he awakened a bit later, he felt uncomfortable. He tossed and turned for a while. His chest, wrapped with a bulky bandage, shot random waves of pain through his body, interfering with his ability to sleep. He closed his eyes and lay still, resting. His mind meandered to the tomato patch, and he relived the last moments of his deed. He felt proud.

A rustling sound at the door returned him to the hospital. He opened his eyes, just a tad, to see what was going on. From a sliver of opening, he saw her. A figure, dressed in Arab garb, her back to him, talking with someone in the hallway. He waited for her to turn around. He was used to the uninviting attire of the local women. *Like a used sack of potatoes washed and hung on the line to dry*, he mused.

But when she turned and looked into the room he saw that she was different. A tall, slender woman in her thirties, he guessed, stood by the door looking at him, then at the boy in the bed near him, then back at him. He watched her clandestinely, through half-open eyelids. Her slim figure was covered from neck to toe but left a visible trace of a sensuous feminine shape.

For the first time in a long while he was alone with nothing on his mind to divert his focus from the sensuous to more immediate challenges. He admired her dark silky hair, barely visible under the headscarf, shining under the bright light above the door. Her deep brown eyes, accentuated by gently drawn eyebrows that echoed her black hair, adorned an olive toned face like twin diamonds on a magnificent necklace. Her exposed face hinted to the continuous flow of her smooth skin deep into the mystery of her black outfit. He took a slow, deep breath, inhaling into his lungs her delicate scent that permeated the room. He sighed. He missed the scent of a woman.

Was he blushing? He tried to suppress his thoughts. At that moment he realized that he had never looked beyond the hijab. He had always looked at Arab women with disdain, failing to explore past the dull darkness of the first impression. Now he reveled in their mystery.

He resolved at once that there were Muslim women who covered their entire body, but their overt attempt to obscure all that was striking did not reduce their skill to hint at charm, sensuality, and beauty. Actually, he thought she was ever so seductive. Or was it his longing for a woman's presence that forced the tempting image into his mind eye?

He glanced again at the hair that cascaded from the Hijab to her olive brow. He thought about Itzhak's review of the great debate in the local Arabic press especially in Filastin and Al Karmil. Both papers had devoted considerable space, a few years back, to argue the pros and cons of traditional Muslim attire for women. He recalled that the entire notion of hijab was based on the Hadith, but could not remember whose Hadith it was. He did, however, remember the gist of it. It was all about the sexual appetite of men. The Hadith put the burden of modesty on women. He was sure that the intent, even though undeclared, was to protect a man from himself. Yossel thought that the whole idea was senseless. Surely man is not so weak as to succumb to his sexual desires whenever he sees a woman's hair. Quite to the contrary, hiding behind shapeless attire only heightens a man's imagination and his sense of hidden possibilities.

He waited for her to move. She lingered at the door, unaware of his thoughts, secure in the knowledge that he was asleep and could neither see nor hear her. She looked at him again and said something to herself as if she was engaged in a conversation rather than a monologue. He watched her lips move. He strained to hear but could not make out what she said.

While his imagination labored in overdrive, his body was calm. He lay in his bed without motion. He said nothing. He kept looking at her as she glided elegantly toward the bed of the little boy, whose life he'd saved only a day earlier.

She sat near the sleeping boy and tenderly combed his hair with her fingers. Yossel noticed her gentle touch. He would have given anything to be in the boy's place. A light tremor zoomed through his body, leaving in its wake a great sense of pleasure.

She looked at Yossel and was captivated by his handsome face. Years of exposure to the local climate had changed his pale skin into a more robust light brown. She adored his red curly hair and delighted in the warm smile that carved his sleeping face below it.

He opened his eyes and met hers somewhere in the middle of the space that separated them. In an instant, she redirected her gaze to the little boy.

"Hello," Yossel said in Arabic.

Her face grew pale. She managed to force a smile. "You speak Arabic? "

"Yes," he answered plainly.

"Thank you for rescuing my nephew," she said in English, hoping that his Arabic was rudimentary at best. She steadied her voice and added, "It was irresponsible of them to bring him into the conflict. I apologize for their carelessness."

He noticed at once that she did not speak like a local person. She did not dress like a local woman, even though her attire was shapeless and boring. Her fingers were adorned with Western-style fingernails. She was way too clean and her skin too smooth. He suspected that she must be an educated woman from the city. But why did she wear the hijab? Why did she not dress like a modern city dweller?

"I thank you for your kind words," he said in Arabic. "I speak Arabic better than English."

He could discern a fleeting and faint expression of discomfort across her face. "Would it be inappropriate for me to introduce myself?" he asked.

"Not at all. Please excuse my manners. I should have done that myself," she answered. "I am Amina Abbasi. I am this boy's aunt."

He marveled at her bravery. "I am Yossel. I have never seen you before. Do you not live in Beit A'yan?"

"No. I am from Al-Quds. The Palestinian name for Jerusalem," she replied from a safe distance behind the sleeping boy.

Many questions swirled inside his head. He was ready to ask the first one when the boy opened his eyes. He rose from his bed, looked around and rejoiced when he saw Amina. He hugged her lovingly. Behind the boy's back Amina put a finger to her lips to signal that Yossel should stop talking with her.

"How are you feeling?" she asked the boy.

"My arm hurts," he answered. "The nurse told me that this man brought me here." He pointed at Yossel.

"Indeed I did, however only indirectly. The people who brought me here also brought you. But I am proud to accept the responsibility for your being here. My name is Yossel. What is your name?"

"I am Ali," said the boy.

"I trust that you are a brave boy and you can handle the pain," he said jokingly.

"I am, aren't I, Amina?" asked Ali, as if he needed a witness to his courage.

"Yes, you are," Amina reassured him, as she signaled Yossel again to hush.

Yossel felt as if he entered a world without possibilities. He and Amina did not talk anymore.

About an hour later Dina came in to take the boy to the examination room.

"May I join him?" asked Amina.

"He will be back in an hour," Dina said. "You may wait for him here."

Once again they were alone together.

Yossel was the first to speak. "I want to be honest. I heard your whisper. What exactly you said I couldn't tell. Did you say something about stealing your land?"

Her eyes grew wide. "Yes, I did."

"One day, I hope, you will let me explain why I am not a thief."

She blushed but soon regained her composure. "Perhaps. You are an amazing man, Yossel. You have risked your life for an Arab boy."

"He is a boy first. He was in a dangerous place at the wrong time. I have paid no attention to the fact that he was Arab. Besides, everyone in Hazohar would have done the same. The Arabs are not my enemies."

"I thought that the Zionists do not like us. We certainly do not like them. We have nothing against the Jews who live among us," she said emphatically, clearly separating the Jews from the Zionists as if they were two distinct People.

She overlooked the fact, Yossel realized, that the Jews she mentioned were a small Orthodox minority, irrelevant to the Zionist's enterprise. Besides, it was apparent that the Arabs did not like the Orthodox either, as evidenced by their recent provocations at the *Kotel* since *Yom Kippur* of the previous year and their murderous atrocities in Hebron and elsewhere only weeks ago.

Yossel was in no mood to argue. He preferred to get to know the gentlewoman who sat at the far corner of the room with a newspaper in hand to protect herself from unexpected visitors. He changed the subject. "Have you ever lived in Beit A'yan?"

"Yes. I was born there," she answered nervously. She glanced at the door and then at her watch. "Please be careful when you talk to me. Other members of the family should be here any moment. Maybe I'd better go." She rose and walked to the door. "I shall come back tomorrow morning," she told him with a hint of encouragement.

He was suddenly sad and alone. Ali and a new nurse walked in. She looked at Yossel with a clear warning gaze. "Yossel, careful!" she addressed him sternly in broken Hebrew. "She is a Muslim woman, it could be bad to speak with her."

"I like her. Please keep the boy out of the room as long as you can when you take him for his examination. And do make some noise when you bring him back."

"Crazy Yossel. I like you. I do what you ask."

Minutes later a woman dressed in peasant garb walked through the door and hugged Ali. She looked at Yossel with a mixture of anger and surprise.

"Who is this man?" she asked the boy. Without waiting for his answer, she stormed out of the room, found the nurse and complained about Yossel.

"My sisters will visit him and they cannot be alone in a room with a stranger." The nurse did not understand. She took the woman's hand and walked back to Yossel asking him to interpret.

"She wants me out of this room," he told the nurse.

"Tell her," she said in broken Hebrew, "many victims of your shooting Jews this week. No room. Your nephew with man who saved his life."

The woman was livid.

She ignored Yossel but grilled Ali. "When she visited you did Amina talk with that man? Was she sitting? Standing? Where?"

"She was with me all the time. She only told him her name and thanked him for taking me out of the tomato patch."

"You must tell me if Amina talks to that man," she insisted.

"Yes, aunty," he said obediently.

She left, never inquiring to the boy's health.

"That was my aunt. I do not like her very much. She is the oldest sister of my other aunt, Amina. She lives in Beit A'yan," he told Yossel, who was already redirecting his attention to his book.

The next morning, Yossel awaited her arrival with much anticipation. He had not felt this way in a long time. He remembered the gentle way Amina's fingers glided through Ali's hair. Goose bumps arose on his skin. He could sense the desire burning within him as his mind conjured up the image of her slender body standing at the door. He sighed.

At last she arrived. She stood at the door looking at the boy. When she was certain that he was asleep she said softly, her voice seeping into his ears like dripping honey, "Good morning, Yossel. Are you feeling better?"

"Better, thank you," he replied. "I am happy to see you Amina." He was eager to resume their conversation.

She floated into the room. Ali awakened, frustrating their ability to converse. She focused on Ali, caressed his hair and talked with him about the family. "It is harvest time. Everyone is working in the fields. So no one can visit. They wish you a speedy recovery. They asked me to tell you that they cannot wait for you to return home healthy." As she hugged Ali, she glanced at Yossel with a tender expression over the boy's head. She caressed Ali gently until he fell asleep. She whispered something in his ears to be certain that he was sleeping. The boy did not react. "We can talk now," she said with anticipation.

"I thought about you last night and wondered if you and your family had moved to Jerusalem."

"Al-Quds," she corrected him, "No, only I." She hesitated a moment then said, "I visit my family on occasion. We do not see eye to eye, and each visit grows more challenging than the previous one."

"Why is that?"

"They are too conservative for me. I grew up in the village until I was eight. I was destined to be a domestic, ignorant woman who would marry at a young age a man my parents chose for me. As a child I was assigned many domestic chores, mostly in the kitchen. I peeled potatoes as early as I can remember. People in the village entertained their family often. Sometimes it took fifteen hours to prepare the food, so all females who could work did so before and after the meal.

"I helped in the preparation of food and the cleaning after the meal. Every day I went to the spring, about a half hour in each direction, to fetch water. I was an expert in balancing a heavy can of water on my head. I think that gave me such good posture." She smiled. "I probably would have spent my entire life in the village, unless I married a man from another village and spent my life in his village, working in his kitchen. Cleaning his house. Doing farm work. In short, I'd have had no life as I know it."

"Domestic life is not easy, but I guess if you do not know any better then it is not as hard," Yossel reflected aloud, even though he felt ill at ease with his comment. "Sorry. I think that was stupid. Of course, everyone can feel hardship. Please forgive me."

She smiled a forgiving smile and said, "I agree." Then she continued. "There was an older man in the village who often visited my father. He was ugly, balding and when he smiled he revealed missing front teeth. He looked disheveled, but he was very wealthy. My sister told me that he was asking my father to save me for him so he could marry me. At that time my father's farm needed a massive infusion of cash. So, after some bargaining, my father was ready to agree."

"At the age of eight?" Yossel exclaimed. "How horrible!"

She smiled. "Probably he would have waited a few years. Luckily, a rich aunt saved me from him. She always liked me and thought that I was a smart little girl. One day she came to visit. She convinced my father to send me to live with her so that I could get an education. It took a nice cash gift to my father to get him to forgo the pending barter with the old man. I know that she also advised him that in this modern age an educated woman can be independent and not a financial burden on the family. Furthermore, she convinced my father that my marriage prospects would be better. My father was a resourceful man and he understood the value of the gift and the benefits of a better prospect in marriage, which translated to a bigger dowry. Besides, he had fewer mouths to feed. So he agreed. Eventually he bartered with the old man: my mean older sister for a nice cash gift. My father did well.

"My aunt sent me to Ramallah to study at the Friends Girl School and later to Beirut to the American University. Now I am an educated modern woman who reverts to the old ways each time she visits Beit A'yan." She laughed gently as she emphasized *modern woman.*

Ali woke up and looked at Amina standing next to him. He hugged her and told her about his aunt's visit. "She was angry to see Yossel in the room," he whispered.

Amina hugged him to hide her expression of disgust, but Yossel saw it. Amina sat by the boy's side completely ignoring Yossel, who was relieved to see the approaching nurse. He knew that the nurse would take Ali to his therapy session, leaving them alone in the room.

Amina rose and walked to the far window and said, "We should be careful when we talk. My sister blames me for her lot. She thinks that I should have married him and she should have gone with my aunt. She hates the old gizzard. I am sure she is already busy spreading rumors in the village. But let us not waste our precious time on my nasty sister. Tell me about your growing up."

"I was born in Kishinev in the *Pale*..."

"*Pale?*"

"Without getting into too much history, let me say this: the *Pale* was an area designated for Russian Jews by Catherine the Great in the mid-18th century. In her overt anti-Jewish sentiments she meant and succeeded to isolate the Russian Jews from the larger Russian society."

"I want to know more about you."

"My parents were Russian of Jewish descent. I was only Jewish in the eyes of the gentiles who rose to belittle me because I lived in the *Pale*. I could safely say that we were indifferent to Judaism.

"One spring day, I was playing on the street of Kishinev with Russian friends, as I had done many times before. Some were Christians and others were Jewish like me, devoid of any meaningful relation to the Bible or the Jewish tradition.

"Suddenly, without a visible sign, the Christian boys lost their mantle of innocence and melted away to reappear as savages in a crowd storming the Jewish quarter and wielding all kind of deadly instruments: knives, spades, axes and clubs. A few were carrying guns, which they held over their heads in menacing gestures. It was a frightening sight, the drunken mob searching for people whom they did not know. People whose blood was the same color as theirs. People, who like them, spoke only Russian. People whose children attended the same schools with their children.

"Blood flowed in the street like a mighty river. I feared for my life and hid in an alley. I cried silently unable to explain to myself why they committed such savage acts on their Russian friends." He paused.

"Please continue. I am interested in your story."

"Many died. Much property was destroyed. It was another alarming event in the life of Russian Jews. Millions fled the Pale. My family moved to Odessa, where I graduated from high school and even started the university."

He stopped abruptly and refocused the conversation on her. "May I ask what you do in Jerusalem?"

"Al-Quds," she chastised him jokingly. "I teach Arabic at the American Colony high school. Since I speak English very well I also assist the Mandatory Authority in verbal and written translations. I love my jobs. They keep me away from the repressive environment of the village. I feel more alive in the city. I can dress in modern attire and be a modern woman. You know I am even working on the first Palestinian Women's Congress to be held later this year. Tell me more about your life, what do you do?"

He was quiet for a while thinking but looking straight at her with an adoring look. She blushed. He was determined to avoid a political discussion.

"Please tell me, what did you whisper when you first visited Ali?"

"Must I?" she replied hesitantly.

"Please."

"I will tell you tomorrow. Now I'd like to know as much about you as I can."

"Okay," he said reluctantly, "I shall do as you ask. I am a farmer."

"My father is also a farmer," she said and burst into laughter.

"So, you are a teacher," he said, "that is a noble profession. My mother was a teacher. She used her extensive library to teach me Russian literature and poetry and how to think independently, but nothing about being Jewish. This I had to learn by myself, a year before I came to *Eretz Israel*."

"Palestine," she said. He decided not to react and waited for her to continue. "That is amazing. We do not study much nor do we have room for independent thinking," she lamented. "In our villages, no one goes to school. Our children grow up without books, without newspapers. They are illiterate and ignorant. In Beit A'yan, there is one semi-educated man. Once a week, after the Friday prayer, he reads the latest news for those who want to know what is going on in Palestine. I was lucky to get out into the open world."

"Jews put enormous emphasis on education," he stated with pride.

"We, and I mean the rural and most of the urban population of Palestine, do not," she replied dejectedly. "Could you go back to Odessa?"

"Sure. I was a first-year student at the University of Odessa, when Russia flew into a rage, again. This time, the entire weight of the Russian Government fell on the shoulder of one person even though he was not the real target. Their aim was clear: Russian Jews. They wanted to squash him and with him their Jewish citizens, as if he was a troublesome cockroach. His name was Mr. Beilis. Do you know his alleged crime?" he asked rhetorically. "They accused him of killing a young Christian boy, draining his blood and using it for a religious purpose; more precisely, for baking the *matzah* for the Passover celebration."

"How awful. Revolting. Stupid," she said with true anguish.

"Yes, but the government prosecuted him relentlessly. Yet he was a Russian first and a Jew by birth only, utterly indifferent to the Jewish religion and to the Jewish people.

"On that day the streets of Odessa pulled me toward my people. I left the university to prepare myself to ascend to *Eretz Israel*. I joined a Zionist group and began to educate myself with everything that was Jewish. I wanted to know who I was not who the government and the mob thought I was."

"And what did you discover?"

"Now, Amina, do you really want to have a political conversation?"

"Yes. If I am to oppose Jewish presence in Palestine, as the upcoming Palestinian Women's Congress will most likely do, I want at least to know whom I am opposing. I do not want to be as capricious as the Russian Government or as ignorant as the Russian mob."

He ignored her statement. Looking at her with a loving expression he whispered, "Amina, I know I may be crossing permissible boundaries, but I must tell you that I have had you on my mind ever since you entered this room; at that time you also entered my soul. I am so happy. I feel as if I have found a new source of energy to fill the void that opened within me when my wife died, almost two years ago."

She blushed. Her expression softened, her voice grew mellower. "Please, Yossel, please not now. I like you very much."

He wanted to reach out and hug her but restrained himself.

They were lost in silence. "Okay," he said. Here is what I discovered on the streets of Odessa. But promise me that you'll tell me later what you whispered at the door."

"I will."

"Our history, as conveyed in the Bible, tells us about a covenant between God and Abraham. That covenant is the birth certificate of the Jewish nation that assures us an eternal ownership of the land of Israel, also known as *Eretz Israel*."

"You do not really believe that?" Amina interrupted him with a discernible amazement.

"I do," he said softly, "just as you believe in the stories of the Holy Quran, such as the one about the Night Journey with Al-Buraq, and the veracity of the Hadith, and organize your life in line with their pronouncements. And just as the Christians believe in the truth of Jesus's resurrection," he replied. "The Quran holds Abraham in high esteem, right?"

"Yes."

"So, if it does, why should you not believe in Abraham's covenant with God, the one that also created the everlasting bond between my people and *Eretz Israel*?"

"Palestine," she said with a mischievous smile then added somewhat apologetically, just as her younger sister walked in, "I need to think about this."

"So this is the stranger whom you see every day?" said Amina's youngest sister, unaware that Yossel spoke Arabic. "He is mighty handsome. How do you talk with him? Do you speak English? Does he speak Arabic?"

"I don't talk with him. And I won't talk with him even if he speaks Arabic, which he does not," she said indignantly. Then she continued her protest, "He is here because there are no empty beds in the hospital. He is not here for me. I am here to see Ali, who has been neglected by most of his family."

"It is harvest time, Amina, people work many hours a day. But tell me the truth: our sister tells everyone that you come here to visit this man, not Ali. Actually, everyone in the village talks about your strange behavior."

"The truth serves no purpose, as you prefer to believe rumors spread by a friendless woman, instead of what I say, which is the truth, so suit yourself, there is nothing more to say."

Yossel looked at Amina. He could feel the pain in her voice.

"Amina, I am your sister, I tell you people speak about you all the time. Even father is agitated by the stories."

"I cannot relate to people who do not think; people who talk behind my back. The hell with them!"

"I would not go home if I was you."

"If I stay out I send them a message that the rumors are true. I think you have accomplished your mission. Maybe you should leave and let me go and bring Ali from his therapy session."

She left in a huff.

The next day was Ali's last day in the hospital. Amina came early, as usual, hoping to continue her conversation with Yossel. But Ali was up. She sat by his side, reluctantly ignoring Yossel, who was pretending to read his book. They talked a little but were mostly quiet as Amina caressed the boy's head. At last, the nurse came to take Ali out. Words gushed out of Amina's mouth.

"Yossel. I fulfill my promise. Here is what I said at the door. Promise not to laugh at me, please."

"Amina, you have been a ray of light that shines on me. Why would I laugh at such a gift?"

"I said, I love you for saving my nephew, but I hate you for stealing my land, my country."

"What a delightful sentiment you convey in the first part. I love it."

"I now can add: I feel like I have never felt before. I think I just love you."

Her honesty surprised her. She was uncomfortable and sought an immediate escape. She walked toward the door.

"Do not leave me, Amina, I love you, too."

They were apart, wanting to fall into each other's arms. She turned around and stepped forward toward him but halted about a foot away. She immediately turned and rushed to the safety of Ali's empty bed. Then she changed her mind and walked back to the door. "I must go now. I shall return later after I regain my composure."

Once again he was alone. He rehashed her three pleasing words, "I love you" in his mind.

Minutes later, she reappeared at the door. "You asked to show me that you were not a thief. Please do." She reflected back on her initial sentiment. "I still think the Zionists stole my land. It is our land," she said. "We have lived here for more than a thousand years. If you think the Palestinians will allow the Jews to settle here, you are wrong!"

"There is plenty of space in this land for two peoples to live in peace side by side," he answered. "Besides, the Arabs have a vast landmass that covers land north, east and south of the Jordan River. Can we avoid politics and talk about us?"

"We can for the time being. But one day we'll have to discuss politics. We must understand each other. So for now go back to Odessa."

"I spent the rest of the year preparing to come here. I studied Hebrew and also improved my agricultural skills. I spent countless hours in debates about the destiny of my people. Those activities and debates always filled me with the sense that my people were awakening from a long, cold night of the Diaspora, and were getting ready to reassert their national destiny."

"Interesting," Amina interjected. "At the same time, Arab nationalism entered its spring. Our people began to think of an Arab state within the borders of the Ottoman district of Al-Sham, that is Syria. We wanted Palestine to be a part of a new Arab state."

Yossel ignored her comment. "At last, I was ready with my people to take our national survival into our hands. With Herzl, the yearning for reclaiming our ancestral land gained strength. The Promised Land and we were on a converging path. But, as many have said, it will not lead to an empty land, waiting to be plowed, irrigated, sowed and reaped. Many Arabs lived in small towns and villages. Nevertheless, we saw the land as our historical homeland; we would accept none other, even though others were offered. Our goal was to end two millennia of continuous yearning and waiting. Ours was a homecoming voyage. *Eretz Israel* was waiting to be reclaimed by her returning children."

He watched her facial expressions and could easily detect a vehement disagreement. He preempted her somewhat apologetically. "I attempted to tell you my story. I know that you disagree with our national direction, but there is plenty of space in the land to allow for two separate national dreams to come to fruition."

"Palestine belongs to the Palestinians!" she declared adamantly.

He knew that if he were in her place he would be angered by anyone who came to settle on what he considered his land. He wanted to avoid an argument. So he said, "Did you not say to me that you want to learn about me?"

"I did."

"Let's converse without anger. I want you to know that Arabs assaulted me three times. I was beaten in Jaffa after I disembarked; I was nearly killed in 1920; and a few days ago I could have easily been killed while I rescued the boy. With all these incidents, I have never been bitter. So I say, eventually we shall have to consider how we may coexist without resorting to bullets and the threats of losing children in the line of fire." He reached out to touch her hand. She shook a little but did not withdraw. He wanted to communicate a gesture of friendship, much the same way he saw Sorke communicate with his friend Itzhak. But inside, his emotions were rising fast.

She was lost in thought, reflecting on what he had just said and done. At last she regained her focus. "Yes, you are right," she said, "If we are to be friends we must be able to converse in peace."

"Today is Ali's last day. I want very much to see you again. Will you permit me?"

"I would like that very much," she replied without hesitation. "Perhaps I could learn a little more about the Zionists. Will you be my tutor?"

Yossel recognized immediately her attempt to hide her interest in him behind a benign veil of a quest for knowledge. His heart leaped from joy.

"You know at the university we had an opportunity to mingle," she told him. "Men and women took trips together and spoke freely with each other. So how about that?"

"I would be delighted and honored to do so. But you must be my tutor on Palestinians issues, such as the planned Women's Congress."

"Agreed," she said with an encouraging smile.

"It may be a difficult exchange and we must keep a friendly attitude no matter what. We can prove that people, regardless of their differences, can be civil and friendly."

"That could be a challenge, but not the only challenge," she replied. "We cannot meet here. The people of the village are too narrow-minded. Should they see us together they will most certainly be very angry. Can you come to Al-Quds? We can meet at the library of the school or perhaps go for a stroll around the city."

He was ready for that. He knew that just being near her might lead to a closer friendship. "I will be happy to travel on Saturdays. Let's meet in the American Colony School next Saturday at noon. Oh, if one of us misses the meeting, then we'll meet on the following Saturday."

She agreed. They were still alone in the room. Their future connection was assured.

Ali returned. This time his mother was at his side. He greeted Amina, who stood by the window. Giving her a big hug, he said happily, "I am going home today."

Yossel looked at the boy and said, "Wonderful news, Ali. How do you feel?"

"My arm is still hurting a little."

"It is better than being killed in the tomato patch," Yossel chuckled. But his subtext was to remind Amina that he was not a foe.

She hugged the boy and kissed his forehead softly saying, "Yossel is right. Promise me that you'll rest at home."

Ali nodded his head.

Then his mother grabbed Amina's arm. "You know the stranger's name," she hissed. "Have you no shame?"

"He saved Ali's life. Why shouldn't I know the name of the man who saved my nephew? You should go to his side and thank him for his bravery. He could have been killed for your son!"

Ali's mother shrugged "He is a Jew. If his people did not try to steal Al-Buraq and the holy Haram, then Ali wouldn't be hurt. I have nothing to say to him. But to you I can say one thing, now I know that what they say in the village is right. You bring shame on us."

"Shame on you for listening to vicious rumors. I have done nothing wrong. I am proud that I thanked the man who saved Ali!"

The mother did not reply. She took Ali by the hand and said, "Let's leave Amina here, she does not belong with us." In a huff she led the boy out of the room to find the nurse.

Amina was embarrassed but managed to tell Yossel that she was looking forward to seeing him in Al-Quds, then she rushed out to catch Ali and his mother.

19 THE FRIENDSHIP BLOSSOMS

"What a great discrepancy there is between what people say and what they do...They sell land and speculate in it... and afterward shout and protest and demand that the Government pass a law that forbids them to sell land."

Khalil Sakakini, Such Am I, O World. p. 158, 163.

On Friday, a week after he was released from the hospital, Yossel did not sleep well. He was too anxious. He was up early on Saturday morning and set out on the long walk to the train station.

He arrived in Jerusalem early. With nothing to do he meandered toward the American Colony House. His head was full of thoughts. *Palestine belongs to the Palestinians! Why do I think of politics when I come to see the one I long for? My love?* But the cause was always there, always preempting his emotions. He remembered *Gershon's indignant statement at the port of Jaffa "This is our* Eretz Israel. *Am Israel is Alive!"* He agreed.

Yossel was aware he was going a bit crazy. Here he was in Jerusalem to meet the woman he loved! And his head was full of thoughts about the cause. He was trying to rid himself from those intruders but they kept coming back. And then all he could think about was Amina. He wanted so much to touch her hand, to bring her closer to his heart. To kiss her lips.

Someone shouted at him in Arabic to watch where he was going. He looked around to find himself walking in the middle of the street. He withdrew to the side and hastened his pace. The time was rapidly approaching noon. He knew he needed to talk with Amina about his feelings, to reassure himself that she felt the same way. But the cause stood in the way of emotion. His whole life was dedicated to the cause. Even his marriage to Rachel was, in part, a union of like minds. He nearly forgot how to react emotionally. He could see the American Colony House some distance ahead. His heart pounded on his chest, screaming for its freedom.

Amina was standing at the gate not hiding her happiness to see him. She was dressed in modern attire that complimented her delicate figure. Her black hair cascaded freely downward. "I am happy you came, Yossel. I am so glad to see you healthy."

"You know, Amina, today is the first time I see you in modern attire. You look beautiful," he said with a smile. "It is such a nice day, Amina, may we walk?"

"My thoughts exactly," she echoed cheerfully. "Oh, thank you for the compliment. I am a modern woman. I see no need to hide behind dreary clothes."

They walked for hours, oblivious to their surroundings. They talked about their childhoods. He told her more about being a child in Kishinev and she told him more about her feeling on the mountains, all alone with the family goats. "At times I miss the open meadows and the mountain air," she said.

"I miss my mother's library of Russian literature. It was a place full of secret pleasures. A refuge from the harsh reality of the streets of Kishinev," he said.

They reminisced about their first meeting at the hospital. "I still blush when I think that you understood every word I said at the door. But I have managed to enjoy my emotion," she told him in a jovial tone.

They thought that the sun had traveled the distance to the western horizon at an unusual speed. It was time to part company and return home. They walked back in silence. Their hands brushed against each other but never paused for a brief purposeful touch.

"I cannot wait for your next visit," she said softly, not looking at him.

"I shall be here at noon next Saturday. Please remember what we have agreed upon in case one of us misses the meeting."

"I remember," she said and bid him goodbye.

He stood there for a moment, watching her disappear behind the curve. He had many soft words that remained on the tip of his tongue; many gentle touches to share with her that had never left his hands. He stood quietly in a stupor of emotional upheaval. Finally he turned around and began his long journey home.

For the next month they met every Saturday. They walked and talked about their lives. About being a Zionist. About being a progressive Arab woman. One day he asked her "What are the sentiments in the village toward you?"

"They have no clue that we meet. I guess my oldest sister has no more rumors to spread. I am sure that everyone is occupied with other kinds of gossip."

Their friendship blossomed but remained platonic. Yossel felt secure in its strength. So he resolved to converse with Amina about her statement at the hospital door. It is time to talk about land, he decided. That afternoon, they sat at a coffee house and sipped bittersweet Turkish coffee.

He looked at Amina and said, "On your first visit you said to me 'I love you for saving my nephew but I hate you for stealing my land, my country.' I know you meant what you said. Over the last month and a half

I have felt that a new man was born inside me. I long for our meetings and cherish your presence. You touch me deeply without ever laying a finger on my skin. You have liberated my imprisoned feelings without ever climbing the barricades. I do not know how you did it or why I feel this way but I am grateful to you. Thank you, Amina, my cherished friend. I want you to love me and I am sad that you hate me because of land. Let me try and explain to you why I am not a thief."

She felt ambushed by his abrupt transition from softness into the avoidance zone but decided to accept his invitation with an air of friendship. "Why do you say that?" she asked. "I am certain that the Zionists are stealing our land. After you told me about the continuous Jewish habitation in the holy cities, I researched your assertion. You were right, but, and that is a big but, they were pious Jews who engaged in religious studies. Land was far from their mind. There was no friction between us until the first Zionist left the walled city of Jerusalem and set foot on our land near Mulabbis."

"They did not simply 'set foot.' They bought the land, and built Petach Tikva. Also, just to be historically accurate, they were those 'pious Jews' you spoke about."

"Thanks for the correction," she said, "but that does not change my argument. After that, a flood of Zionists came into the country and started to settle on the land. Since then they have wanted more and more and more land. That was the seed of our dispute."

"That flood was a trickle," said Yossel, "and many of them could not live in the harsh conditions of the land. They left the country soon after they arrived."

"Yes, but those who stayed encouraged others to come. Palestine belongs to the Palestinian and not to the Zionists who want to change our way of life, to reshape Palestine."

"What way of life, Amina. What Palestine? There is no unity of purpose, no common history on this land among the people who live here. People on the hillside are different from people in the coastal plains. People in the cities are different from the other two, and the Bedouin are different from all three. People's allegiances are to the family, then to the tribes, and there are many of them. Where was the bond with a Palestinian Nation fifty, a hundred or more years ago? How many Arabs dreamed about Palestine? Yearned to return to it from far away corners of the globe? I think none. We are here because the land is our home. The Bible says so; Abraham, whom the Quran adores, says so; the Jews around the world say so; the British Government says so and the Mandate Agreement of the League of Nations says so. Those who live here should continue to do so in the manner they have lived for generations. No one wants to change that."

"You want to take over our holy places in Al-Quds."

"We want nothing of that. We want you to recognize our right to the *Kotel* that is all. Yes, we did try to buy the *Kotel* but failed. No one wants to touch your Holy Haram al Sharif and other holy places that rise on the foundation of our holiest place. Our leaders declared that time and again."

"What about all the settlements that dot our land?"

"They are not on your land. They are on a land that was ours until we were evicted by force. We are buying it with enormous sums of money, not taking it by military might. In fact, Amina, it is greedy Arabs, many of whom live abroad or even in *Eretz Israel* who sell the land to the Zionists. Without these people there would be no Jewish settlements in the country. Without their help, there will be no newcomers. There is not a single *dunam* of land that we stole. Not one!"

Amina looked at him in disbelief.

"Let me tell you something else, most of your villagers do not own their land. They rent it. The landlords are fat, rich Arabs, who most likely live abroad. These rich merchants had been taking advantage of peasants' misfortune for years. Peasants, who failed to pay rent, lost their land. Those are the people who sell land to the Zionists and then cry foul to government officers. Ah, the government, peasants who fell behind on their taxes lost their land to the Ottoman Government. The government had laws against land sales to the Zionists but they rarely enforced them. Greed was all around us."

"I did not know that my people betrayed us for money," she said with visible anger. "Give me a few examples," she demanded.

"I shall," he said, "but first take a deep breath and relax. I cannot bear to see you unhappy."

She sipped her coffee in silence.

"I have always been interested in this subject," Yossel explained. "I collected every bit of information I could find. I remember vividly an editorial in Filastin that said something to the effect that no one should blame the Zionists' advances in the country. The blame was with local notables who sell land to the Zionists. Moreover, some notables and Palestinian nationalists complain often about the duplicity of other notables and nationalists who sell land to the Zionists and then demand that the Mandatory Authorities prohibit land sale to the Zionists. This is the height of hypocrisy!

"Here is a good example of Arabs selling land. The Sursock family who reside in Beirut owned most of the land in the Plain of Jezreel, or as you call it Marj Ibn Amer. They sold it to the Zionists before the Great War for an enormous profit. So why complain that the Zionists are stealing the land when Arabs are the ones who are stealing the land from under the feet of the *Fellahin* (peasants). I can safely tell you that every Zionist Settlement is built on land purchased from Arabs or the corrupt Ottoman regime."

Amina looked stunned.

"You see," he continued, "everyone blames the Zionists for grabbing land where in fact the Ottoman Government and local notables, as well as absentee landlords, have been and are continuing to be the real culprits in this matter."

He looked at Amina. His voice softened and he said, "Amina, you have brought light into my life. I wish you'd stop hating me for stealing your land, because..." He stopped. He wanted to reach out and touch her exposed hand, but the reality in front of him forced him to retract his move.

The afternoon sun touched her gently and gave her time to recapture her composure. She looked at him lovingly and said, "Imagine you are a gazelle. You live in a beautiful valley surrounded by low hills. You roam the land that many generations of gazelles before you grazed in peace. You are happy, content with your lot. There is no need to change the contours of the land or tamper with its vegetation. Everything is just good enough for you. No one threatens your well-being, and no one stands in your way. Without competition you roam the land, delighting in its bounty. When you are thirsty or too hot, irrespective of where you are in the valley, you can go to the spring to drink or cool off.

"One day a group of zebras takes up residence at the edge of the valley. The zebras are no friends of the gazelle. They do not want the gazelles on the land where they graze. They want the rich grasses all for themselves. So they chase the gazelles away when they cross their pasture. Each time a gazelle goes to the spring to drink he must cross the zebra's path. The zebra shows its agitation by jumping and kicking with his hind legs and always succeeds in blocking the gazelle's way. The gazelle is thirsty. He takes a long, circuitous trail to bypass the zebra's place. He reaches the spring exhausted and thirsty, but there stands the malcontent zebra and frightens him away.

"The gazelle can no longer graze wherever he likes. He is thirsty and cannot quench his thirst. He is hot but cannot cool in the refreshing water of the spring. What should he do? Should he abandon the land on which he grazes so happily? Should he crouch at the side of the trail and just die of hunger and thirst? How do you think the gazelle feels?

"The Zionists are the zebras. While the zebras took the land by force, you bought it. But the result is the same. You own the path to the spring.

And you own the spring. So you turn to the *Fellahin* and tell them to go away from your land. They have been working on the land for generations. No one stood in their way even when they did not have a deed to the land. Their landlord, as you have told me, lives in Beirut. Money is all he wants. Some of the land belongs to the government. As long as the *Fellah* pays the taxes to the state or the rent to the landowner no one blocks his way, he is happy with his lot.

"One day a handful of people come to the area. They have never worked the land but they say that many generations before them, their ancestors did. They go to the rich man in Beirut and offer him a generous amount of money for his land. He is happy and sells it to them.

"Then they say to the f*ellahin*, 'You can no longer graze your goats here. This is our land. Go someplace else.' What do you think that illiterate *fellah* thinks? He thinks that the Jews steal his land!"

Yossel was quiet. Deep in his heart he knew that she had a point, but that was not his experience in Hazohar. He said, "When we fenced the spring in Hazohar, we built special outlets for Beit A'yan's herds. We built special outlets for your people to draw water. We understood the plight of the gazelle. And what did your people do? They sabotaged our work and even attacked our guard."

"I plead ignorant to this story. I assume it is true, still it does not diminish the *Fellahin* plight," she retorted. "You fight for exclusive Jewish labor in the agricultural settlements, even though you know that the Arabs are more experienced and demand only rudimentary living conditions and minimal wages. When one buys a *dunam* of land and adopts the idea of exclusive Hebrew Labor, than the *Fellahin*, who have been working on that *dunam* must seek their livelihood elsewhere. The result is fewer Palestinians in the area. The more *dunams* the Zionists buy the more *fellahin* are displaced."

He had always felt uncomfortable with the results of the land-purchasing program but was willing to accept it for the higher principle of Jewish survival and the uninterrupted historical bond with the land. He was convinced that the redemption of *Eretz Israel* meant the transformation of *Eretz Israel* into a Jewish State with a Jewish majority. After all that was the Basel program. No one called it a state, but that was on everyone's mind. That presented an inherent conflict because both People wanted the same land as the destination of their national aspirations. Nevertheless, he had always thought that the purchasing effort should continue, even accelerated.

Yet now that Amina put the brutal reality in front of his face he struggled with his fervent support of the Zionists' enterprise to which he had dedicated his life since departing for Jaffa in 1912. Nevertheless, he concluded that if the Arabs did not like the results, they should put a stop to the land sale. As long as they didn't, Zionists would continue to buy. Their survival demanded it. Survival, not greed, trumps any anti-colonization moral code.

Amina brought him back to the table. "What are you thinking, Yossel?" she asked him gently.

"I like your allegorical story. I actually agree with you. You brought out a problem that has troubled me for years. But I must tell you that, however unpleasant the colonial effort of the Zionists is, the survival of the Jewish people is at stake not that of the Arabs. But, since you are here, we must not, and will never, *steal* your land. We will continue to buy it, work it and evolve as the Jewish nation just as you will continue to evolve as a part of the Arab nation. Regarding the *Fellahin*, they can go elsewhere. People throughout history have moved from place to place. Many Arabs from neighboring countries migrate to Palestine to enjoy the prosperity that the British and the Jewish capitals have brought."

"That is heartless," she protested.

"That has been our way of life for thousands of years. We must learn to live together in peace. There is plenty of empty space in this land, which includes the large area east of the Jordan River. You know, the Hashemite Kingdom of Jordan that the Brits so generously and arbitrarily carved out of your Palestine. If you want us out, direct your fight inward, against corrupt and greedy Arabs."

It was late afternoon. They walked quietly to the American Colony House. After a day of debate, Yossel was convinced more than ever that he was falling deeply in love with Amina. He moved closer to her. Although he knew it was forbidden, he touched her exposed hand flittingly as a bee buzzing an open flower before it settles on the one with the most nectar. She pushed her hand against his. Instantly their hands united in a tender embrace sending a heavenly tremor throughout their bodies. The two hands remained in their gentle embrace for a brief moment then they parted.

Amina and Yossel looked at each other and, in whisper, declared their love. Nothing more was said. They parted company at the gate of the American Colony House.

"See you next Saturday" she called after his retreating figure.

He turned and smiled. "Of course!"

He waited with anticipation all week. Sorke noticed his unending joy as he worked with added energy.

"Be careful, Yossel. What you do may end up poorly."

"I know, Sorke, but I am afraid to break this tie. I am its willing captive."

Early Saturday morning he repeated his usual routine. He arrived at the gates of the American Colony House a few minutes late. Amina was there waiting for him. She invited him in. "Let's sit in the garden."

They sat together enjoying the date-filled cookies she'd bought at the market. They talked and laughed and talked some more. She told him about her feelings, about her happiness. "Thoughts about you consume my day. But a dark cloud hangs above my happiness."

"A dark cloud?" he asked with sadness.

"Yes. What future do we have, Yossel? I wanted to stay indoors because I had a bad dream last night."

"Please tell me."

"I dreamed that someone who is not supposed to be where we are, would be there. And then the stories and the rumors will mount around us, will suffocate us, will drown our happiness."

"Dreams are only dreams, they just reflect our own thoughts. They do not predict the future."

He was a bit disturbed by her dream. He thought about Sorke's words earlier in the week but decided to direct their attention to a less private topic.

"Come, let's go for a walk."

Reluctantly, she agreed.

"Tell me about the upcoming National Women's Congress, Amina."

"I will be happy to, but I want you to know that I talked to a few of our National Women's Congress leaders about what you said regarding land sale. They agreed. One of them even mentioned her husband who, in a fit of anger, railed against 'those hypocritical vipers who poison the Palestinian National interests.'"

"I agree with him. Vipers are present everywhere. We combat ours. But no one among you curtails the activities of your vipers."

They walked slowly, oblivious to their surroundings. She spoke with affection about her volunteer work. She said, "I think that the Women's Congress has its roots with the many charitable societies our women have organized in Palestine. Those serve the need of the people. I have been a member of the Jerusalem Society for a few years. I can tell you that most of our members come from educated, wealthy, urban families. Many of whom are Christians. We do much charity work with orphan girls, village girls and needy girls in general. Our work focuses on educating them in Arabic and preparing them to enter the work force as teachers, government workers and nurses. I am proud to say that one of the girls that I was teaching is now a teacher's helper at the American Colony School.

"In addition we write pamphlets and distribute them in demonstrations alongside our nationalistic menfolk. You can say that Palestinian Women have entered the political fray. Now we are in a supporting role, but I assure you that we will become politically involved in our own right very soon. Our planned Congress will be the first step. We are focused on the support and promotion of the Palestinian National future and cohesion."

"I wonder what will be the congress' main emphasis. Do you know?"

"Yes. I have participated in plenary meetings so I have a good sense of the framework of the final draft resolution. You may not like them, but here are some of our concerns: First and foremost it is our goal to present our demands to the government. To that end, we plan to identify the most pressing nationalistic demands. We are concerned with the incredible tension that emanated from the Wailing Wall incident. Al-Buraq is part of the Haram al Sharif and must be declared as a Muslim property—"

"Pardon me, my dear, but the *Kotel* is already in the ownership of *Waqf*," interrupted Yossel.

"Well, we want to assure that it will remain a *Waqf* property in perpetuity. We oppose the Zionist project in Palestine. We want the nullification of the Balfour declaration, immediate cessation of Jewish immigration and land sale to the Jews. But as a Palestinian National Organization, we declare our support of the decisions of the Arab Conference. Indeed, you will find that many of our demands echo theirs. We are also interested in promoting women's unity, the spread of the Arabic culture, literacy and the end of police mistreatment of Arab prisoners."

"In the spirit of knowledge, or as you once told me, 'If I am to oppose Jewish presence in Palestine, as the upcoming Palestinian Women' Congress will most likely do, I want at least to know whom I am opposing.' Will you come to Hazohar to discuss the Women's Movement and its congress?"

"I will be happy to do so. Perhaps our love and friendship will encourage others to tone down their rhetoric."

As they walked back to the Colony House Yossel reached for her hand. She did not object. She locked her fingers with his, but avoided his eyes. She seemed shy and vulnerable. They walked in silence for a while then Yossel said, "Thank you for your explanation. I hope the black cloud from your dream has dissipated forever."

"Yes, my dear. I feel happy in your company." She squeezed his hand and said no more.

Yossel could sense her racing heartbeat. It matched his. He knew that a good hug would help calm their inner storm, but that was out of the question. Holding hands in public was risky enough. He slowly released his grip. "I love you, Amina," he whispered and rushed to catch the last train home.

20 A FRIDAY OF RAGE

Friday night was always a unique event for the Jews. Throughout many generations in the Diaspora, it was a holy night that separated the mundane from the sublime. It also provided folks with the opportunity to devote themselves to good food and merriment.

At Hazohar, it was also a festive occasion and, in a way, a holy one. For most members of Hazohar *Shabbat* dinner was a time of transformation. It separated the harshness of their workweek from *Shabbat*, a restive day devoted to social encounters, the pursuit of hobbies, occasional trips and most importantly, rejuvenation in advance of the recurring routine.

Most of Hazohar's members were secular, yet they elected to keep their lives connected to the generations that preceded them. *Shabbat* was as Jewish as the aspirations for Zion. It was an important link in the chain that bound Jews, wherever they resided, to the land of *Eretz Israel* and the Jewish nation.

They did away with the blessing and the Bible talk but kept the symbols: candles, wine, and *challah*, conversations, songs, and dances. The evening had always been a greatly anticipated event full of merriment and joy.

That Friday was especially important. Yossel's friend Amina was their guest of honor. She came to speak about the pending Women's Congress. But more importantly, she and Yossel wanted to open a venue to discuss ways to coexist in peace.

Friday was also a holy day for the Muslims. During the day, Mr. Abbasi, Amina's father, his wife and two daughters went to the local mosque to pray. Amina was absent. That Friday was especially poignant for them to show up in public, to quell the old rumors and whispers that had been reignited.

It started a few weeks earlier when Amina and an unknown man were seen on King George Street in Jerusalem. A week later a distant relative spotted the pair at a café in Jerusalem. That person reported his encounter to a friend from Amina's village. He embellished the story and told everyone that his friend saw Amina holding hands with a man and freely engaging in behavior that was unbecoming a Muslim woman. Rumors began to circulate in the village. They grew more and more vicious. Eventually, the family had no choice but to find out the truth. An uncle, who was an officer in the local police department, volunteered to follow Amina the following Saturday. And so he did. He discovered that she was indeed seeing a man. When they parted company he followed the man to Hazohar.

Mrs. Abbasi felt sick when she heard the news. "It was," she confided to her husband "as if our daughter thrust a dagger through my bosom."

Honor was the life blood and the fabric of life in the village. Without it, one felt abandoned, alienated from friends and relatives.

Mr. Abbasi had done nothing about it. His inaction added insult to injury. It was inexcusable.

Amina's unwed sisters were most vociferous in their constant protests. Their potential for matrimony was rapidly eroding. With a continuously expanding red stain on their family honor, their future was eternal confinement to their father's home: a one-way ticket to a miserable life. Not even their great beauty, which they told everyone was a gift from Allah in recognition of their modesty and respect for their parents, could help reduce their shame.

That Friday, the unsuspecting Abbasi family came across a petition signed by many relatives who lived in the village, as well as many who lived in the nearby town of Lydda. The petition, hung on the public wall for all to see, urged the father to restore the honor that had been tainted by Amina's intolerable behavior.

"How long must our innocent daughters suffer the shame of Amina's disgraceful and shameful act? Does Mr. Abbasi care for our family honor? Does he care for our religious and cultural sensitivities? We are all bound by honor. Without honor our family lives in disgrace. How long must we be the subject of humiliation and ridicule because of Mr. Abbasi's cowardly inaction?" asked the petitioners.

The public appeal went on to read: *A family member knows his proud tradition that promotes and respects the honor of the family. We all have daughters who behave in a modest way and honor their parents by their total obedience. A father's request of his daughter is her joy. She obeys his command with devotion and love, especially when it comes to selecting her future husband. A good daughter grows up knowing the meaning of chastity and modesty.*

Later, Mr. Abbasi learned that the same petition was on display in four other mosques in the village. It was the talk of the village after the Friday prayers. It was heard in every teahouse, in every cafe, in the market and at the barber shop.

An uncle, a police officer, approached Mr. Abbasi after the Friday prayer. He whispered in his ear, "Amina is in the Jewish settlement with a man."

There was no excuse to remain inactive. The facts were clear. The honor of the entire family was at stake.

The trip from his home to Hazohar would normally take twenty minutes. That early evening, Mr. Abbasi and his wife made it in ten. They were propelled by an overwhelming sense of rage that blinded their awareness of the road and their movements on it. They were lucky. They arrived at Hazohar before the guard closed the gate for the night. They did not slow down.

Mr. Abbasi pushed the gate and the two entered in the same frenzy. They continued their brisk walk toward the dining hall. The guard spotted them and ordered them to stop. Mr. Abbasi slowed down, but his wife pushed him on. They entered the hall. The air was filled with festive melodies. Everyone delighted in merriment, and no one noticed them. Mr. Abbasi hesitated at the door for a brief moment. The weight of his pending actions jolted his consciousness. Once again his wife pushed him forward. She was consumed with fury, obsessed by her quest to regain the family's honor. She could not let Mr. Abbasi falter. She spotted her daughter at the second table on the right and pushed her husband in that direction.

Mr. Abbasi launched himself toward his daughter with a deafening scream that filled the air with terror. At that moment the guard entered the hall, but he was too late to change the future that unfolded rapidly before his astounded gaze.

Mr. Abbasi assaulted Amina in an uncontrolled frenzy, stabbing her four times before Yossel and other people managed to restrain him. The third blow was a direct hit to her heart. Amina fell to the ground and died instantly.

The weight of his action fell upon him and he stood, unmoving, over the bleeding body of his daughter. Blood dripped from his hand. His gaze fixed at the ceiling, he seemed unaware of the commotion around him.

His wife collapsed to the ground by her daughter's side, sobbing without restraint. She cradled Amina's lifeless body in her arms and rocked back and forth. Lost between grief and pride, she kept on rocking and mumbling, "You destroyed our honor Amina. But your death restored it."

Yossel stared at his beloved Amina. He wanted to push her murderers aside, take her in his arms and speak to her. But Amina was hidden behind a visible curtain of madness. He stood by her side, helpless and dejected. *Destroyed our honor...destroyed our honor...* The words kept buzzing through his ears.

"Why?" he sobbed. "Why?" He looked around in a daze. Everything around him was spinning into nothingness. At last silence descended upon his soul.

A soft voice rose from the silence. "Sit down, Yossel. Please, sit down. You need to rest."

He felt a gentle touch on his shoulders. Someone was trying to lead him away from the gruesome scene.

He did not move. He wanted Amina's blood on his shirt so he could save her forever.

What is Honor? Does it seek death?

There were no answers. Just more and more questions.

After agonizing minutes, Sorke managed to move Yossel away. She led him to a chair and sat beside him, holding his hands. Once again, Yossel sank into deep melancholy.

A few men moved the Arab couple and locked them in a side room. Others covered the body with a tablecloth. Tova went to call the police. A few hours later the police and a medical team arrived to remove the evidence of the horrific action.

Both parents were swiftly arrested and tried. In spite of many calls for leniency from Muslim community leaders the couple was sentenced to death.

The villagers spoke of the evil British authorities that showed no sensitivity to local customs and culture. They praised the Abbasis as heroes, brave restorers of honor.

After months of grief, Yossel, with the help of his friends—Sorke, in particular—began slowly to recover, regaining his vigorous persona.

21 FERMENTING ANGER

"'Half a loaf is better than no bread' is a peculiarly English proverb; and, considering the attitude which both the Arabs and the Jewish representatives adopted in giving evidence before us, we think it improbable that either party will be satisfied at first sight with the proposal we have submitted for the adjustment of their rival claims. For Partition means that neither will get all it wants. It means that the Arabs must acquiesce in the exclusion from their sovereignty of a piece of territory, long occupied and once ruled by them. It means that the Jews must be content with less than the Land of Israel they once ruled and have hoped to rule again. But it seems to us that the drawbacks of Partition are outweighed by its advantages. For if it offers neither party all it wants, it offers each what it wants most, namely freedom and security."

Peel Commission Report, July 7, 1937, p. 394.

"...In November its report was published and revealed that no plan of partition could be evolved within the terms of reference which would, in the view of the members of the Commission, offer much hope of success.. The Peel plan was rejected and two possible alternatives were considered. Plan B would have reduced the size of the Jewish State by the addition of Galilee to the permanently mandated area and of the southern part of the region south of Jaffa to the Arab State. Plan C would have limited the Jewish State to the coastal region between Zikhron Yaaqov and Rehovoth while northern Palestine, including the Plains of Esdraelon and Jezreel, and all the semi-arid region of southern Palestine would have been placed under separate mandate. Two members of the Commission favored Plan C, one favored Plan B. and one declared that no practicable scheme of partition could be devised."

Anglo-American Committee of Inquiry- Appendix IV, Palestine: Historical Background, The Woodhead Commission, April 20, 1946.

"The objective of His Majesty's Government is the establishment within 10 years of an independent Palestine State in such treaty relations with the United Kingdom as will provide satisfactorily for the commercial and strategic requirements of both countries in the future. The proposal for the establishment of the independent State would involve consultation with the Council of the League of Nations with a view to the termination of the Mandate. ... After the period of five years, no further Jewish immigration will be permitted unless the Arabs of Palestine are prepared to acquiesce

in it...The independent State should be one in which Arabs and Jews share government in such a way as to ensure that the essential interests of each community are safeguarded."

British White Paper of 1939.

Somewhere near Kafr Nim, around Passover of 1936, a barrier blocked the road. It was constructed of stones, empty gasoline drums, and tree branches. Four men—disheveled, masked and armed—guarded the barrier. The bus stopped. The driver opened the door as if he had memorized the script of the unfolding drama. Two unkempt youngsters stormed the bus, shooting through the air and shouting, "Where are the Jew dogs?"

Sorke squeezed Itzhak's hand, pressed her body toward him as if attempting to melt into his sturdy frame. "Are we going to die?" she asked.

He had no answer.

Through the side window, they could see two men stopping every car, looting its occupants and scolding those who dared to protest, "Your money is a tax to support our war against the Jews and the British." They waved on cars with Arab passengers to continue their journey. One young man dragged a Jewish traveler out of a taxi. After a few vicious kicks in the abdomen, he left him moaning at the side of the road.

Meanwhile, the two scruffy assailants who had boarded the bus, pushed forward, collecting money and examining each face on their way. They stopped at the sixth row, glowering at two elderly Jews who trembled violently. One man shoved a gun into the ribs of the old man nearest him. He followed his menacing actions with a barrage of curses in Arabic, "Get out, you son of a whore!"

The Jews did not understand the words but reacted fearfully to the ominous gestures and menacing sounds. Passengers' screams filled the air. "Out, you sons of a bitch! Out, you Jew dogs." The young man grabbed his victim's hair and dragged him through the narrow path created by the willing passengers. The second man repeated the act, grabbing the other Jew. Their victims' faces contorted in horror.

Itzhak's instincts prompted him forward to aid the Jews, but a strong hand pulled him back to his seat. "Do not be a fool. They will kill you before you make your second step," warned a middle-aged man in Arabic. Itzhak resisted, but Sorke whispered in a demanding voice, "Slow down, Itzhak! He is right. You will never reach the front of the bus."

After dragging the pair outside, the two men returned to the bus. They stood near the driver and scanned the back seats for another moment before stepping out. Perhaps they were lazy, or satisfied with their prey, or fearful of the inevitable arrival of the police.

Itzhak and Sorke had no time to feel relieved before they heard the four men shout in unison, "Allahu Akbar!" God is great! They sprayed their three crouching victims with a barrage of bullets. In seconds, the gruesome murder was over. The assailants waved the bus on and disappeared into the alleyways of Kafr Nim.

The police arrived long after the sound of bullets had died out. They asked questions. Took notes. Cleared the road. Collected the bodies and promptly delivered them to the Jewish authorities in Tel Aviv.

A few hours afterward, shaken and pale, Sorke and Itzhak arrived at Hazohar. At dinner, they told their friends what had happened.

"This is just another act of intimidation. Those were malicious bandits," suggested Moshe.

Itzhak protested vehemently. "That attack was no robbery. It was a well-coordinated, properly executed harbinger of a new form of Palestinian violence. The Arabs hate us. I have been wrong. My Good-Neighbor principle has done little to abate their animosity. I declare it dead!"

Moshe did not react.

Gershon agreed. "How long will we continue the inefficient Restraint Policy? It is time we meet aggression with aggression!"

Moshe was irritated. He wanted everyone in Hazohar to toe the line of the Jewish Agency (the governing institution of the *Yishuv*). "Hazohar supports the Restraint Policy, Gershon," he admonished him.

"We are still free to disagree, Moshe."

"I agree! If I was armed, would I not act violently against the assassins?" Sorke asked. "Restraint has its limitations."

The discussion died out. No one was in a mood to discuss the issue further.

Next morning, thousands gathered in front of the central synagogue in Tel Aviv to attend the funeral of the victims. Gershon and Tova marched in front of a large contingent that vociferously demanded a retaliatory response to the bus terror. Somewhere along the funeral route, they met up with a larger crowd led by Moshe. It was equally boisterous in support of the Jewish Agency's Policy of Restraint. Tempers escalated.

For a brief moment, Moshe, Gershon and Tova faced each other flushed with anger. Animated voices cut down years of friendship. They were strangers ready to inflict physical pain on each other. People in both groups raised their fists. Hands flailing through the air, searching but subconsciously avoiding the targets that stood inches away. Civility was gone. However, their emotional disposition was fiercer than their physical willingness to fight with brothers. Luckily, the swelling crowd swept them apart.

Jewish anger spilled over into the Arab sections of Jaffa. Rumors of atrocities against Arabs near Kafr Nim passed from one agitated Arab to another. "Jews murdered Arabs near Kafr Nim," shouted one Arab to his neighbor. Roaming bands of youth escalated the tension throughout the night.

Dawn was the harbinger of a dramatic change in the future of *Eretz Israel*. Jews from Jaffa were rushing to work, as they had been doing routinely. A large, belligerent Arab crowd surprised them with unprecedented ferocity. The morning, which started innocuously, deteriorated rapidly into the bloodiest melee in the memory of the *Yishuv*. The streets of Jaffa were covered with Jewish blood.

Later, on April 20, 1936, Sorke wrote, *Britain is the conduit to fulfilling our national aspirations. We must show them that we are law-abiding people. Consequently, the Jewish Agency adopts the Restraint Strategy. The Agency argues that we are good people; we do not avenge atrocities, nor do we engage in preemptive strikes, or random acts of violence. Our actions are passive; we help the authorities to track down criminals and avoid pursuing them. Thus we can demand that the government give us the rights they have promised.*

Restraint? Rubbish! The Arabs translate restraint to cowardice. The policy makes them more audacious, more brazen. Reaction, not restraint must be an antidote to aggression. They cut down our orchards, and we do not pursue the offenders? Bandits torch our wheat fields, and we call the local police to give us justice?

I think Gershon is right; we must become more militant in protecting the Yishuv. Why? A new mode of Arabs' behavior toward us is emerging. They are more organized, better focused, more vicious in their attacks, more purposeful in their protest and more deliberate in their actions. The entire Yishuv is the target of their fury, not a random spot here or there. Itzhak's Good-Neighbor principle has not decreased their antipathy toward us.

***

The bus incident at Kafr Nim was the opening salvo of a well-coordinated rampage against the Jews and the British Authorities. The Great Arab Revolt began. It pushed the Palestinians, the Zionists and the British authorities to the edge of armed conflict. Arab national fervor overtook the docile farmers. Emotionally charged demonstrations, punctuated by murders, strikes, and closure of stores, beset the *Yishuv*. Arabs torched wheat fields, cut down forests and orchards. Irregular Arab militia roamed the countryside disturbing the public transportation and forcing a halt to public work. They threatened, and at times injured, reluctant Arabs, who did not join in the general strike. Overnight, life in Palestine transformed from the mundane to the perilous. Arab demands were unambiguous. Only the complete cessation of the Zionist project would restore the peace in Palestine.

The Arab Revolt brought the unity of the *Yishuv* to an abrupt halt. The rift between the Revisionists, who advocated aggressive response to Arabs' terror, and the majority of the *Yishuv*, who supported the Restraint Policy, had expanded beyond reconciliation. Within weeks, the *Irgun*—the armed underground force associated with the Revisionist Party—began a terror campaign against Arabs and British targets. Gershon, Tova, and approximately ten sympathizers disappeared periodically into the underground. Much occurred during their absence from Hazohar. Anonymous figures firebombed police stations and torched houses in villages near assault sites against Jews. Palestinian transportation was periodically curtailed. Always, a message was left at the scene: "Mayhem begets mayhem. Killing invites killing. Mourning prompts mourning." An ominous cloud hung over the land.

In Hazohar, social cohesion and camaraderie began to dissolve. Moshe and Gershon avoided each other when their paths crossed. A frozen, imaginary line cut through the heart of the kibbutz: the sympathizers of the *Irgun* congregated on one side while the adherents of the Jewish Agency's restraint policy gathered on the other. The divide cut deeply into Hazohar's soul, transforming yesterday's friends into bitter adversaries.

Itzhak maintained a cordial relationship with everyone. One evening he told Sorke, "I sense the imminent breakup of Hazohar."

She responded, "I think you are wrong. Many members of the *Haganah* (the military arm of the Jewish Agency) quietly lean toward Gershon's way of thinking. I am one of them."

The growing rift troubled Itzhak. He was increasingly edgy, unable to control a relentless sense of discomfort that crept into his consciousness *The Zionists' enterprise is under siege from the outside and from within. Nevertheless, it is not the Palestinian Arabs and their Great Revolt that worries me. A new, far more potent power than the Arab menace, a more destructive force than the Arab resistance, is marching across the land, trumping the inherent danger of Arab belligerence. The power is Jewish. The energy is Jewish, and the path it traverses meanders through the soul and the heart of the Yishuv.*

One morning as he and Sorke sipped their coffee, she asked, "I know that you are worried about the future of Hazohar, but is there anything else that causes your continuous gloom?"

"Yes, my dear. I sense a growing split within the Zionist movement; menacing signs of hostility between brothers. A conflict arises from the depth of our soul, to rip apart our project. Thus, possibly achieving what the Arabs had been trying for decades."

Britain was unable to bring the *Yishuv* and the Arab community into a peaceful coexistence. It regarded the mandate as a money pit, a resource guzzler, and a voracious consumer of political capital. And so, in June 1936 the British government created the Peel Commission and entrusted it with solving the problem of Palestine. Once again, commissioners listened to countless words, reviewed maps, and met with angry petitioners. Emotions grew high. In July 1937, the Commission recommended the partition of Palestine, promoted land and population swap between the *Yishuv* and the Palestinian population, and endorsed severe restrictions on immigration and a comprehensive prohibition of land transfer to the Jews.

The reaction in Beit A'yan, as in the entire Arab community in Palestine, was predictable: Palestine belongs to the Palestinians. Reject the partition plan.

The reaction in Hazohar, as in the rest of the *Yishuv*, was swift and emotional. Acrimonious debates over the recommendation erupted everywhere. Gershon summed up his position: "I reject the partition. The only acceptable boundaries of *Eretz Israel* must span the landmass east and west of the Jordan River. I also maintain that the single way to realize the Zionists' project is through armed resistance to the Arabs and the British authority. Furthermore, in light of the deteriorating conditions in Germany, I reject any curtailment on immigration. I find the British position on immigration and land purchases obscene. Actually, we must demand unfettered Jewish immigration and secure it by any means, including illegal immigrations safeguarded by arms, if necessary."

Moshe, without ever looking at Gershon, insisted that Hazohar must continue to toe the line of the Jewish Agency, which firmly believed in negotiation with the British government. "We, in spite of our antipathy to the Partition Plan that awards us a tiny fraction of Mandatory Palestine, settles us with a large number of Arabs and imposes upon us indefensible borders, must accept the principal idea of the partition while rejecting the specifics of the plan. Furthermore, we oppose armed resistance. We believe that it leads nowhere. We must reject random retaliatory actions and continue negotiating with the authorities."

"Moshe is right," Itzhak said. "Permit me to be a bit philosophical. The commissioners reached the right decision. The Arabs and we are two contradictory national movements. Both espouse ownership of the same land, both promote opposing aspirations. The commission was correct to state: 'Neither of the two national ideals permits any combination in the service of a single State.' I think we should conditionally accept the Partition Plan, even though we may disagree over the details."

At the end of the discussion, Hazohar voted overwhelmingly to accept the Jewish Agency's position.

Gershon stared directly at Moshe and spoke angrily, "This decision leaves us no option. It chases us out of our home."

Sorke and others were stunned. They appealed to him to calm down and reconsider his emotional outburst but to no avail. The next morning, twelve of Hazohar's members, led by Gershon and Tova, severed relationships with their home of more than twenty years and left to join the *Irgun*.

The Great Arab Revolt was in full swing when the British Government appointed a new Royal Commission, the Woodhead Commission, to implement the partition plan enunciated in the Peel Royal Commission, a half a year earlier. Hazohar, like the rest of the *Yishuv*, objected vehemently to the proposed partition's details and anticipated with trepidation, the commission's report, due later in 1938.

A few days after the Woodhead Commission issued its report, expressing skepticism on the viability of the partition plan, a member of the *Haganah* Central Command visited Hazohar. He came to recruit Yossel for the Central Command and Itzhak for the new Information Center. In a preliminary consultation with the Hazohar executive committee he told them, "Ominous threats to the *Yishuv* continue unabated. We believe that the possibility of an armed struggle to fulfill the Zionists' goal is imminent. The *Haganah* needs good people, with combat experience as well as the ability to form a trusting relationship with the Arabs. Yossel and Itzhak fit our need. We'd like them to join our ranks."

"If they agree, they are yours," declared Moshe. The others nodded in agreement.

Someone summoned Itzhak, Sorke and Yossel, who joined the conversation. After a detailed discussion of their roles, Itzhak asked in a jovial tone, "So, you want me to be a spy and a weapons depot guard?"

"Precisely. We trust your ability to handle both tasks."

Itzhak reflected on his dreadful experience when the Ottomans came looking for munitions at Hazohar. "That could be a serious business if the British police come looking for arms."

"Indeed," said the commander, "but so can an innocent walk across the street in Jerusalem during any Arab nationalistic furor." They laughed.

"I shall be delighted to work at the Central Command in any capacity you will define for me," said Yossel with pride.

"Moshe, we have an assignment for you also," added the commander.

"Go ahead."

"We want you to safeguard the munitions for the defense of your neighborhood. We also ask that you hide a small factory for armaments in Hazohar."

"We have the perfect structures for a hidden factory—our underground preservation storage—already in place. The munitions can be buried under the chicken coops. So, shall we agree?" he asked the committee.

"Without a doubt," they replied.

"What will be my contribution?" Sorke asked.

"You will teach at the Reali School, and your kids will study there."

"Okay, then, when do we leave?"

"Sometime next week."

Itzhak's family and Yossel spent a few days parting from old friends, "We will keep in touch," they said.

Itzhak rented an apartment in midtown Haifa. During the next few months, he supervised the organization of the new water pump center. Trucks unloaded boxes of merchandise; some were designated to his center and some for the underground arms depository. A special *Haganah* team arrived on designated nights, set up alert stations at each end of Sara Street, and proceeded to unpack and store the munitions.

Once the setup had been completed, Itzhak embarked on a two-week tour through the Arab and Jewish communities north and east of Haifa, in order to reconnect with old clients and establish a relationship with new ones.

The family acclimated to city life, quickly. They made new friends and kept in touch with old ones. Once a month, they met Gershon, Tova and Yossel at the workers' hall in Haifa. They celebrated Jewish holidays at Itzhak's apartment or in Hazohar.

Tirelessly, Itzhak collected information about Palestinian Irregulars, their plans and targets. In addition, he offered, and the Information Center's director accepted, a weekly summary of Arabic newspapers. Guarding the arms depot was a much easier task. Occasionally, a local police officer stopped in the center to check the place. Itzhak was a gracious host. They sat above the depot, sipped tea, and ate biscuits and the officer suspected nothing. They became friends.

***

The announcement of the White Papers of May 1939 transformed the life of the *Yishuv*. Gershon felt relieved and elated. "I tell you, my friends," he said, as he, Yossel and Itzhak strolled along the path to the summit of Mt. Carmel. "The publication of this nefarious book has just hammered the final nail in the coffin of the sterile Restraint Policy."

"I agree," Yossel said with a hint of disappointment. "The three years of the Great Arab Revolt have borne fruit; sweet to the Arabs, but poisonous to us!"

"I am glad we see eye to eye," Gershon reflected gleefully. "This policy paper is the greatest betrayal in our relationship with the British authorities. I have been saying for years, nothing will come of our Restraint Policy. Remember my clash with Moshe after the incident at Kafr Nim? By the way, we have never spoken since, what a shame! Anyhow, over the last twenty-two years Great Britain has managed to erode the value of the Balfour declaration. Now, this policy paper actually kills that declaration. We have been relegated to a subservient people. Our national aspirations were extinguished by London's fear of the continuation of the Arab Revolt while the world is rapidly tumbling toward the fire of Nazi aggression."

"Yes," Yossel lamented, "can you believe that the Arabs secured a veto over the number of people we can rescue from the threat of the Nazi regime?"

"No," said Itzhak, "I never imagined it. Alas, now this is the reality proclaimed in the new policy."

"The audacity of Great Britain has led to this flagrant, calculated move. Shame on us for tying our future to them," Gershon added.

Itzhak was silent. The story of Saadia bubbled once again into his consciousness as he recalled a statement of Mr. Ben-Gurion, the Chairman of the Jewish Agency.

"Somewhere I have read," he vocalized his thoughts, "that Ben-Gurion said, '*We are faced with the breaking of a promise and a surrender to Arab Terrorism. Thursday's demonstration was just the beginning of Jewish resistance.*'"

"Words are cheap. I want to see the actions. I will tell you one thing," Gershon said, "we are engaged in a major effort to bring Jewish refugees from Europe, in a flagrant violation of Britain's prohibition on immigration, enunciated in the White Paper."

"It seems that we are engaged in a similar effort," Yossel revealed.

They continued in silence until they reached the summit where they sat and looked at the bay of Haifa. It was closed to Jewish immigration. Ships loaded with refugees awaiting deportation were moored everywhere.

"Apparently we are not doing as well as we want. Thousands of European Jews are stopped at the gate of *Eretz Israel*, the path to freedom and safety, and are returned back to the talons of the Nazis," Yossel reflected gloomily.

"Sad, but true. Nevertheless we have managed to smuggle many refugees via Lebanon and by evading the naval blockade of our shore," Itzhak pointed out.

"Damn the English," said Gershon, "I think that if Iraq's oil pipeline had terminated in Lebanon, rather than in the Haifa's refinery, Great Britain would have abandoned us many years ago! That would have been good."

No one responded, but both men saw the merit in Gershon's profound but short analysis.

Meanwhile, the *Yishuv* was in an uproar over the White Paper. Stirring debates, angry demonstrations coupled with emotionally charged news articles took center stage in *Eretz Israel*. An adverse reaction to Britain swept the Jewish world.

Sorke observed the events with a keen eye. On June 20, 1939, she wrote, *the Peel Commission recommendations were impractical. The Partition Plan is dead!* The *Arabs' Revolt has yielded a victory of a sort to the Palestinians. They are happy with the latest British White Paper. It killed the Partition Plan, conditioned immigration on Arab consent, restricted land purchases and brought an end to the idea of a Jewish State... homeland? Yes, but within a Palestinian State. Grrr!! To think that Great Britain is our friend on whom we have pinned our national aspirations.*

I support the Jewish Agency. Nevertheless, it is time that we take our future into our own hands once again. We must accelerate the growth of the Haganah. It must become well-organized, properly trained, adequately equipped and achieve the highest state of readiness to fend off any Arab menace.

***

The Second World War obliterated people and material at an alarming pace; England was fighting alone, suffering enormous losses. In *Eretz Israel*, the British authorities ruthlessly implemented the new immigration policy; their coast guard cordoned the beaches and patrolled the high seas. Only a trickle of the thousands who yearned to escape from the conflagration in Europe made their way past the British dragnet. Many were caught and deported to jail-like camps in faraway lands. Others awaited deportation on the ships that brought them to *Eretz Israel*. Freedom was so close, yet so far away.

A short distance away, Yossel huddled with a few commanders of the *Haganah*, planning the implementation of a far-reaching decision by the ruling party of the *Yishuv*; preventing the deportation of the 1900 refugees aboard the Patria.

The liaison of the ruling party provided the background for the decision. "A fierce debate is going on in the Executive Committee," he said. "The activists view Britain's decision prohibiting the refugees to disembark, as a tragic conclusion that must be reversed. The only way to do so is by force."

"What does the opposition say?" asked Yossel.

"They feel that World War II trumps any belligerence against the British. We must negotiate and resort to legal and political pressure. The activists won the debate. Now I leave you to your planning. When you are ready please present your plans to the Executive Committee for their approval."

In the midst of the planning activities, Yossel and Gershon met for dinner. Yossel reminded him of their ascent to Mt. Carmel. "You criticized Ben-Gurion's statement after the issuance of the White Paper. You wanted actions not words."

"I remember. I have noticed that your party is divided. The activists want to ratchet up combat against the British while others continue to promote the defunct restraint policy. I am still waiting for action!"

"One is coming," responded Yossel. "I am not sure I like it, but I am up to my eyeballs in planning it."

"And what is it?"

"You must wait and see."

Gershon smiled. "I understand."

They talked about the land route from Lebanon. "We actively pursue smuggling refugees from Lebanon, but the cost is high and the success stories are few," Gershon said. "It is hard to breach the insurmountable land and sea blockades that the ruthless British authority erected."

"Yes, but I am involved in a plan to do just that," Yossel added cautiously, refusing to elaborate in spite of Gershon's requests.

"I must leave. I shall see you next week at Itzhak's apartment," Yossel said, giving his friend a bear hug before departing.

The first plan was to organize a general strike to protest the British intentions. That failed. The authorities did not alter their plan. They declared their intentions to deport refugees to Mauritius and keep them there until the end of the war. "It is the Government's opinion that they will neither stay in the colony nor be permitted to enter Palestine."

The *Yishuv* was enraged. Even Moshe no longer considered the Restraint Policy effective. He called for a general meeting in Hazohar. At the end, Hazohar's members declared, "We reject the Masada story. We have no desire to commit suicide before our enemies' eyes rather than be captured by them. We are fighting and will continue to fight to win. We insist on reversing the deplorable immigration policy of the insensitive British Government. Our brothers and sisters must be allowed to escape the Nazi threat and live freely in *Eretz Israel*." Moshe followed his declaration with a suggestion to organize a hunger strike to force the authorities' hands.

Meanwhile a rift in the ruling party was also felt in the *Haganah*. Yossel observed that at no point did he witness a complete unity in the *Yishuv*. "There are always competing opinions for every subject," he told Itzhak.

"For sure. But in spite of our differences we have been on a positive growth trajectory ever since we arrived in *Eretz Israel*. That is astonishing," answered Itzhak.

A few days later the planners received the final order from the executive committee; bomb the Patria to prevent the deportation. Yossel did not want anything to do with the plan. He requested permission to step down from the planning team. His request was granted. After a failed first attempt to ignite the bomb, they succeeded.

The enormity of the tragic consequences of fulfilling this order was evidenced after the boat capsized. 257 people died and 172 were injured.

"Did they miscalculate the explosion amount?" Yossel wondered.

The authorities moved the survivors to a temporary holding camp and eventually deported them to Mauritius. The newspapers were mute; they reported the blast, named the casualties but provided no clue regarding the perpetrators of the horrific event. Mourning descended on the *Yishuv*.

22 BROTHER AGAINST BROTHER

"...Lechi men murdered Lord Moyne, Britain's senior representative in Egypt, an act that lost the Zionists the friendship of one of their most important supporters, Winston Churchill."

Tom Segev, One Palestine Complete p. 457.

"To avoid bloody civil war at all costs—this principle, tempered in the sufferings of the 'Season,' we observed years later in the test of blood and fire of the 'Altalena.'"

Menachem Begin, The Revolt: story of the Irgun, p. 155.

The Second World War raged in all its fury but had little military impact on the *Yishuv*. After the Patria affair, the moderates in the executive committee prevailed. The *Haganah* supported the British war effort and avoided arms clashes. Not so the *Irgun*, which continued to attack the Mandatory Infrastructure.

Without any warning, the Mandatory police, in coordination with the army, embarked on a sweep for illegal arms throughout the *Yishuv*. They were aggressive in their pursuit and uncompromising in their deeds. One morning a police lorry pulled in front of Itzhak's center. Seven policemen jumped out. Two proceeded to block the western and eastern exits of Sara Street. One cut the telephone wire, and four approached the door. The sergeant knocked and demanded entry.

Itzhak knew what was on his mind. *I wonder who betrayed us to the police. If I live beyond this search, I want to find that cockroach and squash him under my heel.* He opened the door calmly. The sergeant was polite and asked permission to search the premises. "Sure, help yourself. But you must first have some tea and biscuits," he cajoled the policeman. And so it was, in that tension-filled moment on Sara Street, the group sat together and chitchatted while sipping tea.

Suddenly, the congeniality changed to confrontation. The sergeant overturned the table. Glasses, biscuits and tea scattered all over the floor. He moved into Itzhak's space. "Where is the door to the arms depot?"

"I have none here," responded Itzhak.

The policeman slapped him across the face with brute force. Itzhak lost his balance and staggered backward. The sergeant pushed him toward the wall and hit his stomach with his baton. Itzhak recoiled and screamed with pain.

"The door!" barked the officer.

"No arms here," he whispered through the pain. His mind carried him to the inn in Gordov where, as a nine-year-old boy, he stood up to the disheveled Tsar's policeman. He amassed all his inner strength, resolving to win this confrontation.

The sergeant was furious. "Search the premises, this is a war zone."

They ran through the center, sparing nothing. It took them minutes to ransack the place. They broke the walls, pulled the floor tiles, but found nothing. The sergeant hit Itzhak on his back. This time Itzhak bit his tongue in an effort to remain silent. He collapsed and lost consciousness. Outside, curious neighbors ignored the police guard and congregated in front of the store. When they realized what was going on inside, they began to demonstrate against police brutality.

The sergeant ordered his men out. "We'll be back," he shouted as he exited the shop.

The next day someone ransacked a small police station on the outskirts of Haifa. The two policemen on duty were beaten, hard enough so they could show and tell the story of the attack. It was Gershon with his unit, reacting to the events that nearly killed his friend. He pinned a message to a soldier's uniform warning the British: "Remember! Brutality begets brutality." They never returned to Itzhak's store.

There were rotten apples in the *Yishuv*; people who would sell their soul for the right price. The *Haganah* pursued them relentlessly. When they caught them, justice was swift. On some occasions, the verdict was a warning. Sometimes it was severe lashes. To pay for Itzhak's attack, it would be capital punishment. They searched for weeks and eventually found the stoolpigeon. A special team executed the man.

On November 8, 1944, the relationship between the Revisionist Party and the leadership of the *Yishuv* reached a boiling point. A high British official known for his anti-Zionist sentiment was assassinated in Cairo. The assassins belonged to Lechi, an extreme splinter group of the Revisionist Party.

Davar, the newspaper of the Jewish Agency, greeted the assassination of Lord Moyne with a blistering attack and an unmitigated threat, "Once, we were told that all Jews guarantee for one another...but those who excuse themselves from being a guarantor for the people, those who act against the hope of the people, those who endanger the destiny of the people, exclude themselves from that obligation. The people will reject those who reject the people."

A few days after the assassination, Gershon and Tova came to Hazohar to enjoy *Shabbat* with their friends. Yossel, Itzhak and Sorke came along. Moshe was visibly absent. David and Dina hosted the friends.

They drank tea and munched on biscuits at Dina's flower garden. A wintry crisp day did not chase them indoors, nor did it curtail their conversation.

As usual, they talked about their lives, their families, and general issues of the *Yishuv*. After many pleasantries, Gershon abruptly changed the subject.

He asked rhetorically, "Do you know why I continue to advocate an aggressive posture toward the Arabs and the British authorities? Because both speak to us in militant monologues; both act against us with aggression. Because a militant language elicits an immediate reaction, as was the case of the Great Arab Revolt. Did it not bring them the White Paper that put a death wreath on the Balfour Declaration along with more than twenty-five years of negotiation to implement it? Because they only understand an aggressive response to their aggressive behavior. Did they threaten you again, Itzhak, after I raided their police station?"

"No."

"They got the message."

"At times militant language works, but the latest assassination gave the police the incentive to double their effort to discover illegal arms and disturb our effort to improve the defense force," Yossel protested.

David added, "Your aggression against Arabs and British police increases the internal division in the *Yishuv*. You alienate the British authorities at the time they are fighting Hitler. And you negate the idea that we need the support of the British government and the support of the British public opinion to bring our objective to fruition. By the way, I have heard that Churchill is livid about the assassination in Cairo; it was a militant language, was it not? We cannot afford to lose Churchill's support."

"What has Britain done for us during twenty-five years of negotiation?" Tova asked. "Did they open the gates of *Eretz Israel* to allow us to absorb European Jewry, while it was still possible to escape the German's ovens? How about the last Policy Paper? Did it show friendliness to our cause? No!"

"We know that eventually we will have to fight. However, now, as World War II rages on, is not the time. We must focus on preparation activities: buying arms, producing arms, hiding arms, training future soldiers, etc. That is what I do," said Yossel.

"I agree," said Tova. "That is what you do. You have the means. We do not. So we fill in the void that your wasted energy of pursuing the bankrupt Restraint Policy leaves behind. When will be the time to fight the British authorities? What if the *Irgun* went into hibernation at the beginning of the Arab Revolt and awoke just before the 'friendly'

British government issued the White Paper of 1939. Would that enable the Jewish Agency to prevent its publication? Of course not!"

They continued the conversation in a friendly and respectful manner unlike the general tone of conversation in the *Yishuv*, yet Moshe's absence escaped no one.

When it was time to leave, David pulled Gershon aside and led him to the edge of the garden. There he asked, "Did you read *Davar* on November the 8th?"

"Yes, it hinted at a despicable act that could incite a civil war."

"Moshe told me, in confidence, that there is a formal decision by the Jewish Agency to execute the spirit of that threat by insisting that the *Yishuv* adheres to four demands regarding the members of Lechi and the *Irgun*. These are: One, expel those members from the community. Two, give them no shelter or hiding places. Three, give them neither monetary support nor yield to their threats and blackmail. Four, help the British authority to prevent terror and to dismantle these two terrorist groups."

"Thank you for the warning," said Gershon. On his way home, he told Tova, "A Hunting Season has begun. The public is instructed to hunt us down like animals. The murder of Lord Moyne brought the Jewish world against us. Even so, our method is right. It will force the British to end the Mandatory grip on *Eretz Israel*. They will never break our spirit."

A few days later, members of the *Haganah*, on a voluntary basis, began cooperating with British authorities in finding and imprisoning *Irgun*'s soldiers. Yossel elected to excuse himself from the hunt. He spoke to Itzhak about the need to hide Gershon, Tova and their young boy. Itzhak agreed. On the next day, he contacted the Tova and insisted that they move in with his family. "While I understand the motivation behind this hunt, I think it is a contemptible act. I want your family to be safe. Move in with us. We will shelter you from betrayal," he told his friends.

In three months of an open season on members of Lechi and *Irgun*, the authorities, with an overt collaboration of the *Yishuv*, arrested hundreds of people. Prisoners were deported to jails in Africa. The leader of the *Irgun* managed to evade both the *Haganah* and the police dragnet. From his hiding place, he delivered a stern message to his organization. "Do not resist! We must avoid fraternal war!"

After months of hiding, Gershon, angry but never bitter, resumed his activities with a weaker but not strangled *Irgun*. The *Haganah* was moving rapidly closer to his longstanding position; a war against Britain. It was time to end the British Mandate! The devastated Jewish community of Europe provided the impetus for the accelerated march toward statehood. It was time for the *Haganah* to adopt a stronger, more militarist stance against the authorities.

***

On November 30, 1947, Sorke wrote, *tension in Eretz Israel grew rapidly; the Yishuv, as disjointed as it was, continued to gnaw at the exhausted British authorities. Militaristic actions intensified and so were the diplomatic efforts on behalf of the Zionists' project. Finally, the voice of diplomacy was louder than the guns.*

Yesterday, the Long March of the Jewish people reached its final mile. I was there, and so were Itzhak and the rest of the Yishuv. We walked at the head of the procession; with tears of joy in our eyes, with an exuberant Hatikva on our lips (much like our last day on the boat to Jaffa, in 1912), and the Star of David flag in our hands. We marched on the streets of Tel Aviv, celebrating the United Nations Resolution 181, which proclaimed the partition of Palestine and defined the boundaries of an independent Jewish State.

I can safely say that at no time during the history of mankind had such a march ever been attempted. It was the confluence of a long history of continuous yearning for Zion, our tenacious dedication to reawaken the dormant nation; our indefatigable energy for reviving its land, inexhaustible diplomacy and investment of Jewish capital, and the timely application of hawkish military actions that brought the Yishuv before the United Nations General Assembly, which reaffirmed the birth certificate of the Jewish people that was given to Abraham on his journey to Canaan.

Itzhak's happiness was curtailed by his pessimistic view of the immediate future. "Israel was built for the Jewish people by Jewish capital, political support and labor. Thus, Israel is a Jewish state. Do the Muslim Arabs like us? No! "There will be a ferocious war," he told me. "They will fight us to drain our will or until our strength overcomes them. It will be a war initiated by Muslims against the Jewish people. The mighty will prevail to the end of time."

***

On May 14, 1948, eight hours before the British flag was lowered for the last time, Itzhak and his friends assembled in front of the Museum of Tel Aviv. Itzhak and Sorke were determined to restore the peace between Moshe, Tova and Gershon. They shared their plan with all their friends, who were eager to cooperate. When they saw Sorke taking Gershon's hand in her left and Tova's in her right, they formed a circle around them. Itzhak took Moshe's hand and pulled him into the circle. There he spoke to the three, "Today our dream has become a reality. We achieved it together, and jointly we must defend and nourish its future. I ask that you abandon the bitterness of the past and look forward with optimism. Now is the time to renew and reaffirm our love for each other."

Tova cried and hugged Moshe, who was reluctant at first, but soon returned the love of his friend. The circle closed in on the center pushing Gershon, Moshe and Tova, Itzhak and Sorke into each other's arms. They stood at the center in a strong embrace shedding tears of joy. Past animosity melted away. They were whole again. Then they sat on the pavement crying and laughing until David Ben-Gurion, the newly elected Prime Minister of Israel, read in a voice that quivered with emotion, the Declaration of Independence of the State of Israel.

The country exploded with joy. But it was short lived. The Muslim Middle East did not wait to read the details of the resolution. A moment after the Union Jack was lowered for the last time, Muslim irregulars from the UN designated area for the Palestinian state, and Arabs who resided in the areas of the Jewish state, streamed into the new state of Israel, joining Muslim soldiers from, Lebanon, Syria, Iraq, Trans-Jordan, and Egypt. Saudi Arabia, Yemen, and Pakistan sent expeditionary forces to support them. *Eretz Israel* was once again embroiled in an armed conflict. For the Jews, it was an existential battle. For the Arabs, it was a war to protect the continuity and the Muslim character of the vast territory they had inherited after the fall of the Ottoman Empire.

Once again, the Arab world challenged the existential right of the Jewish people. It protested the partition and the creation of the Jewish state. It rejected the inimitable march of the Jewish people to assert their inalienable rights. Once again the Arabs stood on the losing side of history. They would lose a war they had started and would call their defeat Al Nakba (the disaster). As always, they sought to incriminate others for their persistent failure to choose the right path to a productive future for their people.

***

Shortly before the UN resolution, Gershon sailed to France to train scores of Jews, remnants of Hitler's death camps, who volunteered to join the *Irgun's* push to end the British Mandate. He also supported a clandestine effort to acquire arms and military equipment, and transport it to the *Irgun* forces operating independently within the nascent state of Israel. On June 12, 1948, he boarded the *Altalena,* which set sail to Israel during the first UN supervised ceasefire in the War of Independence.

The government of Israel was embroiled in an intense debate over the future of the *Altalena*. Since Yossel was assigned to the general command, he could hear the discussions becoming progressively heated. At stake was the ownership of the cargo of the *Altalena* "The overriding question," said the commander of the Israeli Defense Force (IDF), "is simple yet complex. Who prosecutes the ongoing war with the Arabs? There is only one answer; one army, under one chain of command, responsible for all the soldiers and armaments they need. That army is the IDF, as commanded by the Prime Minister of Israel. It is that simple. What causes the complexity is that the leadership of the Revisionist Party has other ideas regarding the chain of command and thus the manner of distributing the men and materiel on the *Altalena*."

Yossel's commander instructed him to move to Kfar Vitkin, where he took command of one of the IDF units, which was awaiting the arrival of the ship. His orders, while straightforward, caused him much consternation. "The cargo of the *Altalena* must be surrendered to the IDF."

"This is crazy! What if they refuse? This, then, becomes the shortest path to a civil war. How can I tell young Israeli soldiers to aim their guns on a ship full of Jewish volunteers?" he protested. "Surely we can think of a non-lethal way to take possession of the cargo."

"Suggest one," replied his commander. "You know that we have been negotiating the fate of the ship for days. And what have we to show for our investment? Nothing! Do you think I like to aim my guns at my kin?"

"No. But you command it anyway."

"Correct. We are in a perilous time. We are in the midst of an existential war for the fate of the Jewish nation. The overriding question," said the local commander, "is simple: Who fights the war with the Arabs? There is only one answer: the IDF, not the *Irgun*. Period!"

"I understand and agree. But will you consider the moral implications inside world Jewry, and among the nations around the world when, shortly after Hitler's ovens were extinguished, we continue his murderous behavior by killing even a single survivor of his death camps?"

"I see your point but we can justify this short term aberration for a much greater cause, with a much longer term implications. We also need recognition of the countries of the world. Will they recognize a state that does not have a full jurisdiction over its army? I doubt it. Remember, the prime minister dismantled other irregular units that operated under a separate chain of command and integrated them with the IDF."

Yossel was quiet for a moment. He recalled the debate in Egypt when Trumpeldor accepted a non-combat role. His justification was that there were many ways to serve the Zionists' cause. At last he broke his silence. "What we need is a face-saving solution for the leadership of the *Irgun*. Perhaps we should give them the arms they need to equip their newly formed brigade in Jaffa but insist that once fully equipped they must surrender their equipment and swear allegiance to the IDF?"

"We have tried that but failed. So now we have no choice. We must secure the cargo by any means."

Outside, on the beach of Kfar Vitkin members of the *Irgun* meandered slowly while awaiting the arrival of the *Altalena*. Yossel approached the local *Irgun* commander and said, "The beach is surrounded. All the roads are blocked and there are enough IDF units to ensure the integrity of the cargo and its transfer to the IDF."

"It is our cargo. We have an agreement with the IDF to direct twenty percent of it to our battalion in Jerusalem."

"That is fine if that battalion integrates with the IDF," said Yossel, "but we'll take the rest."

"We raised the money, discovered willing sources, put our men in harm's way to acquire the material, and now you want to take it from us?"

"Yes!" Yossel said. "We will not have an army within an army. There is only one chain of command in any army, anywhere."

Yossel was summoned back. His commander had received new orders from the Israeli Government.

He handed Yossel a new message and asked him to deliver it to the commander of the *Irgun*, who was on the beach. It was an order for an unconditional surrender of men and materiel. It threatened an immediate use of all means at his disposal to ensure compliance. He gave the commander ten minutes to comply with the ultimatum and told him that he alone bore the responsibility for refusing to comply.

Yossel delivered the ultimatum and waited for a reply, but it was not to be. The ultimatum was considered an insult. Uncontrolled anger was followed by recalcitrant voices.

"Tell him no!" A few folks from Kfar Vitkin tried unsuccessfully to calm the angry man. Tempers flared. Someone opened fire. It was not clear who did, but it was enough to open the gates of hell. Brothers were fighting brothers. The fire exchange was short and intense.

There were immediate casualties to both sides. Members of Kfar Vitkin tried again. With everyone in a daze over what unfolded before their eyes they negotiated a ceasefire. The *Irgun* personnel collected their dead, left the wounded with the IDF medics, and withdrew to the *Altalena*, which set sail to nearby Tel Aviv.

Yossel looked at the beach in disbelief. "This must not continue," he told his commander.

"It will if they do not surrender. We must win or we might as well give up the IDF. And with it all the progress we have made toward fulfilling our national destiny. Let's move our forces to Tel Aviv."

They arrived before the ship. Many Israelis gathered on the beach a short distance from the opposing soldiers. They were riveted to the unfolding drama, speculating on the possible fate of the boat. The commander of the *Irgun* issued an order to surrender, but it was too late. The IDF, after receiving an order from the prime minister of Israel, began shelling the boat. One shell scored a direct hit. The boat caught fire. People from the beach, Yossel and his soldiers among them, rushed toward the ship to help evacuate its passengers.

Yossel stretched his hands to accept a body that was lowered from the upper deck. He moved swiftly away from the burning ship. A short distance away, he paused. He looked at the dead man in his arms. A violent, agonizing scream escaped from his mouth, as he stood knee-deep in the water of the Mediterranean. He was carrying the dead body of his friend Gershon, who had come back to a home he would no longer feel or see. At the beach, Yossel collapsed on the wet sand and sobbed uncontrollably.

The great fire consumed the hull of the *Altalena*, as the nation stood a short distance away. Thick, dark plumes of smoke rose to the heavens sending messages of gloom. But from bitterness sweetness came. A last-minute effort to inject sanity into the fruitless dispute united the Revisionists and the Government of Israel. A new message came from the dark plumes: the Nation of Israel lives. A civil war was averted in the middle of an existential war, the War of Independence.

Yossel brought Gershon's body to Hazohar for burial. He stood at the graveside, despondent and morose. Before they lowered the casket, he bent next to it and lingered with his lips on the Israeli flag that concealed his friend. Tova saw his lips move as he cried but heard none of his words.

***

After the war of independence, Hazohar continued to prosper. The kibbutz absorbed immigrants from all corners of the globe. By 1955 it boasted over five hundred adult members and three hundred children and teens, who enjoyed superb educational facilities from kindergarten to high school. Graduates could choose to continue their education at the Hebrew University.

Members worked hard and enjoyed a rich quality of life filled with athletic amenities, cultural and social events, and healthy food. The kibbutz was esthetically beautiful. Gardens filled the public spaces.

Hazohar produced agricultural products second to none: cheeses, butter, fruits, eggs and vegetables.

All the original forty, who started Hazohar in 1913, were marching proudly on the path from middle age to the world of senior citizens. Most of them still resided in Hazohar. Those who lived elsewhere came to Hazohar periodically to visit friends and to partake in the memorial service to fallen comrades. Every two years, just before Passover, the remnants of the original forty reunited for a fun-filled day; sometimes in Hazohar, other times in Haifa, Rishon, or Petach Tikva.

Itzhak and Sorke lived in Haifa. They had two children. The eldest, Baruch, named after a fallen friend, was shot and killed in 1948 during the campaign to defend the Hadassah Hospital in Jerusalem. He was eighteen at the time. Their younger son, Gershon, named after his grandfather, Reb Gershon, who died of natural causes and was buried in Hazohar near his wife Bella, returned to Hazohar after he graduated from the Hebrew University. He married and had three children. Nilli, the oldest, was Itzhak's favorite. So strong was their bond that Itzhak entrusted her with his life story. She was happy to be his confidant and editor.

David and Dina continued to split their time between Hazohar and Jerusalem, where he was the head of the Infectious Disease department and she was the head nurse at the Emergency Room. One of their two children was killed during the war of independence.

Moshe and Alexa remained in Hazohar. They had one child. Moshe worked for the Prime Minister's Office. She headed the Agronomy Department at the Hebrew University of Jerusalem. While not at the University, Alexa maintained Hazohar's green spaces.

Yossel lived in Tel-Aviv. He climbed the officers' ranks of the IDF. As a general he enjoyed a varied and satisfying career. His last assignment was at the office of the prime minister as a liaison between the prime minister and the IDF. He never remarried.

Tova lived in Hazohar. She was in charge of Hazohar's educational institutions. She never remarried. Her only son was killed during the Suez campaign in 1956. He left a wife and two kids.

Ribi and Avram remained in Hazohar. They had three children, all married with kids of their own, all resided in Hazohar. Avram was the chief engineer in a large construction company. Ribi continued to run the food services in Hazohar.

During the war of independence, the unfriendly Beit A'yan became belligerent. It served as a base for vicious attacks on Hazohar and for maintaining the road to Jerusalem under constant siege. Eventually, during the campaign to open the road, the IDF swept through the village.

After a tenacious fight with Irregular Palestinians and the Arab Legion command by Glubb Pasha, an Englishman, the IDF won. When it was over, all the residents were pushed out east and Beit A'yan was bulldozed into nothingness.

23 BUS NUMBER 37

On a late sunny morning, a week before Passover of 1974, Itzhak boarded bus number 37 to the Workers' Hall in midtown Haifa. At eighty, frail but of lucid mind, he went there to meet a few of his surviving comrades, as he had done for years. Nilli accompanied him. Sorke had to do last-minute errands but promised to join the reunion before noon.

They arrived early. No one was there. "You see, Grandpa, there was no need to rush me. I had plenty of time to put on my makeup," Nilli chided him with a broad forgiving smile.

He apologized. "You know how anxious I am to see that everything is ready when my friends arrive. After all, I am the host." She gave him a bear hug and said nothing.

She set up the chairs in a circle, brewed the tea and put out the tea sandwiches on the table alongside the chocolate wafers Itzhak had brought especially for Moshe and Avram. "They are addicted to the stuff," he said and then put an empty plate on the table. He was addicted to poppy seed cake and was sure that Ribi would bring it as she always did.

They sat and examined the familiar surroundings. The paint was peeling everywhere: on the walls, the ceiling, the window frames. Years of dust covered the light fixtures. The shutters were in ill repair, and a few windowpanes were cracked. The stone floor, the chairs, the wall clock and the teakettle belonged to a bygone era.

Yet, with all its blemishes the hall held a special place in his heart. It was a simple, unadorned room, similar to those in Rishon, Petach Tikva, and Hazohar. It served as the center of his cultural, social and political universe during his life in *Eretz Israel*. They were the places for celebrations, dances, and political discussions—sometimes heated and divisive. Wherever he was living, he and his friends gathered at a Workers' Hall to rejoice in their togetherness.

"You know, dear," he told his granddaughter, "these halls were more than friends. They were like family to me and to most of the men and women who pursued the Zionist program in *Eretz Israel*."

The peeling walls had shared in their sad and happy moments, listened to eulogies for departed friends and toasts for special anniversaries. And even though the modern Workers Union ignored the hall, it remained a storehouse of good memories and a monument to enduring friendships.

So many years had passed since he had begun his journey. Many of his friends had capitulated to the difficult reality of *Eretz Israel* and left in pursuit of a better life, an easier life, somewhere in the world, away from the constant hardships. A few died young, but their memory lived on. Lately, an increasing number had succumbed to old age or illnesses. Eventually, their numbers dwindled to a few dozen, now in their eighties.

Aside from sporadic visits, life in the state of Israel kept them apart. But when they retired, in the late fifties, Moshe finally succeeded in organizing their biennial reunions that he'd promised at the end of their first reunion. They had agreed to gather at an alternate Worker's Hall in Hazohar, Tel Aviv, and Haifa once every two years to chat, drink tea, debate and reminisce.

"This reunion month is a special one," said Nilli. "It is your eightieth birthday. That is awesome, Grandpa. Sixty-two years ago you stepped onto the dusty streets of the port of Jaffa and took your first breath of *Eretz Israel*'s air. I am happy for you."

"Thank you."

She smiled.

He acknowledged her smile with a smile of his own and said, "Yes, I remember how light I felt, how joyous, as if two thousand gloomy years of tears, cruelty, ridicule and hate, had dropped off my shoulders. Believe it or not, Nilli, I felt as if I was the Jewish nation, emerging from the cold darkness of the Diaspora, taking its first hesitant step on the shore of the Promised Land. For the third and final time, the Nation of Israel reunited with its land."

"Bravo!" she cheered him. "I love this sentiment." While she knew he would continue, she secretly was hoping that this time he would skip the rest of the story. He read her mind and said, "Abraham is pivotal to the relationship of the Jewish nation with *Eretz Israel*. Without objections, he followed God's command to leave his father's home and follow him. God rewarded his absolute obedience with a covenant. That was the birth certificate of the Jewish nation. On the day they reached Canaan, God reiterated and upgraded his original covenant. He bequeathed the land to the Jewish nation. That was our eternal deed for and the everlasting bond with *Eretz Israel*. That was the first link in the unbroken national chain that is anchored in *Zion*."

"You know, Grandpa," she interrupted his tale, "even though I am not a religious person, I accept the relevancy of that covenant. After all, the Bible is our ethos, our national history, in addition to being our sacred lore. Moreover, both Christianity and Islam consider our Bible as Holy Scripture. They, by definition, must believe in the Abrahamic covenant."

He smiled and continued. "On three occasions, history witnessed the break-up and restoration of that bond. In the first two, God's will alone brought us back to *Zion*. In the last time, after the Romans expelled us from the land, our will and tenacity as people, irrespective of the inordinate obstacles we faced, brought us back. At last, the Jews took their national destiny into their hands. The Jewish nation rose from its deathbed and began the final journey of its national revival. I am a part of that journey."

"I am proud of you, Grandpa. You and your friends, not God, have been at the helm. You, not God, have reawakened the old nation."

"Thank you. I was more like a worker bee tirelessly going through its daily chores to help the building and the growth of the colony."

"Maybe," she said, "but without your sacrifice, your leaders, who spent much time locally organizing the movement or abroad, attempting to raise money and international support for it, would not have succeeded in bringing about the Jewish national reawakening. My generation will not disappoint you. We'll continue what you have started."

Itzhak did not react. He mused to himself. *How perceptive she is. She is our future; the next link of our national chain that binds the Jewish nation to its birth place. I can safely pass the torch to her generation. It understands our story, it's history.*

Sorke arrived just as they concluded their conversation and minutes before people began to trickle in. A few needed the help of a cane; others came with a member of their family. Tova came with her grandson. She looked healthy and strong. Itzhak thought that, considering their age, everyone except Yossel looked good. Yossel looked a bit somber. He brought a large envelope stuffed full of papers.

Itzhak and Sorke greeted their friends. They exchanged warm hugs then sat down and chatted quietly. By twelve-forty everyone had arrived.

Itzhak said, "We should observe a moment of silence for the memory of all our friends, especially Gershon, Kalman, Baruch, and my sister, Rachel. They were honest, dedicated, zealous people, who doggedly pursued the cause and paid the ultimate price for it. They are forever a part of us."

They bowed their heads in silence to honor their deceased comrades. Tova asked Avram to say the *Kaddish* (mourning prayer). At first, he was unresponsive. He seemed to be in another world. When she repeated her request and accentuated it with a light squeeze of his arm, he shook faintly as if returning from a long journey.

"Wha...wha.. what?" he stammered.

"Please recite the *Kaddish*," she asked again.

In a weak voice, he said the prayer. When he finished, everyone said "Amen," and Nilli served the special sandwiches she had made. Their delicious flavor brought everyone back to the present.

Someone started to sing. The others joined. Weak voices bounced off the peeling paint, a bit off-key, but the tunes were recognizable nevertheless. Their faces shone with delight as they clapped their hands to the rhythm of the melodies. Nilli felt that they were magically transformed to a long-gone place when, after a lengthy and arduous workweek, they converged on the Worker's Hall in Petach Tikva or Hazohar, to sing and dance and revel in merriment.

Avram invited Ribi for a dance. They moved hesitantly but happily. Sorke looked upon the couple and thought *they are still in love, how wonderful*. She looked at Itzhak and thought *so are we!* She asked Itzhak to dance. Others joined. After the dancers stopped to rest, she served the poppy seed cake with tea. They all cheered, "Happy Birthday, Itzhak."

In between eating and singing and dancing, everyone took turns telling stories about the early days at Hazohar, their families, and more. Hours of merriment and warm camaraderie had passed, when unexpectedly Yossel became very agitated, as if a floodgate opened to free his pent-up emotions. With a shaking, sad voice, he addressed Tova, "My dear friend," he said, "a terrible secret has burdened my heart. I must reveal it and ask for your forgiveness."

She looked at him anxiously. "Please do not scare me, Yossel."

"I was in Kfar Vitkin, commanding one of the units that fired on the Altalena. Later, in Tel Aviv, I carried Gershon's body ashore. I have suffered for years thinking that I could have been responsible for his death. Please forgive me." He burst into tears. At once a somber mood descended upon them.

"Those were turbulent days, Yossel. There was more than one way to serve the Zionists' project. Occasionally, we clashed. Besides, you did not know he was there. There is nothing to forgive, my dear friend. I have always been proud of our friendship." She rose from her chair and approached Yossel. The two hugged and cried.

There was a sense of relief, but it was short lived. Yossel continued in a gloomy voice, "What have we done? We created a Jewish island in a sea of hostile Muslims. We extricated our nation from the lasting darkness of the Diaspora, just to plunge it into the tight grip of new and potentially everlasting calamitous circumstances."

Itzhak sensed the underlying pain in Yossel's voice. When he felt the light touch of Sorke's hand, he knew that she shared his feeling.

"Why are you so upset my friend?" asked Ribi as she put her hand gently on Yossel's shoulder, pulling him slightly toward her.

"I am sorry," he replied. "Last month I was diagnosed with terminal cancer. The doctor insisted on chemotherapy. I declined. When my time comes, I want to die with dignity. So, please do not say anything about my illness. Since my diagnosis, my past is replaying repeatedly before my eyes. I have been overwhelmed with thoughts about my life in *Eretz Israel*. I put them all down in these papers. Nilli," he turned to Itzhak's granddaughter. "I want you to have them. Kind of an informal history of a friend of your grandparents."

Nilli took the envelope, hugged Yossel and said, "If you only knew how happy you have made me. I shall cherish it. Thank you."

Yossel gave her a loving hug. He turned to his friends and said, "I just want to ask one question. Have we wasted our lives?"

The news was abrupt and hard to swallow. His question startled them. It sounded as if a stranger was talking. He was calm, in a sharp contrast to his agitated demeanor minutes earlier. For a while, they remained speechless. No one knew how to react or what to say.

Alexa broke the silence. She wandered slowly toward the teakettle and said in an attempt to change the subject. "Not everyone wants to engage in this serious discussion. I assure you that I am one of them. Ribi, you have never told us how Avram proposed. Please tell."

Ribi smiled and started to talk when Avram protested gently, "Ladies, Yossel's question deserves an answer. Please do not change the subject." Reluctantly, Alexa withdrew her objection and returned to her seat near Moshe.

Ribi touched Avram's hand and said, "I guess you are saved for now."

Sorke refocused the discussion. "Yossel, you have always been a brave man. Your contribution to the Zionists' program is unassailable. I love you. We love you and will respect and support your decision."

Everyone nodded in agreement. One by one they rose and approached Yossel to embrace him with a hug that carried many years of friendship in its energy. When they returned to their seats Nilli served more tea and chocolate wafers.

Then Sorke continued. "I will not lie to you. I, too, am troubled by the relentless belligerence of the Arabs, but I assure you that the 'calamitous circumstances' you speak of are manageable. Even though the local Arabs have terrorized our life for nearly one hundred years, our nation managed to grow in spite of their nefarious deeds. Look around you and marvel at our cultural, intellectual and economic achievements. We have done well. Be proud: you have done well! You do not need to question the value of your life."

"I'd like to add a few words," said Dov. "First, I'll stress the positive. We have resuscitated a dying nation, and given her a center that garners the loyalty and love of Jews everywhere. We have forged a new Jewish character. But, somehow, I share your sentiments, Yossel. We are still under constant threat from the Arabs and, to add insult to injury, we remain the victims of the Chosen People Syndrome. You are right. We escaped one threat to find ourselves in the cauldron of another. However, I am still not convinced that you stand on solid ground with your doubts."

"What have we done? Did I waste my youth? These are indeed serious questions," said Itzhak.

Before he pressed forward with the rest of his thoughts, Nilli interjected, "Please wait, Grandpa, I apologize for cutting in, but can you explain the idea of the Chosen People Syndrome?"

"Sure. Here is the idea behind the Chosen People and its syndrome. The Bible is specific about the concept. It says something like this: 'You are holy to God, and God chose you from all other nations.' I am not sure exactly where it is but you'll find it somewhere in *Devarim* (Deuteronomy). The prayer book reinforces this idea on numerous occasions.

"With the privilege of being Chosen came a number of moral obligations. For example, possessing an exemplary moral code, combatting human greed, lust, violence and more. In short, becoming a beacon to the nations.

"Jewish mysticism expands the scope of those obligations. It perceives the status of humanity as a broken vessel in need of repair. It charges the Jews with the responsibility of mending it. Indeed an awesome task. The Jews have never been in a position that enabled them to fulfill those obligations. For us, those remain spiritual goals.

"The non-Jewish world reacted in many ways to the Chosen People notion of the Jews. These reactions, Dov calls them the Chosen People Syndrome, have been mostly negative, full of hate, and unimaginable atrocities. Another aspect of this syndrome shows a great deal of hypocrisy as is clearly visible in the promotion of a different moral yardstick to assess Jewish behavior than the one the non-Jewish world adopts for itself. Have I answered, Nilli?"

"Yes. Thank you, Grandpa. Can you provide an example?"

"Here is one example of an extremely lopsided application of the moral code. The Arab world has never forgotten the unfortunate bloody event at Deir Yassin in 1948. It always reacts to it with horror and condemnation. So do many non-Arab people. Let us ignore the fact that the circumstances under which that horrible incident occurred have been factually ambiguous. We shall accept it as a real massacre. Now I will ask, where is the civilized world's display of horror and indignation regarding Arab massacres of Jews, for instance, at Hebron and Safed in 1929, at Gush Etzion in 1948, at the Haifa Oil Refinery in 1947, at the bus of Ma'aleh Ha'akrabim in 1954? I tell you, it has been muted.

"I believe all killings are horrific. But the responses are grossly uneven. The Jews are judged in line with a higher moral code than the Arabs."

"Interesting," said Nilli, "I must go and study those events in more detail."

"Me, too," said Tova's grandson.

Itzhak redirected his thoughts. "Let me tell you emphatically, Yossel, we have not wasted our youth! Here is why: We answered the distress call of the Jewish people. I am convinced that from the outset, the Zionists' project enabled our people, outside *Eretz Israel*, to coalesce around a common cause. Indirectly it gave them the necessary pride and strength to withstand overt and covert anti-Semitism. I assure you that *Zionism* endured while other movements like the Bund and the Jewish Enlightenment failed and became historical relics.

"Moreover, Dov has suggested that we've built a center; I tell you, we've built an anchor for the Jewish people."

Avram said, "Here is what I think, Yossel. Even though it may appear that we have failed because we were unable to help European Jews during the Nazi regime, I maintain that we did not waste our youth. We overcame Ottoman ill will toward us, the British retreat from the Balfour Declarations, and Arab belligerence. We overcame the British prohibition on immigration and land sale. And yes, we endured the atrocities of the Nazis. None of that halted our long journey for reclaiming our historical homeland; none caused a mortal wound to our national survival. At the end, we triumphed. We are here!"

"Indeed," said Alexa. "We all agree, now can we return to the conversation about our life? After all we have not seen each other in a long time."

"Not yet," said Sorke. "I cannot imagine the fate of Judaism if our enterprise had collapsed during any one of the adversities that befell us. Our effort was not in vain; on the contrary, our time was well-spent. We created the State of Israel for the Jewish people, a shoulder to lean on in times of hardships and a friend to love in times of peace. I am convinced that if the Nazis rose to power today, the little state of Israel would play a pivotal role in combating their abhorrent regime."

"I agree, Grandma," said Nilli. "The Nazi regime severely affected your achievement. However, we must remember that we are here and Hitler is in hell. We are an independent state, and I know that you have contributed immensely to this reality."

Tova's grandson added, "I agree with Nilli. We have learned in school that the Jew of the Diaspora was weak, passive, oppressed, and unwanted. He meandered from place to place, mostly because local governments pushed him around. He always waited for a heavenly-induced redemption while rejecting the assumption of responsibility for his destiny. God, in His time, would redeem him from the horrors of the Diaspora. You changed that narrative. In the process, you forged a new Jewish character. You accepted responsibility for your fate and opted to restore the glory of the Jewish people as a nation like all other nations, an equal member of the family of nations. We are no longer the Chosen People—meek, apathetic, waiting for God to act on our behalf. Yossel, you must agree you did well."

"I like it, Danny," said Nilli. "I think you speak for our generation!"

Danny had a proud smile across his face.

Before Yossel had a chance to answer, Moshe interjected. "I agree with the younger generation. But I want to add this; we did not come to *Eretz Israel* merely because we wanted to escape the vulgarity of the Diaspora or to seek personal security. We came here to rescue the Jewish nation from assimilation and eventual destruction. And we did. I say we succeeded beyond all expectations."

"My dad is right," said Moshe's son. "The Zionists' call to action reflected the existential will and tenacity of the Jewish people. Yossel, you lament the newest trouble, the sea of hostile Muslims. So let me suggest this: First, you rejected the choice of going to America or Uganda. You came to *Eretz Israel*, which was already settled by a sea of hostile Arabs, to reclaim our historical ownership of the land. Uganda, unlike *Eretz Israel*, was not ours. It was a meaningless geographic entity, devoid of emotional attachment and history. Besides, if we were there today, a sea of hostile natives would have surrounded us as well. You have taken the right path and by doing so you have brought an end to two millennia of national darkness and yearning. In the process you helped establish a first-class democracy in a region full of oppressive autocracies."

"I like that!" exclaimed Nilli.

"I think," said David, "that we pushed a whole nation out when we moved in. If we examine Yossel's question from this perspective, I could say, morally speaking, we have wasted our life."

"Wait a moment!" retorted Moshe. "Your point begs the following question: What nation? The Palestinian?"

"Yes."

"Interesting. Who are the Palestinians? What national history do they have in *Eretz Israel*? Under the Ottomans, as late as the twilight of the 19th century, the few Arabs who were vocal in Palestine wanted to be a part of an Arab nation anchored in Damascus. Until then, Palestinian nationalism was not part of their psyche, history, or loyalty. While we struggled for the survival of the Jewish nation, they were paying homage to family and tribe, not to a nation.

"Caliph Umar conquered the land from Byzantium. But a thief who steals from a thief is still a thief. Their claim to *Eretz Israel* may be vocal, but it emanates from no national entity. Their affinity to the land comes from their continuous habitation on a conquered land. That in itself is not enough. After all, they were technically squatters on a land that was not theirs. Possession does not trump legitimate ownership. There is no statute of limitation on ownership. Remember, before Israel became a state, we bought every *Dunam*, worked it and made it more productive. After a war we did not start, we have retaken what was ours."

"Well, according to your logic we are thieves, too. We took the land from the Canaanites!" retorted David.

"Technically, you are right. However, the Canaanites are not here to claim their land. They did not survive the turbulence of history. We did!" replied Moshe.

"So, you accept the notion that might is right," David pressed on.

"Possibly," retorted Moshe, "but our might was without guns."

There was a long pause, then Itzhak broke the silence, "Our might was perseverance! Unlike many other nations that have vanished from the demographic map of the world, or were pushed by stronger nations to the margin of existence, we survived. We had the will, the commitment and the culture. With the birth of *Zionism*, we acquired the political and economic capital to strengthen our national existence. We applied our peaceful power and began the slow, expensive and arduous process of reclaiming our land. Yes, it was might that made it right. However, unlike the greed and superior armies of all colonial powers in history, our might was our existential will. We also had history on our side."

"I agree with Grandpa," said Nilli. "Do you think that if the Inca had our power and tenacity, they would not have reclaimed their land? The same could be said about many marginalized nations. We are the only example in the history of mankind to possess the national ingredients necessary to right a wrong. So, Yossel, you did well. You did not waste our life."

"Okay," said Yossel, "but today the Arabs are still hostile and find new ways to randomly terrorize our life. Is this not worse than the pogroms in Kishinev? Do you call this success?"

Sorke replied, "Yes I say their bark is stronger than their threat to our survival as a nation. That aggression is manageable. In spite of it, we are moving forward to an ever better future, while they, because of it, regress, spoil their present, and sacrifice their future."

Yossel seemed ready to abandon his original thought but not yet prepared to join the confident rhythm, the one that most of his friends pursued. He shifted direction. "Half our people live in peace, free of anti-

Semitism in the USA. They are fully integrated in the American society. The Jewish Problem does not exist anymore for them. I am not convinced that my life was better spent pursuing the Zionists' project."

"No, Yossel, there is no need for doubt. We did well," Moshe admonished him with a friendly smile. "I say we created a new Jewish nation: a nation like all other nations. A part of it is good, and a part of it is bad—but, I repeat, it is ours! Indeed, I submit that the Jewish masses that went to America, would have been assimilated long ago if we did not build this state. Think how much money and political capital they have invested to ensure our success. I am convinced that our sacrifice was worth every tear and every drop of sweat."

"Even though I agree with my friends, my reply has a different slant," Dina said. "Last month my granddaughter gave me a book. It was by Khalil Gibran, a Lebanese writer. In one of the articles, I found this line: 'Are you a politician asking what your country can do for you, or a zealous one asking what can you do for your country?' This line is very appropriate to Yossel's question. The point is, if we think about the quotation, we can easily identify ourselves. We were the zealous ones. For us, the nation was above all. The nation was the essence of the cause, the reason for our sacrifices. Our entire effort was to resuscitate the dying Jewish nation. *Zionism* set out to highlight the primacy of the nation in our lives. It succeeded beyond our wildest dreams. Look around you, and you can see a free, vibrant people. The Hebrew language is flourishing. Jewish culture, literature, education and science are world class. But all of this is in danger because Nilli's generation is much more selfish than ours. They expect to receive not to give, and that tendency is growing. Should it become the prevailing attitude of the new generation, my answer to Yossel's question will be a definite 'yes, we have wasted our youth.' For now, however, I believe that the trend is still weak, so I reply with a hesitant 'no, we have wasted nothing.' I am not yet ready to concede that Yossel is right, although I feel myself closer than ever to his position."

Nilli and Danny were fidgety. She wanted to speak, but David preempted her. He said, "Let me shed a simpler light on the issue. Last month I visited my son in New York. We walked around Times Square. Stores flooded the street with colorful lights displaying the latest fashions for men and women. Well-dressed people rushed up and down the sidewalks as if driven by an invisible power that proclaimed, 'Time is money. Move on! Do not block my way.' Newspapers announced the latest political scandal, complained about drug use among the young and showed unflattering photos of the president. I thought I was walking here on Herzl Street where everyone only thinks of himself, where consumerism is king. Unlike Dina, I am certain that the age of selfishness is upon us. I think that I am inching closer to agreeing with Yossel."

"I disagree with both you and Dina," said Nilli. "My generation was, is and will always be ready to put the nation above self. Conditions change. We react within the circumstances of our time. Your sacrifices made our environment more comfortable. There is no reason to revert to the hardships of your life in order to have a strong existential will.

"Perhaps," lamented Yossel, in an attempt to bolster his initial doubt with new ammunition. "But I agree with David and I am more pessimistic than Dina. We are a little America. We dress like Americans. Everyone sings American songs; 'Hi' and 'Bye' are everywhere. Fewer and fewer people say 'Shalom' nowadays. The news of drug use and political corruption are all over the daily papers. Everyone rushes. Everyone flaunts the latest American fashion and smokes Marlboro cigarettes. People are no longer looking at the nation as the essence of their lives. The collective interest was pushed aside to make room for egotism and selfishness. Everyone is engaged in a blind pursuit of personal riches. Was our sacrifice in vain? I answer my own question with a 'yes.' Our sacrifice was in vain."

"Hold on," protested Nilli. "Lest we forget, it was my generation that fought the *Yom Kippur* war last year and faced a mortal danger to our existence as a nation. It was my generation that eventually prevailed. If that was not putting the state before the self, what is?"

"Nilli is right, Yossel. I disagree with your conclusion," said Danny. "I know that there is good and bad in our generation. There is egotism and consumerism and, most visibly, we seem to have lost the primacy of the nation. But I am convinced that it is only transitory. If our existential reality is threatened, as you warned, the primacy of the nation, the will for national survival, will be restored in a heartbeat. Look on the positive side, Yossel, there is much more tangible good than bad. We are not perfect. Nobody is."

"Our existential reality is threatened by our own deeds," David retorted. "We have lost our moral compass. Look at what we do in the occupied West Bank. Is that a way for a Jew to behave? We are arrogant; we behave as if God sanctioned our expansion into Palestinian land: a new twist of the Chosen People Syndrome. Shame on us."

"Come have some tea and poppy seed cake, leave the moral compass to the politicians and the Messiah," suggested Alexa in a vain attempt to give the conversation a lighter tone.

"David's point deserves an answer," said Tova. "I agree. We could do better. We should not have expanded beyond the armistice lines except when we reunified Jerusalem. We should not build homes and villages there on a large scale. But you say that our behavior is shameful? Really?" Her voice filled with excitement. "What standards do you use to render such an accusation? Are we subjected to the standards embedded in the Chosen People Syndrome as Itzhak outlined earlier? Nilli," she turned to the young woman, "this is another example for you. I thought we came here to liberate ourselves from that yardstick that hypocritical nations use so conveniently. Is our behavior without precedent?" A tense hush engulfed the room.

Tova, cognizant of the impact of what she was going to say, continued with a heightened intensity. "Show me one case in history when a moral code prevented a nation from looting another. Look at the behavior of the nations of the world in recent history. King Leopold of Belgium oppressed and exploited the Congolese. He used the Congo as his personal treasure chest, as did the British in Matabeleland (later Rhodesia), South Africa and the rest of their colonies. I can go on and on. The interesting thing is this: none of the actions I enumerated or alluded to came in response to any existential threat. It was born by greed, grandeur or political expediency.

"Have we committed such egregious violations in the West Bank? No!" Her voice quivered with anger. "Yet they all rush to judge our behavior toward the Palestinians. Shame on them!

"Let's talk about the Palestinian Arabs. They are not our friends. They have never been our friends. Please remember, we do not educate our children to hate. They do. We do not nurture terrorists. They do. We do not harbor any wish to destroy them and push them into the sea. They do. Did we take anyone's land by force before 1948? No! We bought the land from greedy Arab merchants and community leaders. Why is it that Palestinians always directed their wrath at us? I heard people protesting that we presented the poor, ignorant peasants with eviction notices once the land was ours. We did. But show me a place anywhere in this world where you buy land or any other property and then cannot use it. Besides, did Itzhak's Good-Neighbor policy toward Beit A'yan bring any positive attitudes toward Hazohar?

"I remember going with Gershon to Jerusalem in 1929. Why did he nearly die? Did we threaten the Haram al-Sharif? No! All we wanted was to pray freely at our holy shrine. Besides, let us never forget that they, as arrogant conquerors, built their temple on the ruins of our sacred temple."

She paused. Everyone felt the passion in her argument. No one interrupted her, not even David, who was the target of her emotions. She took a deep breath getting ready to continue. She was no longer speaking to her friends. Her mind's eye took her beyond the walls of the Worker's

Hall. She was speaking to the world. She was shouting at the hypocritical Arabs and their supporters.

"When Churchill carved Jordan out of what was perceived as Palestine in Balfour's promise to the Jews, he created a Palestinian state. No one protested the fact that Great Britain unilaterally gave land for Abdullah's own kingdom. But when Great Britain gave the Jews a promise—not the physical land for a homeland, not a state, not even the homeland, just a promise for a homeland—the Arabs shouted foul. How hypocritical was that? Yet the Jews accepted successive reductions of the promise. Then came the Partition Plan that further eroded the size of the promised Jewish landmass. The Jews reluctantly accepted the partition plan. Not so the Arabs. If they accepted the UN's Partition Resolution and refrained from attacking the *Yishuv* they would have had no refugee problem and most of the land west of the Jordan River would be theirs.

"But no. They marched to war expecting to win, to put an end to the Jewish national aspiration. They almost succeeded. But at the end they lost. Their reckless behavior created an enormous refugee problem. Not only a Palestinian problem. In fact, the combatant Arab states pushed out close to a million of our people from their homes during and after the War of Independence. Did we scream to high heaven expecting the UN to pay for their resettlement in the new state of Israel? No! The Jewish people took care of them."

There was silence in the room. The only sound, other than her voice, was the occasional creak of a chair.

"The Arabs rejected their brethren. They treated them shamelessly, settling them in temporary refugee camps, never to integrate them in their societies. Somehow the Arabs managed to create a Palestinian refugee problem and an agency in the UN to sustain it. Since that time the Palestinian refugees are the only refugee group in modern history that have their own UN agency that pays them, their children and their grandchildren, a quarter of a billion dollars annually. Do they use these funds to improve their life? To develop a first class educational system for their children? Health system? Housing and green spaces? Industry and agriculture? No! They channel the money to bank accounts of greedy leaders and toward the purchases of aggressive weaponry because they are bent on our destruction. And for that we should trust them and extend our other cheek?" Her voice grew louder, more intense and her body was more animated as if to stress her points.

"Yossel, since the sword is the only language they speak, we must maintain our strength and reject their hostility. In other words, manage their aggression to minimize our damage. From the Jewish perspective *Eretz Israel* was ours in the past, is ours now, and will remain ours in the future. I feel comfortable in telling you, my friend; we have not wasted our youth."

Everyone in the room applauded. "Brava, Tova. Well-said!" She smiled, sat down exhausted but quickly rose and said, "One more thing. I agree that we pushed them off some of their land during the war, but show me a war in which civilians, who are in the line of fire or occupy strategic positions, do not escape or are forced out. After all that aggression they want to return home? What about our million or so refugees? Should American Indians reclaim America? The Inca, reclaim Peru? No need for more examples. Besides, as many Palestinians that left or were forced out, a similar number remained behind and they are citizens of Israel."

Tova's grandson interjected, "Go ask them if they want to be included in the state of Israel if a peace treaty is signed, or be transferred to the control of the Palestinian Liberation Organization (PLO)."

Tova patted him on his shoulder and continued, "The Palestinians and the rest of the Arabs have never wanted us here and did all they could to get us off the land. Have we ever blown up their busses on route from one civilian destination to another? No! I agree that we treat them poorly, but they are not our friends. They are our enemies, by their own deeds, verbal and written declarations. Should we let them walk freely to our towns and cities when they indiscriminately bomb busses, coffee houses and restaurants? Of course not!

"We have not lost our moral compass, David. Yes, it has been tarnished, but it is still intact. We exercise much more care when we respond to belligerence or threats to our national existence than most nations. Or for that matter, the Palestinians themselves, who always choose random targets for their murderous activities. The world must judge us with the same yardstick that is used to judge every other nation on earth. We shall manage the Palestinians' threat."

"Well-said," Itzhak said and gave Tova a big hug. "I can only add one thing. It took me years to reach this conclusion. There is no absolute morality. But if there is, existential resolve will trump it any time. Of all the nations that have abused other nations, and there are too many to enumerate, we have built this country to assure our national survival. I agree with Tova. I am neither ashamed of our life's toil nor see our life wasted."

It was late in the afternoon. The sun was racing toward the Mediterranean. The workday was over. The streets welcomed thousands of Israelis who streamed to the sidewalks from office buildings. Passover meal was a day away.

The friends were tired. It was time to go home. Their conversation ended. One by one they rose. Their companions folded the chairs and stowed them in the closet Nilli collected the cups and plates and brought them to the sink, washed them, and returned them to the dish cabinet.

They trudged toward the door, hugged each other, and said, "Have a happy Passover." Two more steps and they were outside, on the packed sidewalk, where restless people rushing to get home quickly, swallowed them.

Then the hall was quiet.

"Grandpa, Grandma and I have to buy a few things for Passover. We shall see you later. Do not forget, we are going to dinner tonight. Oh, will you take Yossel's manuscript home, please?" Nilli said apologetically as she handed him the envelope without waiting for his answer. Then she hugged him and disappeared with Sorke in the crowd.

Itzhak tidied up the room and turned off the lights. For a brief moment, he lingered between two worlds. Behind him were the peeling walls, the old teakettle, and memories of a bygone age. He could still hear echoes of their discussion. He disagreed with Dina, David, and Yossel. But they were, and always would be, his friends, his family. His head was flooded with thoughts of the past; thoughts about their story, about his story.

He took another look at the old place, "I hope to see you again," he whispered to the empty space. "We did have some great times, you and me. No! I have not wasted my youth!" His face lit with a joyful smile. He locked the door behind him.

Outside, a new Israel moved at an alien rhythm. A new generation led the nation. It moved to its own beat. It carried new slogans, sang new songs, danced with new steps, and changed the existing Jewish narrative. Nevertheless, this generation had added a new link in the unbroken existential chain of the Jewish peoples.

Modern Israel overwhelmed his frail disposition. It was rushing to and fro before his eyes. The sidewalks were wide, amply lit, and alive. New buildings proudly displayed their architectural persona at the back of the sidewalk. Wide boulevards, forever clogged with cars that seemed to go nowhere, stretched before his eyes. He looked at the shoppers, office workers, and children rushing home.

The new Israel is moving on a path that he helped carve. It will guard and evolve its own destiny.

A multicolored blanket of blond, red, black and brown hair covered the sidewalk in undulating waves that embraced and swept him forward. Itzhak was tired but happy. He reached the bus stop, sat on the bench and waited for the arrival of no. 37 to Achuza.

When the bus arrived, the familiar elbowing of people who wanted to enter first to get a seat, brought a smile to his face. It was a hallmark of Israel's public transportation. He pushed his way forward and took a seat in the middle of the bus. He closed his eyes and tried to recollect the earlier conversation. *Have I wasted my youth? I once read Arnold Toynbee's assertion that the Jews were a 'historic fossil, not dead, true, but also not really alive.' I laugh at him now. In fact we all should laugh at him. Why? Because we are alive. Because we are a world-class democracy, a world-class nation. Our effort was never in vain.*

A few stops later a young man boarded the bus. He was neatly dressed, shaven and well-groomed. He moved cheerfully to the middle section, whistling a happy tune and took a seat near Itzhak, saying politely, "Good evening."

Itzhak replied with a nod of his head and returned to his thoughts about the earlier conversation. *Did we waste our youth?* He was convinced that he had not. But the question kept reappearing then lingering in his head. The bus moved at a snail's pace through the clogged streets of Hadar. Unexpectedly the driver stepped on the brakes in front of a pedestrian. Nili's envelope flew from his hands, hit the floor and scattered paper all around him. Itzhak attempted to bend and collect Yossel's manuscript but to no avail. It was hard for him to bend. The young man reacted swiftly. He crouched on the floor of the bus, collected the papers and with a broad smile handed them to Itzhak.

"Thank you very much, young man. You saved me from a major scolding."

The bus continued at a slow pace. Before the turn into Carmel Center, the young man rose slightly to reach the chain and pulled it to request a stop at the next station. He said goodbye to Itzhak and stepped into the aisle. When the bus stopped he moved gaily, in quick steps toward the exit, paused at the door, turned and shouted, "Allah is Great!" A powerful explosion followed.

Blood splashed on the twisted metal of the bus frame. Body parts flew randomly, some to the street, through the shattered glass; others stuck to the mangled metal. The wailing of badly burned people rose to heaven in protest to God's inaction. Groans and moans of the injured attacked the eardrums of the few pedestrian who rushed to aid the disoriented living.

Sounds of sirens filled the air as first responders rushed to the scene through the evening rush hour. It was a horrific scene. The living walked around in a daze. The blood of strangers oozed from their exposed skin. Blood and body parts of people who had sheltered them from the power of the explosion covered their clothes. Those who died to give them life; strangers, who happened to sit next to them before the blast, or blown off a remote seat and came to rest on the body of a person they knew not.

Many of the passersby lay injured on the sidewalk. Flying glass or metal shrapnel cut short their evening plans. It was an inexplicable carnage; a young man with a lucid mind had changed, with one barbaric act, the lives of so many people who had done nothing to him. Many were killed, and scores were wounded.

24 A GENERATION OF SMALL DEEDS

גּוֹי קַו קָו אֲנָחְנוּ! מִקַּו לָקָו קוֹמְמוּ
שְׁמָמוֹת עוֹלָם וּבְנוּ בִּנְיַן עַד!

Hayim Nahman Bialik, Blessing the People.

Nilli and Sorke returned home in time to freshen up and go to a neighborhood restaurant. As Nilli opened the door she called out, "Hey, Grandpa, it is time for dinner." No one answered.

"Check the bedroom, he must be taking a nap before dinner," suggested Sorke.

Nilli walked into his bedroom, hoping to find Itzhak there. Alas, the room was empty. The bedspread was undisturbed. She looked around and saw no sign of Yossel's manuscript.

"He isn't here," she called and wondered aloud where he could be. It was unlike him to meander alone. Nilli felt a rising tension, *perhaps he lingered on at the Worker's Hall,* she reasoned to herself. A persistent ring interrupted her thoughts. She rushed to the kitchen, stood in front of the telephone, hesitating to pick the receiver up. Her hands trembled. A frightening thought flashed through her mind, *bus 37*.

She frantically lifted the receiver. A serious sounding voice said, "Good evening, Mrs. Hacohen." Nilli suspected something was wrong. "She is unavailable. This is her granddaughter. May I take a message?"

"This is Dr. Jacobs from Rambam Hospital. There has been a terror attack on bus 37. We have admitted Itzhak Hacohen at five this afternoon. Please come to the Emergency Room."

Many images flashed through her mind. *Perhaps he is lightly wounded? Critically wounded?* A strong tremor shot through her body. Whatever it was, she took solace in the fact that he was alive. She stood silently, holding the receiver in her hand, listening to the monotonous end-of-call sound.

"Nilli, who called?" asked Sorke.

"There was a terror attack on bus 37, Grandma. Grandpa is in the hospital," she said urgently, unable to control her emotions. "We must go to Rambam." Sorke collapsed. Nilli hung up the receiver and rushed to her side. "I am okay, Nilli," Sorke said. "Help me up. Let's go."

The two left in a hurry. Outside they waited for a few minutes that felt like hours. When a free taxi drove by, they flagged it and were on their way.

The reality of his condition confronted them as soon as they entered the Emergency Room. Nilli sat near the bed. Sorke sat opposite her, disoriented. Nilli held Itzhak's hand and looked at him with love and sadness, as if this might be the last time she would see him. She touched his head gently. He looked pale and fragile and was attached to numerous life support machines. She was crying but didn't bother to wipe her eyes, allowing tears to stream down her cheeks to his hand. "I love you, please do not leave me, Grandpa," she murmured. But there was nothing she could do.

Grandpa was her favorite pal, always happy, always ready to cater to her every wish. She adored him, especially when he told her stories. She recalled the story of Saadia, his favorite. "Taking responsibility for one's action," Itzhak often said, "is what that young boy taught me. And that was the way I lived my life."

She walked around the bed to embrace her grandmother. "Let's hope for the best, Grandma," she whispered. Sorke nodded with teary eyes.

During the night Itzhak teetered between Heaven and Earth. Nilli never left his side. She sang to him softly "Anu Banu Artza Livnot U'lhibanot ba..." then whispered in his ears. "Yes, Grandpa, you came to this land to build it and be reformed by it! You and your friends have given us a most magnificent gift: a free nation in our ancient land. I know that at times you have felt that we did not fully appreciate your sacrifices. So, on behalf of my generation, I say thank you for all the things we take for granted. I shall treasure and protect your gift..."

His hand suddenly turned cold. Nilli stopped talking and rushed to summon the nurse. Sorke hugged him, kissed him, and tidied up his hair with her fingertips. Tears streamed down her cheeks. Her hand reached for her lips to prevent a growing anguish from bursting into a scream. Seconds later, the doctor arrived. He pronounced the obvious. "Itzhak has passed." The room filled with their anguished cries.

Nilli touched her grandmother's shoulders and said, "It's time to go home, Grandma." The grieving woman rose slowly, wiped her tears and whispered, "Goodbye, my love."

***

The following Sunday, at the funeral, Nilli and Sorke stood silently by Itzhak's grave, facing the Mediterranean; the same sea whose moody disposition, earlier in that century, had tormented young Russian pioneers on their torturous journey to the Promised Land. The sea was calm. Modern Israel squeezed the small cemetery. High-rise buildings looked down at the graveyard from three sides. Yet, to the west, it still commanded an open vista of the sea, perhaps a symbolic gesture to the many pioneers who had made this small plot of land their own, forever.

How strange must that sight have appeared to the few old timers who stood quietly at the gravesite, lost in time and carried far away by memories? Frail, their faces carved with deep marks of a rugged life, they were mere shadows of their youth. They gazed passively upon the tombstones, resigned to the reality that they, too, would soon join their resting comrades. The men were dressed khaki pants, the women in khaki dresses. Both wore white shirts, a clear reminder of the modest life they had never abandoned. Their attire contrasted with that of the other members of the family, particularly the youth, who dressed in trendy designer clothes.

Nilli wondered, *how many Jews knew of the Herculean effort that went into building modern Israel? How many sacrifices were demanded unconditionally by the growing nation? Lives? Comfort? Health?*

She stood before the very people who, at a young age, left behind the pursuit of education, commerce, and comfort. *These are the people whose words, actions, and tears were the seeds of the renewed nation. They are the anonymous ascenders who built a new national identity, a Jewish State whose welfare, defense and economic destiny are, for the first time in two thousand years, back in Jewish hands. From time to time their spirits sagged, their morale reached its nadir, doubting their contribution to the Zionist enterprise Bialik, the Jewish national poet, came to their aid, uplifting their spirits with his poem Blessing the People, 'We are,' he consoled them, 'a generation of small deeds! With small acts we cultivate desolated land and build a lasting structure!'*

Sorke's gentle touch returned her to the reality of the moment. It was her turn to eulogize him. She began in a shaky whisper.

"My grandfather, Itzhak, could have been your father or your grandfather. His story was the story of the men and women who were jolted out of a long slumber by the rising voices of *Zionism* and the atrocities of the pogroms.

"He emerged from the *shtetl* of the *Pale* at the age of eighteen and by his small deeds helped transform the ancient *Zion*-centric whisper of the Jewish people into a majestic reality. My grandfather and his friends, some of whom are here with us, were the spokes that sustained the accelerated motion of the Zionists' wheel. They were the bulldozers that carved roads; the furnaces that forged the plows, and the defense tools to protect the land; the poets who elevated the sagging spirit of their comrades; the philosophers who raised the notion of 'work' to the height of religious fervor; the corpses of dreamers that had been cut down prematurely by violence.

"He, alongside the women and men of his generation, worked in malaria-infested fields, dug water canals, built fences; erected settlements; guarded the meager possessions of others while acquiring none for himself." She paused. Looked at the Tova and Yossel and the rest of Itzhak's friends. Her voice gained strength and she continued.

"He was the worker bee of the Zionist Enterprise. His life was unadorned. He gave no speeches and received no awards. He never traveled abroad to represent the *Yishuv*, yet without him and his friends the Zionist cause was doomed. They possessed few assets, sketchy education and an iron will to turn a backwater land at the southern planks of the Ottoman Empire into the Jewish homeland.

"Whatever the cause demanded, he performed selflessly. The cause was the fuel that sustained his life, until the two fused into a new being: a Jewish character divorced of two millennia dominated by religion, oppression, and marginal existence. He was strong, free, and willing to tackle any challenge.

"His tenacity and dedication triumphed over hunger, unemployment, deplorable living conditions, and emotional desperation to restore the Promised Land to its former glory; to lay the foundation for a Jewish state where everything is both Jewish and possible.

"In the process, his family might have had less of his attention, less of his presence, but undeniably, as remote as he might have been, his example went a long way to forge his children's character.

"He responded to the existential yearning of the Jews: a tenacious sound, if somewhat a whisper, that reverberated from all corners of the globe, year after year, for nearly two thousand years. It proclaimed: 'Next year in Jerusalem.' There had never been a force known to men that silenced that sound, even though many men devoted their lives to the discovery of such power. Today, the Arab Muslim world is trying to achieve what many before it could not. It refuses to acknowledge our historical right to this land, to the *Kotel*. They kill us at random, as they murdered my grandfather, thinking that their action will compel us to retreat to the darkness of the Diaspora. To them I say, never! My grandfather's murder has not severed the chain that sprouted on this land a thousand years before Omar conquered it and made it Muslim."

Her voice grew stronger, more determined.

"I declare proudly, I am the extension of my grandfather's generation. I am the new link in that chain. It is longer and stronger than ever before. I will continue to build and brighten the Jewish future, all the time stretching my hand to my Muslim neighbors. Come; live side by side with us. Acknowledge our inalienable rights to this land. The choice is yours—peace and tranquility that lead to a prosperous future, or perpetuation of hate that will soil your present and destroy your future. Israel is here to stay. It is strong, industrious, possessing highly developed science, culture, commerce, and education." She paused. Looked at the four generations of Israelis who surrounded the gravesite and exclaimed joyfully, "Am Israel Chai! The nation of Israel is alive!"

IMPORTANT WORDS

Al-Buraq. A steed that carried the prophet Mohammad from Mecca to the faraway mosque. Muslims believe it to be Jerusalem.
Aliyah. Literally means Ascend. In the context of Zionism, it means to immigrate.
Am Israel. Literally means the People (Nation) of Israel.
Am Israel Chai. The Jewish people or the Jewish nation is alive.
Babushka. An old woman, a grandmother in Russia and Poland.
Bakshish. Bribe.
Blood Libel. The Oxford Dictionary of the Jewish Religion describes it as follows, "the accusation-frequently leveled in the Middle Ages, during the nineteenth century, and propagated again during the Nazi period that Jews use the blood of a Christian for their religious rites..." (Blood libel is the subject of the Prioress's Tale in Chaucer's Canterbury Tales.)
Challah. Traditional Jewish bread specifically baked for Shabbat (Saturday).
Devarim. Deuteronomy.
Dunam. (Pl. Dunams.) A unit of measure for land, roughly a quarter of an acre.
Erev. Evening.
Ezra. Literally means help. A German philanthropic society.
Eretz Israel. A term referencing the land of Israel prior to the establishment of the state of Israel. Also known as Palestine.
Fella. (Pl. Fellahin.) Arab farmer.
Gesher. Bridge.
Gaon. Genius.
Goy. A term used in the Bible for any nation including Israel. It subsequently came to mean a non-Jewish person. 'Goyim' is the plural of Goy.
Haganah. The underground military organization of the Jewish Agency—the governing body of the majority of the Yishuv, 1930 – 1948.
Habonim. The Builders.
IDF. Israel Defense Force.
Irgun. The underground military organization of the Revisionist movement in *Eretz Israel*, 1931 – 1948.
Kabbalah. Literally means to receive. According to the Kabbalah Center, Kabbalah is an ancient wisdom that reveals how the universe and life work.

Kasher. Also pronounced as Kosher. Literally means, proper, correct, according to Jewish dietary law.
Kiddush. Literally means Sanctification. It is a blessing recited over a cup of wine and bread before the meal, expressing the sanctity of the Sabbath or of a festival.
Kaddish. The mourner's prayer.
Kotel. Also known as the Western Wall, or the Wailing Wall. It is the only standing remnant of the outer perimeter of the Second Temple in Jerusalem which was destroyed by the Roman in 70 C.E.
Kol Nidre. The opening prayer of Erev (evening of) Yom Kippur (see below).
Lovers of Zion. A precursor to the Zionist movement.
Marranos. The Oxford Dictionary of the Jewish Religion explains, Marranos are "crypto-Jews" of Spain and Portugal, forcibly converted to Christianity in the fourteen and fifteen centuries...some became sincere Christians, while others continued to adhere to Jewish practices in secret.
Mazal Tov. Congratulation.
Matzah. Unleavened bread baked and consumed during the Passover holiday.
Oy. A Yiddish expression used especially to express exasperation, joy, or dismay.
Pale of Settlements. A section of western Russia that was declared as the only Russian territory permitted for Jewish habitation.
Pogrom. The United States Holocaust Museum states: Pogrom is a Russian word meaning to wreak havoc, to demolish violently.
Reb, Rabbi, Rebbe. A religious teacher and a person authorized to make decisions in matters that are subjected to Jewish law.
Ritual Killing. See Blood Libel.
Shabbat. Also pronounced shabbes. The seventh day on the Jewish calendar. (On this day God rested after the six days of creation. Respect for Shabbat is commanded in the Ten Commandments. Shabbat begins on sundown, Friday and ends on sundown Saturday.
Shtetl. A village or a small town with a large Jewish population.
Talmud. The Oxford Dictionary of the Jewish Religion defines Talmud as "...compilation..., in which are collected the teachings of the major Jewish scholars who flourished between 200 and 500 CE."
Tishah Be'Av. A day of mourning in commemoration of the destruction of the two temples in Jerusalem.
Torah. The Oxford Dictionary of the Jewish Religion defines Torah as a term applied both to the entire corpus of sacred literature and to the first five books of the Hebrew Bible.

Waqf. According to Merriam-Webster dictionary, the Waqf is an Islamic endowment of property to be held in trust and used for a charitable or religious purpose.

Yeshiva. (Pl. Yeshivot.) The oldest institution for higher learning in Judaism, primarily devoted to the study of Torah, Talmud and related religious topics.

Yid. (Pl. Yids.) A derogatory reference to Jews.

Yishuv. Hebrew term that refers to the Jewish community in *Eretz Israel* prior to the creation of the state of Israel. There is the Old Yishuv and the New Yishuv. The old Yishuv references Jews who settled in *Eretz Israel* prior to 1881. The New Yishuv is associated with Jews who settled *Eretz Israel* during the Zionist era.

Yom Kippur. The Day of Atonement. The most solemn occasion of the Jewish calendar.

Zion. The Oxford Dictionary of the Jewish Religion declares, "... in the language of the Prophets and Psalms (and in later rabbinic, homiletical, and liturgical usage), *Zion* was synonymous with Jerusalem... The prophets speak of *Zion* to refer to the entire Jewish kingdom (Is. 1.27) or the people of Israel (Zec. 2.14). In the image of a forsaken spouse, *Zion* symbolized the fate of the Jewish people in distress (Is. 49.14), while in prophecies of redemption; *Zion* is depicted as the mother of the reborn Israel (Is. 66.8)... *Zion* has been a symbol of Jewish restoration throughout the ages."

Zionism. The Oxford Dictionary of the Jewish Religion describes the term as "The return of the Jewish people to its own land (*shivat Tsiyyon*), poetically called Zion, is deeply ingrained in Jewish religious thoughts... It became imprinted in all forms of religious expression... Zionism emerged at the end of the nineteenth century as a political movement with mostly secular leadership, but its roots were religious and historical.

www.ingramcontent.com/pod-product-compliance
Lightning Source LLC
Chambersburg PA
CBHW061425040426
42450CB00007B/904

* 9 7 8 0 6 9 2 9 6 0 8 5 1 *